THE HISTORY

OF THE

CHURCH OF THE HOLY APOSTLES

(PROTESTANT EPISCOPAL)

Ninth Avenue and Twenty-eighth Street, New York, N. Y.

THE HISTORY

OF THE

Church of The Holy Apostles

(PROTESTANT EPISCOPAL)

1844-1944

by

LUCIUS A. EDELBLUTE, M.A., Rector

PUBLISHED BY THE RECTOR

CHURCH OF THE HOLY APOSTLES, NEW YORK, N. Y.

1949

CHURCH OF THE HOLY APOSTLES, 1880

DEDICATED

to

Miss Sophie R. Olmstead and Mrs. Anna C. C. Carll, in affectionate gratitude for their enthusiasm and unfailing devotion.

SOPHIE RICHARDS OLMSTEAD
Born, October 8, 1863
New Haven, Connectcut
Graduate of Mount Sinai Hospital,
Class of 1891

ANNA C. C. CARLL
Born, January 6, 1867
Upsala, Sweden
Graduate of Upsala University, 1885

CONTENTS

ILLUSTRATIONS

ILLUSTRATIONS

FOREWORD

This is a story of a church in Manhattan which has ministered in one locality for more than a century. It has witnessed neighborhood changes and outlived the aftermath of wars. Many of its sons and daughters have given their best to church and country. From the altar of the Church of the Holy Apostles in Chelsea Village have gone forth much vital labor and spiritual strength, and as members of its parish have made new homes in other parts of Greater New York, the influence of the church has spread throughout the city. Four other Episcopal churches came into being through the enterprise, sacrifice, and ministration of its rectors: Rev. Robert S. Howland, D.D. (1847-1869), Rev. George Jarvis Geer, D.D., Co-Rector 1858-1866), and a devoted layman, Mr. Herbert McCallion (1908-1916).

My qualification for writing the history of this parish lies largely in the fact that I have been its rector for thirty-one years. This circumstance, however, would have gone for nothing in producing the work if it had not been for the interest and financial helpfulness of two devoted members, Miss Sophie R. Olmstead and Mrs. Anna C. C. Carll, the latter giving her diamond engagement ring to help defray the expenses of its publication.

The idea of such a volume was suggested to my mind as we approached the One Hundredth Anniversary Service on November 19, 1944. It occurred to me that however stimulating this celebration might be to the fellowship of that time, a more lasting tribute was called for to those who had brought the parish into being in 1844 and to those who had contributed since then to its usefulness. In the nature of things, the ceremonies of a day or a week, while fitting in themselves, could hardly do justice to a hundred years of devotion and service.

1

Having witnessed the varied effects of two wars upon the parish and the neighborhood of Holy Apostles, I felt all the more the need of an adequate history of this church on the West Side of New York at Ninth Avenue and Twenty-eighth Street. It could not be told in an anniversary sermon or in a short sketch, such as was published under the auspices of the Brotherhood of St. Andrew in 1894. I am naturally indebted to the forty pages of this short "Historical Sketch of 1894," but I am far more under obligation to the carefully preserved minutes of the vestry, standing committee reports, and historic letters and documents. I am also thankful to those who have read the manuscript and have made suggestions, and I acknowledge with gratitude the interest and helpfulness of Mr. and Mrs. Stanley J. Cypher and Miss Lillian G. Stafford.

In the account of my own ministry from 1918 to 1949, I have spoken of myself in the third person as "rector" or "Mr. Edelblute," for I wished to keep my narrative quite objective. Then, too, I realize that as the years passed by, my ministry would be recognized as an integral part of the whole period.

The preparation of this book has been a great pleasure and labor of love, and its completion a lasting satisfaction. I wish I might have had more time for setting forth details, but the arduous duties of a city rector preclude such fullness of treatment. Whatever imperfections or omissions one may find within its pages, let them be charitably attributed to the busy life of a clergyman.

LUCIUS A. EDELBLUTE

INTRODUCTION

The Church of the Holy Apostles in the Perspective of 100 Years

It has been said that the first hundred years are the hardest. That may be so, and surely the last fifty years of this parish have been anything but easy. The constant and accelerating change in this immediate neighborhood, beginning shortly after the Civil War, has had its discouraging aspects. Whereas the population of the city was ninety per cent Protestant in 1860, today barely thirty per cent are Protestant, and of these possibly only five hundred thousand persons would claim any church affiliation.

An unusual rector may create a church in any neighborhood, but ordinarily it is the neighborhood that creates both the church and the success of the rector. In Dr. Howland's time (1847-1869), the neighborhood called for a chapel on West Twenty-ninth Street; in a few years during the same rectorship, the chapel was found unnecessary and the needy chapel people were invited to the mother church. Later on, as the wealthy left the water front and moved toward the center of Manhattan, Dr. Howland followed them and built up the Church of the Heavenly Rest. In a trying downtown situation, a young, energetic rector may do better than an old, set-in-his-ways rector, but there is a limit to his efforts unless he draw from good church members living elsewhere.

During the last fifty years, ten Protestant churches, between Fourteenth and Thirty-fifth Streets from Broadway to the North River, have closed their doors or withdrawn to other areas. During one summer (1926), a Roman Catholic parochial school dropped in enrollment from 1,300 to 900. On the other hand, four Orthodox Greek Church bodies are today maintain-

3

ing places of worship in the same neighborhood. A church can help, of course, to create a neighborhood, but that usually requires large endowments, a live vestry and congregation, and an extraordinary rector.

Throughout the century, there has hardly been a time when this parish has not been struggling with its budget, interest on loans, and indebtedness. Again and again, the leaks had to be plugged somehow to keep the ship from sinking. This is not the history of a church which has always had smooth sailing, where all the rectors were saints and all the brethren— angels. Rather it is a record of sacrifice and devotion, of facts and realities, of a measure of hard-earned success. For the faithful ones, the Lord be praised!

Chapter I

THE TURN OF THE CENTURY—1795-1836

Chelsea in the City of New York

Back in 1750, Captain Thomas Clarke, a British soldier and veteran of the French and Indian Wars, built a house on a hill overlooking the Hudson and called it Chelsea. It stood opposite to what is now London Terrace, south of West Twenty-third Street. Captain Clarke named his house "Chelsea" after a then pleasantly situated village of the same name on the Thames, London. The Chelsea Royal Hospital, a retreat for old and invalid soldiers, was located there, and the spacious and beautiful grounds surrounding the hospital extended to the river's bank. Each veteran had his own private room where he slept and ate. A communal hall accommodated the six hundred pensioners, where they met to redeploy that "thin red line."

In his American Chelsea, Captain Clarke hoped to spend the rest of his life in retirement. From this home on a hill, overlooking the Hudson, Chelsea Village got its name. But soon after its erection a fire occurred and the house almost burned to the ground. Ill at the time, Captain Clarke was carried some distance to a friend's home, where he soon afterwards died. His young wife rebuilt the house and lived there with her two daughters. After Mrs. Clarke's death in 1802, the estate finally became the property of the grandson, Clement Clarke Moore, the author of the celebrated children's poem, "A Visit from St. Nicholas," more familiarly known by its first line, " 'Twas the night before Christmas."

Young Clement Moore studied for Holy Orders in the Episcopal Church, but never presented himself for ordination.

5

The city block, now called Chelsea Square at Ninth Avenue and Twentieth Street, upon which the General Theological Seminary is built, was given for a seminary through the munificence of Clement Clarke Moore in 1822.

At the turn of the nineteenth century, about two miles south of Chelsea, was little Greenwich Village, said to be the second oldest habitation of white men on the Island of Manhattan. New York at the end of the island was now over-reaching Greenwich and making it a suburb. Broadway since its earliest days was the "handsomest street" and soon to become the great thoroughfare. It was eighty feet in breadth, ending in the broader Bowling Green near Battery Park, which was then half the size it is today. Above Canal Street, at an early time, Broadway was known as the "Middle Road" which extended to a fence across a dirt road at what is now known as Astor Place, the fence at the northern end being the southern boundary of the Randall farm, some years later deeded for an endowment to the Sailor's Snug Harbor. The "Middle Road" in 1800 was still a difficult succession of hills. Its highest elevation in the city was at what is now Worth Street, where it rose precipitously over a steep hill and then descended abruptly to the valley at Canal Street. To a slight degree this elevation and declension may be noticed today.

Three years before the turn of the nineteenth century, an English actor, John Bernard, wrote regarding New York:

It resembled a large fair or a cluster of inns rather than an abiding city, all its inhabitants looking like birds of passage, with the exception of a few aboriginal Dutch who had not been swept away by the European flood to their yellow brick dwellings on the banks of the Hudson. But these kept themselves distinct even from the other natives, regarding the entire body as a variety of Arabs who had been expelled from Europe for their robberies.

They maintained their houses like fortifications, their doors and windows were closed and barred, their garden walls armed with glass bottles in the bed of mortar, and they sitting on their "stoops" so dilated as not to leave room for a cat to pass, and rolling waves of smoke from their melancholy pipes to warn the stranger off. They were a marked contrast to the spare but muscular proportions of the other residents, the eternal restlessness of the foreigners, or the splashing, sprawling progress of the Yankees. The world seemed to be standing still with the one; the others seemed to be carrying all the world before them.

The habits of the New York merchants reminded me of my friends at Guernsey. They breakfasted at eight or half-past, and by nine were in their counting houses, to lay out the business of the day; at ten they were on their wharves, with aprons around their waists, rolling hogsheads of rum and molasses; at twelve at market, flying about as dirty and as diligent as porters; at two back again to the rolling, heaving hallooing and scribbling. At four they went to dress for dinner; at seven, to the play; at eleven, to supper.

At the beginning of the year 1800, very little of note seemed to be occurring in the future metropolis of the Western world. New York was still little more than a village of sixty thousand inhabitants in contrast with the magnificent proportion of the city of today.

Water was originally obtained from public or private wells. Later on, about 1800, it was conveyed through wooden pipes (bored logs) running three feet under the level of the streets. From deep wells or springs water was forced up by steam engines into a reservoir at Chambers Street, which stood fifteen feet above the level of Broadway. In 1806 an order was issued removing the old wells and pumps, several of which stood in the middle of Broadway, and establishing others at the sidewalks. The Croton aqueduct was not completed until June, 1842.

The lighting of the city at this time was by oil lamps 114 feet apart, placed angularly on the opposite sides of the streets. In 1825, the first gas pipes were laid along Broadway from Canal Street to the Battery on both sides of the street. Later on, other streets were lighted by gas from these mains. For a time the city took on a weird appearance, with some blocks well lighted by gas and others dimly lighted by the oil lamps. Many of the citizens, fearing that explosions might occur from gas, would not permit it in or near their buildings. It seemed more revolutionary to the people of that day than the introduction of electricity in our own time. With the improvement of gas lighting along Broadway, south of

Canal, that street was soon to dig its roots into the hearts of New Yorkers as outstanding among the great streets of the world.

On the East Side of the city was Bowery Lane, a rival of Broadway. Soon after 1800, however, the "Lane" was over-shadowed by the increase of business along the "Broad Way" and the transferring to that street of the fashionable hotels and shopping marts. The Bowery nevertheless continued to be an important street, connecting at its upper end with the old Bloomingdale Road and going on into the country along the Sound. The vortex of business life at this time was still centered at Bleecker, Pearl, Cliff, John, and Cherry Streets. The population of New York in 1814 was 92,000, of whom one thousand were Negro slaves. On July 4, 1827, Governor Tompkins' immortal recommendation was adopted—that "slavery should cease forever in the State of New York."

On the West Side of the island, leading out of the old city, was Greenwich Road, skirting along the Hudson. This road was like any other dirt road—in dry weather quite endurable, but in rainy conditions, especially in the region of Lispenard salt meadows near the present Canal Street, almost impassable.

The "potter's field" was along the Greenwich Road at the junction of the Albany Road. The keeper of this burial place was paid six shillings a day. In 1800 the city officials, deeming the potter's field "too near public thoroughfares," selected a more remote place—the present site of Washington Square at the southern end of Fifth Avenue. It was not until 1823 that a new potter's field was located farther uptown at Fortieth Street between Fourth and Fifth Avenues. Two-thirds of the old potter's field was then leveled for a park (Washington Square) and one-third was sold by the city for building lots. It soon became a center of social life instead of what it formerly was, a place of death.

In the early years of the nineteenth century, Broadway at

Fourteenth Street was "far uptown," and there was much open country above Union Square. In 1807, while Marius Willett was mayor, many far-reaching improvements were planned for the city. One of these, and by far the most important, was the planning for the metropolitan city of tomorrow. The parallel streets and broad avenues from Fourteenth Street to the upper part of the island were then decided upon, in contrast to the crooked lanes of fashionable and exclusive Greenwich and downtown New York.

After the War of 1812, and the treaty of peace signed on February 17, 1815, when tranquillity was restored to the city, leading citizens began to urge the city forward to a new era of prosperity, and the hum of industry was soon heard on every side. The success of Robert Fulton's trip in the "Clermont" from New York to Albany and his return, in defiance of wind and tide, turned far-seeing minds to water commerce, even though the farmers along the Hudson saw only "the devil on his way to Albany in a sawmill." By October, 1811, Robert Livingston Stevens put into operation the first steam ferryboat, which plied between New York and Hoboken. In 1817 the first regular line of packet ships to Liverpool, known as the "Black Ball Line," was established. A little later, other lines of steam and sailboats were plying the "seven seas" and many of them were dropping anchor in New York harbor. The second great event in 1817 was the planning of the Erie Canal, and its completion in 1825 again put New York first among the seaports of young American commerce. The city had now grown to 166,000 inhabitants, with its "cradle days at an end, and the vigor of metropolitan greatness in its blood."

The year 1824 saw 1,600 new houses built below Fourteenth Street, mostly two-story wooden or brick structures. A correspondingly great increase took place in the value of real estate, especially in the northern areas of the city. Many new schools were built between Rivington and Grand Streets. The Manumission Society, which since Revolutionary times had fostered freedom of slaves and free education, changed its name to the Public School Society—sponsored by Mayor De Witt Clinton. However, it was not until 1853 that all the rights and belongings of the old Public School Society passed into the hands of the Board of Education of today.

One's mind immediately goes back to the fostering of education by Trinity Church in King's College, now Columbia University, and her mothering care of churches almost from the time of her charter in 1697 when granted the land at the head of "Heere Wegh"—Wall Street. The first church was totally destroyed by fire during the Revolutionary War. The second church, built in 1788, was consecrated by the Rt. Rev. Samuel Provoost, its rector and first Bishop of the State of New York.

The citizens of the Province of New York before the Revolution were mostly Protestants, many of them Waldenses and Huguenots, who had fled from the religious persecutions in Europe and sought haven under the tolerant Dutch government. When in 1807 Trinity Church built St. John's Chapel, now torn down, in Varick Street near Canal, it was considered so large and so far uptown that people wondered when the time would come that a congregation could fill its pews. By 1825 St. John's Chapel had become the center of an exclusive neighborhood which had gathered about St. John's Park opposite the chapel—"a spot in the city, beautiful to behold."

Now the "youth" of the city had passed. The progress of New York was becoming more metropolitan and rapid, a time when "she began to sit up and take notice." The first railroad out of New York (the New York and Harlem) was built in 1836. Water and lighting were provided, and sewers were planned and laid through downtown streets. The time was ripe for the invention of multi-dwelling houses, afterwards named flathouses. The first local stagecoach line, started by Kipp and Brown, was running by 1838. This line ran from South Ferry and Broadway to Twenty-third Street and Ninth

Avenue. There was also a stage line along Eighth Avenue.

The Village of Chelsea had not been forgotten by this march of the city northward along the Hudson. Owing to better roads and the stagecoach line, Chelsea's isolation had quite ceased by 1835. Detached mansions, which had once stood on estates, mingled with new and smaller homes. Quaint little houses with pretty gardens and iron fences graced many of its streets. There were also many open spaces and shortcuts from one place to another, but in a few years these too were built upon. By 1845, west of Ninth Avenue on Twenty-fourth Street, a row of little houses with their curiously designed iron fences, colonial doorways with brass knockers, and diamond-paned windows, was known throughout the City as the "Chelsea Cottages."

But now a new force had to be reckoned with in the life of New York—*immigration*. For all practical purposes, immigration was no factor at all in American life until after 1830. During the period of 1831-1840, however, more than half a million white immigrants flocked to America. New York City and Chelsea were among the areas affected. The vast majority of the immigrants were of British descent. Many of them settled in the upper regions of the City on the cheap land above what is now Thirty-fourth Street. The need of these families and their children led to the forming of the "Eighth Avenue Sunday School" by devout church men and women, who lived as far south as Christopher Street.

In 1830 the Protestant Episcopal Church was a small affair throughout the country, but by 1840 it had become a force to be reckoned with in American life. In ten years it had made an advance such as it had never known before. The number of its clergy had doubled, and for the first time in its existence its influence began to be felt somewhat generally in every community east of the Mississippi. Dioceses had increased from nineteen to twenty-seven.

Now the Episcopal Church has become acclimatized in the best sense of that word. While during the Revolutionary War and the War of 1812, the Protestant Episcopal Church was looked upon with suspicion (as Tory) or as an offspring of the Church of England and the British Government, by

1835 it had adapted itself to its new environment and had become "one of the many" of the Protestant churches of the country. However, even amid misunderstanding by some, it held fast to the Episcopate, the Priesthood, Infant Baptism and Confirmation. It had also instrumented its life by its ancient and timetested gatherings, such as Convocation, calling it now the "General Convention." Thus it streamlined itself to the new country and for a new day in which they were to serve.

It should also be noted that most of the immigrants, possibly 80 per cent, were from the United Kingdom of Great Britain—England, Ireland, Scotland and Wales—coming to our shores with a similar background of common law, representative government and the rights and duties of free men, even though they spoke some variety of the English language.*

The field in all parts of our city, in Chelsea and in the isolated uptown regions above Chelsea, was "white unto the harvest."

---

* *Immigration and Growth of the Episcopal Church.*—*Walter Herbert Stowe,* 1942.
Reprinted from Historical Magazine of the Protestant Episcopal Church 1942.

Chapter II

THE EIGHTH AVENUE SUNDAY SCHOOL

On Sunday, July 11th, 1836, a few devoted men and women, seeing the need of religious training among the children living north of the Village of Chelsea, gathered them into a Sunday School. They were assisted by Daniel Cobia, a student at the General Theological Seminary, and, as time went on, by other students of the seminary. For a year or more, this Sunday School was a wanderer in the neighborhood with no settled abiding place. Houses were few in number and generally widely scattered. Marius Willett, when Mayor of New York (1807), had planned streets and avenues for the upper West Side, but these were still like country roads.

The shore line of the Hudson was just west of Tenth Avenue at Twenty-eighth Street; it then took a sweep west to a rocky point at Thirty-fifth Street to about Eleventh Avenue, making a marsh in the cove thus formed. At Thirtieth Street, between Eighth and Ninth Avenues, arose a rocky ledge, extending almost to Forty-second Street. The rather abrupt elevation near Ninth Avenue at Thirtieth Street became known as "Strawberry Hill," to which access was gained by "Stony Lane." The expanse north was, for the most part, made up of small fields and rocky places with many squatters along the river shore.

No attempt had yet been made by the municipal authorities to illuminate this part of the city. Visitors to the scattered homes in this district often carried lanterns at night. Of course there were no sewers, and drinking water came from shallow wells or springs. During the summer of 1836, the Sunday School was under the care of Mr. John Smith, who lived on

West Thirtieth Street, assisted by Messrs. Jesse A. Spencer, John Snowden, William Snowden and Miss Fearnhead, who afterwards became Mrs. James Blackhurst. Mr. Alonzo R. Cushman early became interested in the school.

During the summer, the school met in a room of the "Twelfth Ward Hotel," situated at Eighth Avenue and Thirty-seventh Street. Then a house was hired back in the fields between Seventh and Eighth Avenues at Thirty-fifth Street. The school remained there for about six weeks, then moved to another house in the fields, and so on. But soon it became known as the "Eighth Avenue Sunday School."

The little band of teachers visited the sick and needy, gathered in the neglected and isolated children, gave them books and started a lending library. By September, these services were so important that Mr. Jesse A. Spencer took the leadership as superintendent, while Mr. Alonzo R. Cushman acted as treasurer and began to make appeals for help in this work to the church people of New York.

There were no public libraries at this time. Gifts of books and money were solicited. Hardly a week went by without some help being received.

Swords, Stanford & Co. in 1836 gave a donation of sixty books for a library, and this library continued well on into the twentieth century as an integral part of the work of the Church of the Holy Apostles.

Others at this time contributed money as well as books: C. C. Moore, Cornelius Oakley, John H. Mott, Charles A. Lee, Edward D. West, Robert Ray, T. Whittimore, John Smith, J. P. Stagg, W. M. Benjamin, N. J. Seaman, B. A. Hatch, J. B. Sutton, Alonzo R. Cushman and Mr. Barrow—all prominent members of our city's churches.

All but eight of the forty-seven clergy of the Episcopal Church lived below Fourteenth Street at this time. Bishop Benjamin T. Onderdonk, the Bishop of the Diocese of New York, lived at 15 Whitehall Place.

In 1832, Bishop Onderdonk stressed the importance of awakening the interest of neighborhood parishes in home missions. Again and again in subsequent Diocesan Conventions, the Bishop urged the need of missionary zeal throughout the Diocese, which then embraced the whole state, but particularly did he emphasize aid to the missionary stations here in the city. "I would earnestly commend our city missionaries, stationed and itinerant," he said, "as the best agents for the charities of the Church."

Bishop Onderdonk approved the efforts being made by the Eighth Avenue Sunday School, and placed the direction for clerical administrations under the Rev. Hugh Smith, Rector of St. Peter's Church—the nearest parochial clergyman.

The Sunday School session was at 9 A. M. every Sunday, and opened with a short service of hymns and prayers. The lessons were the Church catechism, with public examinations on its contents. The older pupils learned the collects for the day. On the first Sunday of the month, books were lent by the library. Teachers' meetings were arranged for each month. The offering made by the pupils went toward the expense of the school, and at times amounted to not more than 12½ cents, rarely more than 31 cents.

Just one year after the inception of this work, the school saw both its saddest and one of its brightest periods. The optimistic beginnings were seriously blighted by the panic of 1837, one of the worst panics the country has ever experienced, and it was feared that the school would have to be abandoned. Mr. Cushman, the treasurer, sent out "An Appeal," May 27, 1837.

The Eighth Avenue Mission, corner of 8th Ave. and 35th Street, is in need of funds for necessary expenses, for better accommodation of scholars and to induce their parents to attend. The whole of the first floor has been hired and because of favorable situation, the school has agreed to give $125 per annum. The school is in a flourishing condition. Its members are increasing every Sunday, last third and fourth Sunday about 50 in attendance. It rests with Church people who have helped so much to give toward the work in this destitute neighborhood. The school is also in need of sufficient benches, chairs, etc.

Mr. Cushman tells us of the bright side in 1837:

The response was so generous and the need of the work so vital that by September of the same year, a lot located in 36th Street was leased (from a Mr. Twitchens) for $30 a year, upon which a small frame building was contracted for to give the school a permanent home.

He further states:

In the short space of six months we were obliged to move three times, greatly to the disorganization of the school. We were forced to put up with interruptions, sometimes not unaccomplished with insults—each case —money was unhesitatingly extorted from us. We trust steps to build will not be considered imprudent or uncalled for. No other city missionary work extends so far uptown on the west side.

As a further amelioration of distress, ladies connected with the work formed, in the fall of 1837, a Sewing Society, the object of which was to aid the poor and destitute of the neighborhood along Eighth, Ninth, and Tenth Avenues between Thirtieth and Fortieth Streets. Of great help to them, stated their appeal, would be garments to be made over—shoes, stockings, calico—and supplies such as thread and needles. This Sewing Society made many appeals for their work till the coming of the first rector, the Rev. Foster Thayer.

In a public letter dated August 24th, 1837, Bishop Onderdonk commends the work of the mission to the church people of the city as follows:

It gives me pleasure to learn that the efforts are making for the erection of a suitable building for the use of the Sunday School, situated in the Eighth Avenue at a distance from any other school and from any church.

A Building Committee elected by the teachers on September 2, 1837, issued this report:

We are convinced that this is an important and deeply interesting field for labor and exertion. Here as in the suburbs of all cities, the poor and destitute more especially reside. Far removed from any place of public worship and without anything to remind them of the weekly return of the Lord's Day, they very soon forget to render any homage to that great and good Being, who commands all men everywhere to repent. This neighborhood is constantly increasing by the accession of immigrants and the continued growth of our city. The inhabitants are all poor, even if they had the will in these days of deep depression to erect a building of this description.

This paper was signed by Reuben Spencer, City Surveyor and Treasurer of the Building Committee, John Smith, Jesse A. Spencer, Superintendent, and Alonzo R. Cushman.

The building planned was to be a frame building of the country school-house type—"22 ft. front by 60 ft. deep on the leased lot, north side of 36th Street," 250 feet east of Ninth Avenue—to be used as a Sunday School and as a place of worship for adults. It was completed by December 9th, 1837, at a cost of $750. The building was lighted by lamps and heated by a coal stove. The benches used in the building came from the Sailor's Mission in West Street, where seminary students assisted in the work among seamen. To meet all obligations upon the completion of the building, it was necessary to negotiate a loan of $300 to pay off the balance on the contract with the builders.

At the time of the erection of the building, eleven of the leading men of the mission called a meeting at the residence of Mr. Reuben Spencer to form a Standing Committee. Those elected were Messrs. John Smith, Reuben Spencer, Thomas Hardcastle, John Snowden, and W. R. Wadsworth. The Rev. Hugh Smith was ex officio Chairman and Rector.

The Reverend Kingston Goddard (being present) was then called to the chair by a layman, Mr. John Smith, chairman. He stated that "it would be necessary to obtain the consent of the neighboring clergy before a new church could be formed." As some doubts were expressed about the Rev. Mr. Smith, Rector of St. Peter's Church, giving consent, a committee of two was appointed to wait upon Mr. Smith and ascertain his disposition toward this objective. The whole idea of a new mission being formed came as a shock to many, but a resolution was passed:

> That Rev. Hugh Smith be respectfully and affectionately invited to still extend his pastoral care over the mission, which existed prior to his departure for Europe. And to express to him that never has it been the most distant idea of doing anything or taking any measures which might meet with his disapprobation.

John Smith and Jesse A. Spencer waited upon Dr. Smith and on January 9, 1838, thus reported his feelings in this matter:

> We found the Rev. Hugh Smith favorably disposed toward the school and desirous to promote its welfare. He was perfectly acquainted with the apparent incongruity of the present name and its connection with St. Peter's. He also expressed his willingness to the holding of public worship at all times when a suitable clergy could be provided, it being however perfectly understood that such ministration shall be exclusively for the benefit of the population resident near the school and not of those who attend St. Peter's and this approbation of lay reading by the superintendent when he should deem it necessary and expedient, he to visit the school as often as possible or convenient.

Thus the mission was definitely placed under the pastoral care of the Rev. Mr. Smith, who had also kindly acceded to the wishes of the Bishop in this matter. But the mission was, in all respects, an independent work, carried on by a group of men and women on their own responsibility and wholly maintained by them at their own expense. Conventions and amenities in the church were more strictly adhered to and more strictly enforced in 1838 than in our own time. When Bishop Onderdonk, for example, stood firmly for the division of the State of New York into two separate dioceses—Western New York with its own Bishop and New York—factional strife broke out which partly led to his suspension in 1845.

On December 12, 1837, for the first time in their new building, was held the eighteenth regular meeting of the teachers of the Sunday School. There was much rejoicing of heart and thanks to God. The superintendent reported an enrollment of 139 pupils, with twelve teachers. The minutes tell us that Jesse A. Spencer was superintendent; Alonzo R. Cushman, secretary; and Robert Heasley, librarian. The teachers were named as John Smith, John Gregory, John Linsey, Miss Georginna M. Nance, Miss Judith Brickill, Miss A. Dodds, Miss H. Ward, and the three Hardcastle sisters—Misses Eliza A., Margaret, and Susan F. All these persons had been in the work since 1836.

In February the teachers planned two sessions of the school, one at nine o'clock and another in the afternoon at two. Two delegates were appointed to represent the mission at the "Board of Managers of the New York Protestant Sunday School Society," also an assistant superintendent was found necessary. During March a general visitation in the neighborhood was undertaken by the teachers, who reported:

We found the people in general in favor of the Sunday Schoool and twenty more pupils promised to attend. The parents were very thankful to hear that there was preaching there on the Lord's Day, a great number of them not being able to get to the village Church. It was almost heart-rending to witness the poverty, distress and sickness in this neighborhood at the present inclement season. Oh! How profitable might a fortune be spent in the service of Him who gave all, if His servants were so disposed.

The offerings reported at the afternoon services, when adults attended, was usually about $1.50. During this time the nation was still suffering from the depression—the "panic" of Van Buren's administration. By June of the same year, the financial condition of the school was in a deplorable state. There was no money in the treasury, with a note due for $360. Appeals were made to church people for help, which were acknowledged in "The Churchman" by Mr. Cushman as Secretary. At the June meeting of the teachers, "thanks were tendered to Mr. Cushman for his diligent and faithful attendance to the finances of the mission."

It was now deemed necessary to rent the building during week days. The Public School Society was approached, but no agreement could be reached at that time. The mission then rented the building for $60 a year to a private school taught by a Jonathan Morrow. Mr. Morrow failed when the neighborhood did not support his venture, and after a few months he moved elsewhere, leaving all his personal effects in the school building.

The Sunday School, kept alive through this difficult time by gifts of friends and the sacrifices of those most vitally interested in the work, was now to suffer a great loss. Partly because of poor health, partly because of studies at the Seminary, its beloved Superintendent, Jesse A. Spencer, felt compelled to withdraw. His letter of resignation follows:

Seminary, N. Y. City, Dec. 6, 1838.

Fellow Teachers:—

It is not unknown to you that we have labored together in the same portion of our Master's vineyard for more than two years, and I think I may venture to say we have taken sweet counsel together in this work of love, which, next to that of the divinely constituted pastor himself, is the most important office that can engage our attention or be committed to our trust. I rejoice in being able to bear testimony to the zeal and fidelity you have displayed, and for your uniform kindness to myself you have my most sincere thanks. Be assured you shall not be forgotten. Allow me the privilege of one who has so long stood as your Superintendent, and let me urge upon you to increase your diligence and your care in the Master's service. Work while it is called today, give your whole energy to your duty as teachers, by setting the scholars a godly example of virtuous sobriety, of calm, consistent Christian deportment, of careful regard to those "little things" which go so much to stamp either favorable or unfavorable impressions. We cannot be too careful to avoid even "the appearance of evil"; we cannot walk too circumspectly in our intercourse with a crooked and perverse generation.

My beloved fellow teachers, it is the last time,—and I take this opportunity as one of solemn import to offer these remarks. Bear with me, and let my words sink into your ears, not because they are my words, but because they came from God:—He that winneth souls is wise. He that is slow to anger is better than the mighty; and he that ruleth his spirit than he that taketh a city. Verily, I say unto you, inasmuch as ye have done it unto one of the least of these my brethren, ye have done it unto me.

You will, I doubt not sympathize with the feelings under which this communication is made. After serious, and I trust prayerful, consideration,

I feel it is an imperative duty to dissolve the connection which has so long subsisted between us and the reasons for this course are such as I dare not disregard. My health at no time since my entrance into the Seminary has been what is usually termed good. The duties moreover required of me by the institution are such as demand close application and are indeed more arduous than perhaps I could make evident by any attempts to describe. Since my return from the west, I have found my health gradually getting worse and worse and my studies increased in a three-fold ratio; so that I am forced to the conclusion that I must, however reluctantly, resign my station as Superintendent of the Eighth Avenue Sunday School, inasmuch as the actual toil of body and mind on the Lord's Day in addition to the other days of the week is more than my present state of health will permit, and because it is of great moment to my future prospects that I should not for the sake of the present advantage run the hazard of unfitting myself entirely for the discharge of that high and holy office I have in view. From these considerations, my beloved co-workers, I doubt not you will readily see the necessity of the course I have adopted; but be assured that at all times and in whatever station, the recollection of the hours we have spent together will be sweet and comforting. Commending you to the especial protection of our Heavenly Father and the Son of His love, I remain in the bonds of Christian regard, yours etc.

J. A. SPENCER.

The leadership of Mr. Spencer was sorely missed, and now that the Mission Sunday School was securely housed, interest among church people who had sustained the work turned to other urgent appeals—and the mission congregation to their privileges. Mr. George S. Gordon, another seminary student who succeeded Mr. Spencer, soon resigned, and Mr. W. W. Whithers carried on the work for a time. Mr. Cushman made many appeals for the liquidation of the debt on the building, but with little result. The expense of buying a bell for the mission and hanging it caused much criticism. The standing committee then tried drawing up a set of bylaws for the teachers. Frequently debated was the question: "Who is now directing the work and is responsible?" The financial problem was fast becoming a great and ever-present burden. As a last resort, the standing committee proposed a fair to be held in Easter week, Monday and Tuesday, April 1 and 2, 1839, in a large room in the Public School at the corner of Grove and Hudson Streets. The women of the Mission and the Sewing Society and

others of the congregation proffered their services. The exact
results of this fair are not stated, but it may be assumed that
the proceeds were suffcient to liquidate all indebtedness, as
no more is said of a debt on the building.

The standing committee meeting on the last of April was
a stormy one and feelings ran high. As in many other such
fairs, no one had become really responsible for the moneys
expended or received and so no accurate accounting could be
made. Mr. Cushman, the prime mover of the fair, had been
advanced thirty dollars for the purchasing of necessary articles
and at this meeting the treasurer requested of him "to give
an accounting of all expenditures and receipts." As excitement
increased, Mr. Cushman, as secretary, was requested to deliver
all the books of the standing committee. A number of resignations followed; however, Mr. Cushman remained a member
of the finance committee, and the teachers expressed their
appreciation and thanks to him for his services and interest in
the school. Now teachers' meetings occurred less frequently,
the Sewing Society stopped their work, and the year ended
in deep gloom. After the storm came a dead calm. So human
and so trivial are these upsets, yet so disruptive of God's work!

Though the calm was felt by the teachers and all others
connected with cause, those vitally interested kept on in the
teeth of difficulties. The Bishop now appointed Mr. F. E. White
as leader, with Mr. Brand (both of the Seminary) as an
assistant. Soon thereafter Mr. Brand by a "viva voce" vote
became the superintendent. Mr. White meanwhile had taken
up parochial work at All Saints' Church on the lower East
Side.

The year 1840 closed brightly, as the building had been
rented to the Public School Society for use as a day school
for $90 a year. Financial worries were at an end. Moreover,
adult attendance at the afternoon session had increased, and
British immigrants were still settling in the neighborhood of
the school. During the next few eventful years, the Sunday

School was to become a parish.

The City of New York was putting into execution the new Croton water system, bringing good, fresh water to all parts of the city below Fifty-ninth Street. Gas and sewage conveniences were being developed. When the water was admitted into the receiving reservoir in Central Park by the city dignitaries, a monster celebration followed in October, 1842, the like of which had not been seen in the city's history up to that time.

The increase in immigrants and the city improvements below Fifty-ninth Street had much to do with the ever-growing need for a parish, which finally, in 1844, emerged as the Church of the Holy Apostles. Although changes now came more frequently in the personnel of the Eighth Avenue Sunday School, the work went on and became stronger. During 1841-44, as the rentals from the building covered the expenses of the school, teachers' meetings became less frequent and the standing committee met but twice. The whole district of the school was now divided into four sections, each of which was to be covered by a different visiting teacher so that there would be no overlapping.

Mr. John Smith, on July end, 1841, presented to the teachers and congregation the Rev. Donald Fraser, who was to take over the infant congregation if consent from the Bishop and the Rev. Dr. Smith could be obtained.

The Standing Committee signifying their readiness to transfer their title of the premises to a vestry when formed, and that vestry to assume all responsibilities, Rev. Mr. Fraser would labor to create a parish, but by December 1942, he had failed to gain sufficient support and so had to retire to another field.

Upon the retirement of the Rev. Mr. Fraser, Mr. Nichols of the Seminary was appointed superintendent and lay reader by the Bishop. Mr. Nichols, in turn, asked Mr. Charles Sands to take over the leadership of the school.

At a later meeting he asked if it would be more conducive

to good feeling to take their vote in this instance, which they did—and Mr. Sands was placed in office as the last lay Superintendent of the Eighth Avenue Sunday School, then in a most flourishing condition.

At the sixth and last annual meeting of the teachers of the school, on April 12th, 1844, held at the home of Miss Hannah Brickill in Christopher Street, the following officers and teachers were present:

Mr. Sands, Superintendent; John Brandigee, Secretary; John Snowden, Treasurer; James Blackhurst, Librarian. The teachers, Messrs. John Gregory, Tillotson, Fetters and Misses Hannah Brickill, Caroline Hardcastle, Elizabeth Fearnhead, Georginna M. Nance.

The Standing Committee: Messrs. Charles Sands, John Smith, Reuben Spencer, John Gregory, Thomas Hardcastle, John Snowden and Alonzo R. Cushman. The school was now often referred to as the "Thirty-sixth Street Sunday School."

The standing committee, since the failure of the Rev. Mr. Fraser to form a parish, had been looking toward a new building and parish organization. At their May, 1844, meeting, Mr. John Smith called upon Mr. Cushman to make a statement to this effect.

He (Mr. Cushman) had received a proposition to organize and receive the services of a clergyman, who, he stated, "could bring $800 or $1,000 toward carrying out the pecuniary demands on a vestry, toward a building, etc., if deemed necessary." He further stated that "the individual had not given permission to use his name at present." A committee was appointed to obtain the Bishop's advice in the matter.

In August, the committee reported the Bishop's opinion that he desired to see a congregation grow out of the school in that neighborhood, which, he thought, required it; but he did not and could not approve of the investment by a clergyman of funds belonging to himself personally in a church as an inducement for his being received as the clergyman of the same; and if such was the fact, he would advise not to accept the offer made. For the present, he said, while you cannot support a clergyman, I would recommend you to pursue a course like this, viz., Call upon a number of the clergy through the city and state the situation of your school, and obtain their consent to preach for you, if not all day, part of the day—in that way, you will make the people acquainted with the services and get them in the habit of going there, and also you will be able to know when there is strength enough to support a church, should you organize.

A clerical supply committee was then organized.

At the next meeting, September 4th, 1844 (at the home of Mr. John Gregory), Messrs. John Smith, Charles Sands, and Dr. John Snowden being present, the chairman stated that they were gathered to hear the proposition which the Rev. Mr. Thayer wished to make. He had been invited to preach for them.

Rev. Mr. Thayer stated that he had been invited by Dr. Snowden to call upon the Bishop, who heartily concurred in his going to the school. That he had been up there and preached and was surprised to find a school of something like one hundred in attendance; that he had been in the neighborhood, and thought a regularly organized church much called for in that place. If, he said, a number of gentlemen who were interested would immediately organize, he had hopes that they could attain something in the neighborhood greatly to the advantage of the location; and at any rate, he could promise them the cooperation of friends who stood ready to support him in whatever portion of the city he should locate himself. Rev. Mr. Thayer further stated that should this committee consent to transfer the building of the Thirty-sixth Street Sunday School to a vestry, when formed, he could get enough money to enlarge the present building or raise enough money for another in another locality.

There was a division of opinion as to whether it was necessary to consult the Rev. Dr. Smith before organizing, as the Bishop had already given his consent that the Rev. Mr. Thayer be in charge of the school. On motion, it was resolved that the standing committee transfer to the vestry when formed, with the consent of Dr. Smith, all their rights to the building; the vestry to assume all the liabilities of the same.

Dr. John Snowden and Charles Sands, the superintendent, were appointed to consult the Rector of St. Peter's, and found Dr. Smith in no wise adverse to the organizing of a church in Thirty-sixth Street, "provided that after a trial of four, five or six months, they found an organization could be effected with fair prospects and were satisfied that a church so organized could live."

On October 16, 1844, a full report was made, all the committee being present, and it seemed that everything that had so far been done was acceptable to all. The first step toward the organization of a parish took place in the Sunday School building at a general meeting, but encountered considerable opposition by a Mr. Sands and a number of families under his influence.

Nevertheless, those interested in creating a parish met for worship with the Rev. Mr. Thayer at his home in West Fiftieth Street. There, at the morning service on October 20 and again on October 27, Mr. Thayer gave notice that on Friday evening, November 1, 1844, a meeting of the male members of the congregation would be held for the purpose of creating a church organization by the election of wardens and vestrymen.

Thus, despite objections, difficulties, and prolonged agonies, the Eighth Avenue Sunday School gave birth to the Church of the Holy Apostles.

OFFICERS AND TEACHERS

OF THE

"EIGHTH AVENUE SUNDAY SCHOOL"

1836-1844

REV. HUGH SMITH, *Ex-officio Rector and Advisor*

SUPERINTENDENTS

DANIEL COBIA—G.T.S.	1836-1836
JESSE A. SPENCER—G.T.S.	1836-1838
GEORGE S. GORDON—G.T.S.	1838-1839
WILLIAM E. SNOWDEN	1839-1839
F. E. WHITE	1839-1840
WILLIAM F. BRAND—G.T.S.	1840-1841
JAMES WITHERSPOON—G.T.S.	1841-1842
GEORGE H. NICHOLS—G.T.S.	1842-1843
CHARLES SANDS	1843-1844

TEACHERS—MALE

JOHN SMITH	1836-1838	MASTER JOHN CUSHMAN	1839-1839
JESSE A. SPENCER	1836-1838	JOHN CARTER	1839-1839
JOHN LINSEY	1836-1838	F. E. WHITE	1839-1840
JOHN SNOWDEN	1837-1841	JAMES WITHERSPOON	1839-1839
		HUGH CURRIE	1839-1844
ALONZO R. CUSHMAN	1836-1839	WILLIAM F. BRAND	1840-1842
ROBERT HEASLEY	1837-1841	JOHN BRANDIGEE	1842-1844
HORATIO CARR	1838-1838	L. FRAZER	1842-1842
WM. W. WITHERS	1838-1839	GEORGE H. NICHOLS	1842-1843
JOHN GREGORY	1838-1840	CHARLES SANDS	1843-1844
D. McILVAINE	1838-1839	JAMES BLACKHURST	1843-1844
GEORGE S. GORDON	1839-1840	FETTERS	1844-1844
WILLIAM E. SNOWDEN	1839-1839	TILLOTSON	1844-1844

TEACHERS—FEMALE

GEORGINNA M. NANCE	1836-1844	E. HUGHES	1838-1839
JUDITH BRICKILL	1836-1841	TURNER	1839-1840
ELIZA A. HARDCASTLE	1836-1844	MARY A. CARTER	1839-1840
MARGARET HARDCASTLE	1836-1839	E. CARTER	1839-1840
SUSAN F. HARDCASTLE	1836-1842	JANE DRAPER	1839-1840
A. DODDS	1836-1839	ELIZABETH FEARNHEAD	1840-1844
HANNAH BRICKILL	1838-1844	CAROLINE HARDCASTLE	1840-1844
H. WARD	1838-1839	C. FRAZER	1842-1844
A. SELKREG	1838-1840	MARY HARDCASTLE	1843-1844

LIBRARIANS

ROBERT HEASLEY   JOHN SNOWDEN . . 1839-1839
                    1837-1838-1839-1840   HUGH CURRIE . . . 1840-1843
D. McILVAINE . . . 1838-1838   MISS GEORGINNA M. NANCE
WM. W. WITHERS. . 1838-1839   1840-1841
ALONZO R. CUSHMAN   1839-1839   JAMES BLACKHURST . 1843-1844

SECRETARIES

ALONZO R. CUSHMAN   1836-1839   JAMES WITHERSPOON . 1839-1843
JOHN SNOWDEN . . 1839-1839   JOHN BRANDIGEE . . 1843-1844

TREASURERS

REUBEN SPENCER . . 1836-1838   JOHN SNOWDEN . . 1844-1844
JOHN GREGORY . . 1838-1844

STANDING COMMITTEE

OF THE

"EIGHTH AVENUE SUNDAY SCHOOL"

JOHN SMITH 1836-1844   JOHN SNOWDEN . . 1838-1844
THOMAS HARDCASTLE . 1836-1844   JOHN GREGORY . . . 1838-1844
ALONZO R. CUSHMAN   WILLIAM ED. SNOWDEN   1839-1839
           1836-1839-1843-1844   WM. W.. WITHERS . 1839-1839
REUBEN SPENCER   F. E. WHITE . . . 1840-1842
           1836-1838-1839-1844   JAMES WITHERSPOON . 1840-1841
W. R. WADSWORTH. . 1836-1838   JOHN BRANDIGEE . . 1842-1844

SECRETARIES OF THE STANDING COMMITTEE

JESSE A. SPENCER . . 1836-1838   JAMES WITHERSPOON . 1840-1843
ALONZO R. CUSHMAN   1838-1839   CHARLES SANDS . . . 1843-1844
WM. W. WITHERS . . 1839-1840

TREASURERS OF THE STANDING COMMITTEE

REUBEN SPENCER . . 1837-1838   JOHN SNOWDEN, M.D. 1842-1844
JOHN GREGORY . . 1838-1842

Chapter III

BACKGROUND AT THE CALL OF THE FIRST RECTOR, 1844

The Founding of the Church of the Holy Apostles—1844

To all those of whom it might be said—as WAS *said—*

As we have seen, a group of persons of both sexes, favorable to the design of organizing a Protestant Episcopal church in the region beyond Thirty-fourth Street, had been worshipping in the house of the Rev. Foster Thayer. On the two Sunday mornings previous to the meeting of the men for the purpose of establishing the new parish, "regular notice as required by the statue, in such case made and provided, was given by Mr. Thayer for Friday evening, November 1, 1844."

The meeting was held in the room where the congregation had worshipped because of opposition to their purpose at the "Thirty-sixth Street Sunday School." On motion, the Rev. Foster Thayer was called to the chair; Worthington Romaine was appointed Secretary; Messrs. Christopher D. Varley and Henry Onderdonk were selected as the two witnesses who were to testify to the proceedings of the meeting. The following gentlemen were, by a majority of voices, elected Church-wardens and Vestrymen:

WARDENS

JOHN SMITH   ELIAS G. DRAKE

VESTRYMEN

JOHN SNOWDEN, M.D.	CHRISTOPHER D. VARLEY, M.D.
FRANCIS MANY	JOHN BRANDEGEE
WORTHINGTON ROMAINE	JAMES BLACKHURST
ALONZO R. CUSHMAN	HENRY ONDERDONK

It was then moved that Monday in Easter Week be hereafter the day appointed for the annual election of churchwardens and vestrymen. It was further agreed in due form that the name and title of the Church be known as:

THE RECTOR, CHURCHWARDENS, AND VESTRYMEN OF THE CHURCH OF THE HOLY APOSTLES IN THE CITY OF NEW YORK

The proper certificate was here signed and witnessed. On November 2nd the Certificate of Incorporation of the newly born Church was duly filed with the proper municipal authorities, and may be found recorded in the Register's Office in the city, in Liber No. 2 of Religious Incorporations, page 79.

Though the members of the infant church had found a shepherd—a tried and experienced missionary—in the Rev. Foster Thayer, it almost seemed that they had taken too much upon themselves in organizing a parish, for crippling divisions and resignations plagued them at once. A number of the workers in the Eighth Avenue Sunday School belonged to other nearby churches and now felt obliged to give up their connection with the newly formed parish. Even members of the vestry had church interests elsewhere. Mr. James Blackhurst was a vestryman of the Church of the Advent and soon resigned. Mr. Henry Onderdonk had been actively engaged in church education in the Diocese of Maryland and removed to that State. Mr. John Brandegee, a student at the General Theological Seminary, felt the pressure of his studies too taxing to continue in the parish work. Finally, Mr. Thomas Hardcastle and his family, who had been interested in the school from the very beginning and who had often opened the doors of their home at 139 West 17 Street to the teachers' meetings, left the city.

The discontented Sunday School teachers, led by Mr. Land, refused to acknowledge the authority of the vestry. The financial committee, however, through Mr. Cushman, had already secured the bond on the mortgage from a Mr. Vail for $20.

During the brief absence from the city of Mr. Thayer, the Rev. John Ireland Tucker was prevented from holding services in the school building because of the disturbances caused by Mr. Land and his followers. Members of the vestry were forced to vacate the premises through threats of forcible ejection by the opposing faction.

They left peaceably protesting their rightful title of the building, because of the presence of the young. Mr. Watson Haynes, attorney, was engaged by the vestry to obtain their lawful right to the Sunday School building on West 36th Street.

During the interim, services were held at the home of the Rev. Mr. Thayer. The following protest voiced the opposition among the teachers:

October 16, 1844.

Gentlemen:

We the subscribers, Teachers of the Eighth Avenue Sunday School, earnestly desiring the good of the school and the peaceful performance of Divine service in the building, regret that you have made the transfer of the property to any legally formed vestry, and that you make some immediate arrangement that orderly and properly conducted religious worship be held there, in accordance with the wish of those deeply interested in the welfare of the same.

Signed: MESSRS. JOHN SNOWDEN, JAMES BLACKHURST,
MISSES GEORGINNA M. NANCE, HANNAH BRICKILL
AND ELIZABETH FEARNHEAD.

* * * *

The vestry sent this reply:

November 11, 1844.

To the Standing Committee and Teachers:

The undersigned have been appointed a committee of the Vestry of the Church of the Holy Apostles to request from you the transfer of the school building in West 36th Street to the said Church, thereby placing it and the school under the pastoral care of the officiating Clergymen of the Parish. It will be the object of the Vestry to have Divine Worship celebrated in it at regular and stated periods, etc., thus promoting, it is earnestly hoped, the spiritual welfare of the neighborhood. These objects and aims are so desirable that we beg leave to subscribe ourselves your Christian brethren.

Signed: FRANCIS MANY, HENRY ONDERDONK,
WORTHINGTON ROMAINE, Clerk of the Vestry.

* * * *

While waiting for a solution of this problem, the vestry appointed a committee to confer with the authorities of the Blind Asylum for the use of their chapel. At the second meeting of the vestry, November 19, 1844, committees were appointed to draw up "Rules for the Vestry" and the "Order of Business." On November 26, the Rev. Foster Thayer was called as the first Rector of the Church of the Holy Apostles. The teachers were requested to retain their connection with the newly formed church, and Dr. C. Dixon Varley was named temporary superintendent until the teachers should duly reorganize and elect their own choice for that post.

At the December 1844 meeting of the vestry, a special committee reported:

> That from January 1st, 1845, an agreement has been made between Nicholas Dean and Hamilton Murray of the Board of Managers of the New York Institution for the Blind, at West 34th Street and Ninth Avenue, and a committee of the Vestry, Messrs. John Smith, Elias G. Drake, A. R. Cushman, for the use of the Chapel of the Institution as a place of worship, every Sunday morning and afternoon, on Good Friday, Ash Wednesday, Christman Day and a part of Thanksgiving Day. . . . All alterations (made for religious services of the Episcopal Church) for a desk or pulpit, altar and altar rail, shall come under the direction of the Board of Managers of Institution, and all costs and changes were to be paid by the Vestry. It is also agreed that pupils shall occupy the rear ranges of seats in the chapel and that no collections shall be taken up in the chapel and this arrangement is to terminate by January 1846.

At the last meeting of the vestry in January, the letter of acceptance of the rectorship by the Rev. Mr. Thayer was read:

December 17th, 1844.
To the Wardens and Vestry of the Church of the Holy Apostles:
A communication was placed in my hands inviting me to the Rectorship of the Church of the Holy Apostles signed by Worthington Romaine, Esq. It would have received earlier attention, but my engagements prevented action, and moreover I was solicitous to see what degree of interest would be felt in building up a Church in this section of the city. As our arrangements are now fixed for a place of worship for some time to come, I hereby signify my acceptance of the Rectorship of the Church of the Holy Apostles now worshipping in the Chapel of the Institution for the Blind. My letters of transfer from Bishop Kemper are in the hands of the Bishop

of New York.

My object in accepting the Rectorship in this incipient state of the parish is that I might act with more efficiency in promoting its interests and giving it permanent prosperity. I also do it in the hope that the Gentlemen who have stood by me so nobly in carrying out the principles of the Church of Christ will continue so to do until a brighter day shall dawn upon us and a little one shall become a thousand.

A Church is much needed in this section of the city, and by persevering labor and earnest prayer our object by the blessing of God may be accomplished. I remain,

Yours truly,

FOSTER THAYER.

* * * *

The Church was now organized and had a resident pastor. Within six months (in April 1845) the vestry was offered a building site at Ninth Avenue and Twenty-eighth Street, and, in less than a year (on March 31, 1846), the cornerstone was laid. But the Bishop of the Diocese, who had shepherded this flock, was not present.

The Rt. Rev. Benjamin Tredwell Onderdonk, the Bishop of New York, was under suspension, convicted by his peers (on trumped-up charges) of impurity and immorality. The Ecclesiastical Court's decision went against him by one vote, seven to six. He would not appeal to the secular courts. He refused to retire. His reply was:

I hereby protest, before this Court, and before Almighty God, my innocence of all impure or unchaste intentions. . . . Brethren, solemnly protesting as I have protested, and do now protest, before Almighty God and the honest judgment of this Church, I believe that the unjust sentence of this Court will neither be ratified in Heaven, nor sustained on earth, after the light of reason and truth shall have dispelled—as it surely will dispel—the mists of prejudice and passion.

The Bishop stood out boldly against the unjust sentence to the day of his death. He had been a "firm, untiring administrator of the concern of the great diocese, since his election as Bishop of New York in 1830. He claimed and sought for the Church the same progress which distinguishes our land at large, and it was a part of the patriot's duty, which he thought himself called upon to fulfill, to aid in the progress."*

Bishop Onderdonk had organized the New York City Mission Society in 1833 "to provide churches with free sittings for the poor who were unable to pay pew rents." By 1838, as we have seen, he had divided the State into two dioceses—Western New York and New York. In the face of bitter criticism in 1843, he had dared to ordain to the ministry the brilliant student, Arthur Carey, who, at his examination for Orders, asserted that the Church had always taught the doctrines of Baptismal Regeneration, Apostolic Succession, Justification by Works, and Transubstantiation (the doctrine of the Real Presence of Christ in the Holy Communion).

In one of his addresses to the Diocesan Convention of New York, he had said:

> Protestantism is being riven to the center with internal dissension, covering with its name every variety of schism, and every bold and wicked innovation of heresy, forming an unholy alliance with the veriest infidelity. . . . The rejection of Christ's Priesthood, the rejection of His Sacraments, every species of schismatic organization, every kind of erroneous and strange doctrine, every grade of heresy, is called by the name Protestant . . . and vaunts itself as the legitimate result of the great privilege of private judgment, and the bounden duty of casting off the degrading and sinful yoke of papal despotism and corruption.

This made sorry reading for stalwart Protestants in the church. He further declared:

> The true blessings of the Reformation are to be found not in departure from Rome, but in return to Christ; to the principles, faith, and order of His One Holy Catholic and Apostolic Church. . . . So thought the brethren who have been termed the "Oxford Divines."

The Bishop could not be cowed by the Low Church Party or "anti-Episcopal" group, a term that connoted to these factionists that "no mere Bishop could lord it over them." Resent-

---

*"Bishop Onderdonk," *Historical Magazine*, 1948, E. Clowes Chorley, D.D.

ment increased against the Bishop and came to a head at the General Convention at Philadelphia in October, 1844, "with the sentence of Indefinite Suspension from the Office of a Bishop in the Church of God." "After his death in 1861, the sentence was recognized as neither just nor equitable."*

Bishop Onderdonk asked the Diocese of New York for an investigation of the "threats made and the action against myself in view of nothing short of my official destruction. Most industrious efforts were made to injure me by false reports, and by statements which I was not allowed to see." He was classed as a "Puseyite"—with all the innuendoes behind that term.

A "Puseyite" at that time (1840-45) was one who stood up while reading the *Psalms,* the *Te Deum,* or the *Creed,* and turned to the Altar at the *Gloria Patri;* the reason for these actions seemed by some about as valid as to others—of the young man who did not stand, saying he considered Sunday "a day of rest." The early Forties was also a time of controversy over the "free church," i.e., one without rented pews, versus those churches with rented pews. One argument against free churches, published at the time, was that "families would be scattered in the congregation."

Bishop Philander Chase, of Ohio, the President of the Ecclesiastical Court, said, "Even if the charges were true, the facts failed to support the charge." He went even further and apologized for the decision of the court. Bishop McCoskry commented, "The sentence of suspension should be altogether remitted and terminated." Bishop Delancey stated, that "imprudences do not imply immorality."

But the ban was never lifted.

Bishop Onderdonk secluded himself entirely from all appearances in the public eye. His life was spent, during those long and lonely years, in his library, with his pen and his books. He went daily for prayer through the quieter streets to the Church of the Annunciation. Through the subsequent

*"Bishop Onderdonk," *Historical Magazine,* 1948. E. Clowes Chorley, D.D.

years, he cherished the hope of restoration to the work of the Christian ministry.*

Both the Rev. Mr. Thayer and Dr. Howland, the first two rectors of the Church of the Holy Apostles, voted that the Trustees of the Episcopal Fund pay over to the Bishop the sum of $2,500 annually, commencing October 1, 1846. On October 13, 1858, the following resolution was adopted by the vestry:

Resolved, that the delegates of this parish, at the next Diocesan Convention, be requested to present the question as to the propriety of the restoration of the Rt. Rev. Benjamin T. Onderdonk, and to sustain the same.

Again, on September 20, 1859, the vestry adopted the following:

Whereas, the Vestry understand that measures are now being taken by influential clergymen and laymen, both of the former opponents, as well as friends to Bishop Onderdonk, to secure his restoration, Resolved: That the Delegates from this Diocese to the next General Convention are hereby directed to cooperate with these measures and to take such further steps as their judgment may dictate to accomplish that desirable end.

This measure was carried triumphantly through the General Convention, but failed in passing the House of Bishops at Richmond, Va., and the final result was heard by the vestry "with the deepest sorrow."

Resolutions were at once passed and forwarded to Bishop Onderdonk, sympathizing with him and expressing the hope that he would yet be restored to the exercise of his Episcopal authority. His touching reply was directed to be entered on the minutes, but has since been lost to the parish.

Bishop Onderdonk died on April 30, 1861, and the standing committee of the parish records:

It is with much sorrow that we have to record the decease, during the

---

*Op. cit.

past year, of our beloved Diocesan, Bishop Onderdonk, a sorrow much increased by the fact that he was taken away before the suspension was removed, and he had been restored to the discharge of his Ministerial and Episcopal duties. It is pleasant for us to remember that he appreciated the kind feelings of our Parish toward him and ever spoke of us with an affectionate regard and interest.

The "Historical Sketch of the Church of the Holy Apostles" affirms that "Bishop Onderdonk chose this as his Parish Church."

The Rev. Dr. Samuel Seabury, Rector of the Church of the Annunciation, Bishop Onderdonk's oldest friend and confidant, gave the funeral eulogy at Trinity Church, taking as his text *St. John* V:35;

He was a burning and a shining light: and ye were willing for a season to rejoice in his light.

A fitting epitaph is carved on his tomb:

Here lies the once powerful, most amiable and much beloved Bishop of New York.

May God be praised for the common Christian charity displayed by the rectors, vestry, and members of the Church of the Holy Apostles toward their Bishop, who had given fatherly care to them when they were a struggling mission and infant parish. They must have had him in their thoughts and prayers at the laying of the cornerstone and the consecration of this Church by his good friends, Bishops McCoskry and DeLancey.

THE REVEREND FOSTER THAYER

1844-1847

BISHOP OF NEW YORK:

THE RT. REV. BENJAMIN TREWELL ONDERDONK, D.D.

1830-1861

1846—The Mexican War.

Chapter IV

THE REVEREND FOSTER THAYER, 1844-1847

Early Struggles

The Rev. Foster Thayer was Rector of the Church of the Holy Apostles at a time when the church people of the diocese were much agitated over the reports as to the conduct of their bishop, the Rt. Rev. Benjamin T. Onderdonk. It is to the credit of the Rev. Mr. Thayer that he was not swept away by prejudicial emotions. Two other vexing problems confronted the new rector; the lawsuit over the ownership of the parish property on West Thirty-sixth Street and the constantly recurring dispute as to whether the new church was to be a free church or one having rented pews.

At the time of the organization of the Eighth Avenue Sunday School in 1836, Mr. Thayer was a missionary at St. Paul's Church at Waterloo, Seneca County, N. Y. The following year he was ordained Deacon by the Bishop of New York, and after his ordination to the Priesthood he was called as rector to St. Paul's Waterloo. Shortly after commencing his work there, he wrote the Bishop as follows:

Immediately after commencing my labors here, I succeeded in establishing a Sunday School of 60 scholars and six teachers. I have recently established a course of pastoral visitations, united with biblical instruction, by meeting different families once a week at their dwellings.

The first rector of Holy Apostles was thus a missionary in the truest sense of the word. Before he was to undertake the work of this parish, he understood that it was to be a "free church." It was just this missionary zeal for free churches that was to cause the termination of his rectorship here in the short time of two years and five months.

41

In 1838, Mr. Thayer was a missionary at St. Paul's Church, Angelina, Allegany County, N. Y. Then, during the following year (1839), he left the Diocese of New York and was received into the Diocese of Connecticut under the Rt. Rev. Thomas C. Brownell, where he did missionary work at St. Paul's, Huntington, and at Stratford, Conn. He then became a missionary at Mishawaka, Indiana, now the See City of the Diocese of Northern Indiana.

In the same year (1842) Bishop Brownell gave him a letter dismissory to the jurisdiction of the Rt. Rev. Jackson Kemper, Bishop of Missouri and Indiana and other states in the great Northwest Territory. Bishop Kemper at this time was affectionately known as "The Bishop of All Outdoors." While under Bishop Kemper's jurisdiction, Mr. Thayer did work at Trinity Church, Niles, Michigan. Bishop Samuel Allen McCoskry was then Bishop of Michigan; in 1846 he laid the cornerstone of Holy Apostles. At Niles, Mr. Thayer was most successful. During his first year there, the interior of the church was repaired and beautified. From Niles he came to New York in 1844, after spending a few months at Vincennes, Indiana. Bishop Kemper reports in 1844:

Rev. Mr. Thayer, I presume, does not intend to return to the Diocese, although he has not yet asked for a transfer. But during the following year, Bishop Kemper transferred him from the Diocese of Indiana to the Diocese of New York.

The Rev. Mr. Thayer's letter of acceptance of the rectorship of the Holy Apostles was dated December 17, 1844, and was formally placed before the vestry of the parish at their January meeting, 1845. His salary from the first of January was placed at $500 yearly, half of which was the responsibility of the vestry, the remaining half to be made up by personal contributions from his friends. At the same time the sexton's salary was fixed at $50 per annum. Up to that time Mr. Tunis Bennett, the sexton, had received no salary.

The distressing conditions at the Thirty-sixth Street Mission forced the newly organized church to find temporary shelter elsewhere. By negotiations with the authorities of the Blind Asylum, the chapel of that institution was leased for one year. The removal of the congregation to its new home, with an enthusiastic missionary priest as leader, made an appeal to the imagination of church people throughout the city and especially in the immediate neighborhood. Mrs. Thayer was most helpful in the new work. By June, 1845, through her own efforts and the help of friends, she had purchased a "Communion Sett in Case" ($172) and presented it to the parish. This was a large sum in those days, and the task of raising the necessary fund for the set was not completed until a short time before the rector's resignation. On each of the five pieces in the set is engraved a Latin cross with the words *"A cruce salus"* followed by "The Church of the Holy Apostles, July, 1845." Her letter on this subject was as follows:

May 3, 1847.

Gentlemen: The indisposition of one member after another of my family, I offer as my excuse for the tardy manner in which I have proceeded in this undertaking. I am happy, however, to say that Providence has smiled upon my humble effort, and the object is accomplished. I therefore, present you with Gale & Heyden's receipt. A few other receipts in behalf of your parish, I have already delivered to C. D. Varley, M.D.

That Heaven will bless and direct you in the furtherance of your undertaking is the wish of yours,

Most respectfully,

MARY THAYER.

P. S. I am about to retire to the interior of Pennsylvania for the summer, and I will be glad to aid you further on my return. Please acknowledge the receipt in the *Churchman* and *Protestant Churchman* for the satisfaction of the contributors only.

* * * *

In acknowledgment the vestry sent the following:

Resolved, That the Clerk communicate the thanks of the vestry to Mrs. Thayer and through her, to the other contributors for her handsome silver communion sett procured by her exertion.

May 4, 1847.

In May of 1845, Mr. Robert Ray and Mr. John A. King made a liberal offer to the vestry of four lots (opposite the Ray estate) at Ninth Avenue and Twenty-eighth Street, "provided a Church of brick or stone be erected thereon within a year," and added to their offer a subscription of $1,500 for the erection of the church. An appeal was now made to the public and Trinity Church for assistance in this venture. In the appeal it was stated that the vestry hoped to have a "Choir of the Blind" on the plan somewhat similar to the one in Liverpool, England. An additional lot on Twenty-eighth costing $1,200 was also purchased at this time for a rectory at six per cent interest. This foresight enabled the vestry to enlarge the church in 1854; the lot was never used for its original purpose.

Soon a committee (Messrs. A. R. Cushman, C. D. Varley, and F. Many) was appointed to confer with architects for a suitable plan. The church to be erected at this time was definitely to be one of the free churches of the city, an idea close to the heart of the rector and many parishioners. There were then in the City of New York forty-one Episcopal churches, of which only eighteen were free, i.e., without owned or rented pews. By July, the rector reported that he had obtained $2,810 for the erection of the church. Mr. John Smith reported seventy children enrolled in the Sunday School, with seven teachers.

An appeal for the free church read:

The idea of a Free Church is: Remedies for welcome. Remove the doors from the barricaded pews. Open the doors of the Church daily from morning till evening for prayer. Support your Church through free-will offerings of the congregation, not by pew rents or owned pews.

The first plans submitted by Mr. Le Fevre, the architect, were for a stone church to cost $18,000. A stone spire was estimated to raise the expense to $22,000. The drawings were referred back to the committee with instructions to secure plans for an edifice whose cost should not exceed $18,000, and which should be sufficiently ample to accommodate eight hundred persons.

The Rev. Mr. Thayer, who strongly favored a free church, advocated collecting the funds on a strictly voluntary basis. Dissenting from this view, however, were Mr. Cushman and Mr. Baker of the vestry.

Again a request was made to Trinity Church for $15,000 to enable the vestry to proceed with the erection of the church, but Trinity felt unable to lend so large a sum at the time. Dr. Berrian, Rector of Trinity Parish, had estimated that the gifts, loans and grants made by Trinity to other parishes totaled two million dollars—an enormous sum for those days.

At a special meeting of the vestry, December 17, 1845, the Committee on Plans presented a new design by Mr. Le Fevre for a church on the Tuscan order, without galleries, at a cost of $11,000. On a motion of Mr. John Smith it was resolved "that the plan now submitted, in the place of the plans formerly adopted by the vestry, be approved; also, "(1) that the cost of the same should not exceed $11,000; (2) that a mortgage can be secured on the Church and lots for $4,000; (3) that the committee shall have procured the title of the property from Mr. Ray before commencing."

The church as now planned was to be a brick exterior with a wooden spire, without transepts or chancel, and the interior pillars of wood were to be covered with plaster. Thus the church form was a parallelogram with pillars and clerestory windows, about twenty-five feet shorter from east to west than it is today. The dimensions were set at eighty-nine feet long by fifty feet wide, having a chancel recess of ten feet. The spire of wood was to be 160 feet high. At this time it was hoped at some future day to replace the spire by one of larger size and of more durable material. The contract was let early in 1846 to Wm. S. Hunt and Lorenzo Moses, builders, whose work was to be completed by February, 1847.

The cost of the building so far was to be secured partly by

subscription, partly by a loan from Trinity Church, and partly by a mortgage on the lots upon which the church was to be erected. On agreement with the vestry, Trinity Church promised a loan on a mortgage of $4,000, and a gift of $2,000, the loan to fall due in 1850.

Other difficulties cropped up at this time. Intent on securing money for building the church, the congregation had forgotten the rector's salary, now in arrears by $189.16. Another distressing notice came to the vestry from Mr. Hamilton G. Murray, Chairman of the Chapel Committee of the New York Institution of the Blind, stating that the chapel would be occupied by another denomination for the ensuing year, according to the rules of the Institute, which prohibited the use of its chapel for more than a year to any particular denomination.

However, the congregation did not remain long without a home, for now the rector offered the first floor of his home—the Martine house of Fitzroy Row on West Twenty-eighth Street. A temporary altar was erected at the far end of the double parlor, and the congregation met there for services until May, 1846.

Sunday services, including morning prayer and sermon, were held at 10:30 a. m. The Sunday School met at 3:30 p. m., and an evening service with religious lecture and instruction was held at 7:30 p. m.

During this period, the following interested priests of the Diocese preached: The Rev. Dr. Edward Y. Higbee, the Rev. Prof. Turner of the General Seminary, the Rev. J. M. Forbes of St. Luke's Church, the Rev. Dr. Taylor, and the Rev. W. Morris.

The meetings of the vestry in the rector's home on West Twenty-eighth Street were largely given over to gloomy financial matters.*

Mr. Ray declined to give the deeds to the lots, until he

---

*See Appendix K, Item 1.

was sure the full amount for the building of the church should be subscribed. The vestry again appealed to Trinity Church, especially in regard to the arrears in the rector's salary and Trinity responded at once with a yearly grant of $300 toward his stipend.

After a while, the problem of a suitable location again engaged the attention of the vestry as it was found inconvenient to worship at the home of the rector. Eventually, the upper part of a red building situated on the rear of a lot at the corner of Twenty-seventh Street and Ninth Avenue was secured as the only available place in this immediate neighborhood. The first floor was used as a blacksmith's shop, and the windows opened upon a coal yard.

The altar, altar rail, lectern, and font, all formerly used in the chapel of the Institute for the Blind were moved there. A rude vestry room was formed over part of the stairway. Services were continued there until February 27, 1848, as furnishings for the new church were delayed by want of funds.

In March, 1846, the rector stated to the vestry that Bishop McCoskry had designated Tuesday, March 31, at 5 p. m. for the laying of the cornerstone. Invitations were issued to the clergy, wardens, and vestrymen of the City, Brooklyn, and Williamsburgh, and the professors and students of the General Seminary to attend the ceremony of the laying of the cornerstone. Dated March 27, the invitations were worded in these terms:

Notice is hereby given that the Corner Stone of the PROTESTANT EPISCOPAL CHURCH OF THE HOLY APOSTLES will be laid by the Right Rev. S. A. McCoskdy, D.D., on Tuesday next, the 31st inst., at 5 o'clock P. M.

You are respectfully invited to be present on that occasion. The Reverend Clergy, and the Wardens and Vestrymen of the other Episcopal Churches in this City will assemble at the residence of the Rector, The Rev. Foster Thayer, in 28th Street, between 8th and 9th Avenues, at half past 4 P. M., from whence the procession will move to the corner of 28th Street and Ninth Avenue.

The Reverend Clergy are respectfully requested to bring their surplices with them.

On behalf of the Vestry,

A. R. Cushman and Francis Many, Committee.

In connection with the foregoing, this resolution was adopted:

In the box in the cornerstone, there shall be placed a Bible, Prayer Book, Church Almanac for 1846, last report of the Bible and Prayer Book Society, last report of the New York Institution for the Blind, and on a parchment the title of the Church, the names of the Rector, Wardens and Vestrymen, Architect and donor of the church lots.

According to schedule, therefore, on Tuesday, March 31, Bishop McCoskry of Michigan, acting for the Bishop of New York, attended by many clergy and others, and in the presence of a large number of people attracted to witness it, performed the ceremony of the laying of the cornerstone of the church to be erected to God under the title of the Church of the Holy Apostles in the City of New York, at the corner of Ninth Avenue and Twenty-eighth Street.

The form of service used on this occasion was that set forth by the Bishop of the Diocese, Bishop Onderdonk, A.D. 1836, and since commonly used. The procession with the clergy present mostly habited in their surplices, moved from the house of the rector in Twenty-eighth Street, headed by the Bishop. The Psalms occurring in the services were the anthem "Laudate Nomen" from the Institution Office and "Jubilate." They were chanted by the choir from the General Theological Seminary to a Gregorian tone, as were the Responses and Amens. An address was delivered by the Rector.

The knotty question whether the new church was to be free or not was cropping up every few months, and now became a real divisive factor among members of the congregation. In April, 1846, Mr. Cushman sponsored a resolution that "the Free Church be and is hereby rescinded." The Rector and Mr.

John Smith countered the resolution and had it laid on the table. By June 2, 1846, the matter was again brought before the vestry with a similar result. As a direct consequence of this dissension, Warden John Smith resigned about this time and the Rector followed his example the following year.

Although the vestry once more declared for a free church, the dispute was finally settled the other way in November, 1847, during the rectorship of Dr. Howland. Under the great financial strain of completing the building, the idea of a free church definitely had to be given up. The attendance at the services during this time had gradually dwindled until at the close of Mr. Thayer's rectorship there were left but twenty communicants on the church's list.

All property owners along Twenty-eighth Street were now assessed for the grading and paving of the street between Eighth and Ninth Avenues. The Church petitioned the city authorities that "if this Church be assessed for the building of a sewer along Ninth Avenue, the Community Council grant them relief from said assessment." It was granted (1846-7).*

The difference between the rector and the vestry as to policy was now so acute and the financial outlook so gloomy that in April, 1847, the vestry signified to the rector that "they could not bind themselves to give any salary to him for the present year."

Whereupon, Mr. Thayer reminded the Vestry that the arrears for his salary were now $337.67 since January, 1847, and stated then his reason for his resignation:

To the Wardens and Vestrymen of the Church of the Holy Apostles:
  Being satisfied that a Free Church would not be sustained and having labored to secure a large amount of funds for the building of the Church, as was possible under present circumstances, and considering the embarrassed state of finances, I hereby tender my resignation as Rector of the Church, to take effect, May 1st, provided the salary due me to the 1st of May, 1847, shall be paid. Up to the 1st of January, I believe it is $125.

Yours,

(Signed) FOSTER THAYER.

*See Appendix K, Item 2.

P. S. The Finance Committee may recommend what amount shall be paid from 1st of January to May 1847. I think if possible, the proportionable amount should be paid.

After leaving New York, the Rev. Mr. Thayer went to Vergennes, Vt., where he was installed as rector of St. Paul's Church by the Bishop of the Diocese, the Rt. Rev. John Henry Hopkins, who preached to a large and attentive congregation, which had been without a rector for nearly a year.

During the following year (1848) the Rev. Mr. Thayer reported to his Bishop:

I am happy to report, this second year of my rectorship, a marked improvement in the condition and prospects of this church. The number of attendants has steadily increased, and as far as I can judge much harmony prevails among the congregation. I have made pastoral visits during the winter, at the houses of the members of the Parish on a strictly religious nature—reading of the Scripture, exhortation and prayer. They have been attended by those of the immediate neighborhood, which, it is believed, have been blessed by the Holy Spirit—been invigorating in faith, and refreshing to piety.

The improvement in the Church approved by the Bishop, at my suggestion; simply consists in the removal of the altar to the center of the Church with the pulpit and lecturn outside the rails;—an arrangement more appropriate and better fitted for the performance and understanding of the whole service.

The Rector deeply laments his many failures in duty,—the excessive prevalence of a worldly spirit, and alarming religious insensibility to the great salvation among many dear to him, and for those souls he is bound to watch as one who must give an account. Still, he is encouraged to believe that some are growing in Christian virtues, in love and faith, daily commune with the Maker, and are preparing for the only state, while their cooperation with him in his official labors, and their heartfelt sympathy with him under severe private afflictions, from which by the blessing of God he is now entirely relieved, have incited him to fresh ardor in the discharge of his duties as a minister of Christ, and awakened brighter hopes for the future.

Respectfully submitted to the Diocesan,

Foster Thayer.

* * * *

In 1850, the Bishop of Vermont, reports: "The Rev. Foster Thayer, who has not been laboring in the Diocese for the last two years, had decided to renounce the ministry, and has been displaced from the ministry accordingly."

CHAPTER V

THE REVEREND ROBERT SHAW HOWLAND
1847-1869

BISHOPS OF NEW YORK:

The Rt. Rev. Benjamin Tredwell Onderdonk, D.D., 1830-1861

The Rt. Rev. Jonathan Mayhew Wainwright, D.D., Provisional Bishop, 1852-1854

The Rt. Rev. Horatio Potter, D.D., Provisional Bishop, 1854-1861, Bishop, 1861-1887

1848. Gold discovered in California at Sutter's Mill.

1853. Perry's trip to Japan, resulting in commercial relations between the United States and Japan.

1855. First Atlantic cable.

1859. Darwin's *Origin of Species* published.

1860. Pony Express begun.

1861-1865. The Civil War.

1867. The United States purchase of Alaska from Russia.

1869. The Suez Canal completed.

1869. First Lambeth Conference of Anglican Bishops.

1869. Completion of the Union Pacific Railroad.

ROBERT SHAW HOWLAND
Rector 1847-1869

Chapter V

THE REVEREND ROBERT SHAW HOWLAND
1847-1869

A Golden Age

It would almost seem that this chapter in the history of Holy Apostles should be devoted to two outstanding men, the rector, Rev. Robert Shaw Howland, and his assistant, Dr. Geer. They, as yokefellows, created the aggressive usefulness of the church in this neighborhood and its spiritual influence beyond its borders. They labored side by side for fifteen years, for at times, during the absence of the rector, his assistant did the actual work of the parish. This fact does not signify that Dr. Howland was not always vitally interested in and keenly alive to the needs and opportunities of the parish. Illness often took the rector away, but because of his sincerity, friendliness, and candor, the parish never lagged. Dr. Howland besides was a man of considerable means, which he lavished on the parish and its work. His family prestige, his own dignity, and his sacrificial concern for his flock kept the congregation ever conscious of his leadership. The Rev. George J. Geer was called as his assistant on October 17, 1852. He lived in the immediate neighborhood at 229 West 27 Street, and so was in close contact with the parish problems and those of its people.

On June 2, 1847, the Rev. Mr. Howland was unanimously called as rector "at a salary of five hundred dollars per annum, until the finances of the parish warranted an increase of the same." He lived on Twenty-third Street, near Ninth Avenue in what was then known as "The Chelsea Cottages."

The Rev. Robert S. Howland, D.D., was born in New York, November 9, 1820, the son of Gardiner G. Howland. His father was a New York merchant of the firm of Howland and Aspinwall, and was an active member of charitable organizations. Robert received his primary education in France and was graduated at St. Paul's College, Long Island, in 1840. He took a partial course at the General Theological Seminary, New York City, but his studies in theology were intermitted for three years. About eight months of this time were spent in Maryland, where he assisted Bishop John B. Kerfoot in organizing St. James' College, and the remainder of the three years he spent in foreign travel, visiting Europe and the Holy Land.

Upon his return from Europe, he completed his course at the seminary and was ordained deacon by Bishop Thomas C. Brownell of Connecticut, at New Haven, on October 27, 1845. A year later, he was ordained to the priesthood at St. Luke's Church, Hudson Street, by Bishop Levi S. Ives of North Carolina. His first ministry was as an assistant to the Rev. Dr. Forbes, Rector of St. Luke's Church. It was from St. Luke's that he was called as rector to the Church of the Holy Apostles. Dr. Howland was thus a man of culture and traveled experience, possessed of a keen mind, great dignity, and spirituality. Columbia University conferred upon him the honorary degree of Doctor of Divinity in 1863. His wife, Mary Woolsey Howland, was well known as a poet.

At the time he accepted the call to the parish, June 2, 1847, the congregation was still worshipping on West Twenty-seventh Street, near Ninth Avenue, while the new church was in course of erection. The outlook was indeed gloomy for the little congregation, for the communicant list had fallen to about twenty persons, funds were almost nil, and there were many financial difficulties ahead. The floating debt had steadily increased since the organization of the parish. Then, too, many members who had so valiantly assisted in the mission Sunday School were no longer connected with the parish; and others had joined in mission endeavors to the north of Chelsea. The enthusiasm of creating a church had now more or less waned, and especially so after the misunderstanding with the first rector. The financial burdens of the infant parish seemed almost too much for the remaining few to bear.

All things considered, the rectorship of the Church of the Holy Apostles, if one were to judge from a purely worldly standpoint, was anything but a desirable position. This can be gathered from the extracts of the letter sent by the Clerk of the Vestry to the Rev. Mr. Howland, informing him of his election:

New York, June 2, 1847.

Reverend and Dear Sir:

At a meeting of the Vestry of the Church of the Holy Apostles, held June 1, 1847, it was unanimously Resolved, That the Rev. Robert S. Howland, be and is hereby called as Rector to this Church.

Resolved, That the salary of the Rector be Five hundred dollars per annum (including the amount ($300) granted by Trinity Church) until the finances of the parish warrant an increase of the same.

I have been requested to inform you that by a resolution of the Vestry the sittings in the Church now in course of erection are to be free to all who may desire to worship God there, an object which will doubtless commend itself to your Christian feelings. The Vestry do not think that they would be acting in good faith toward you did they not state that the finances of the parish are at present, in an embarrassed condition, and they would therefore request you to call upon the Treasurer, Mr. A. R. Cushman, 261 Pearl Street, who will cheerfully give you any information that you may desire.

With sentiments of respect and esteem, I remain Yours, etc.

FRANCIS MANY, Clerk-Vestry.

* * * *

The Rev. Mr. Howland's acceptance soon followed:

July 28, 1847.

Gentlemen:—I accept the Rectorship of the Holy Apostles in this city. In sending this acceptance, I desire to add my thanks for the good opinion of me which your invitation implies. God grant that I may never prove unworthy of confidence.

The cure of souls is a most weighty and responsible charge, and I want therefore to ask your prayers and hearty cooperation — and a consistent recognition of the position—of an ambassador of Christ, "a watchman who must give an account," who is burdened with the responsibility of spiritual things, because they are properly under his direction.

May He who has blessed our efforts to erect the outward edifice, bless also our endeavors of pastor and people to raise a spiritual temple holy and acceptable in the day of the Lord.

I am, gentlemen, now and always, yours in the service of the cross, and in the love of Christ.

R. S. Howland.

o   o   o   o

When the Rev. Mr. Howland accepted the call as rector, he was twenty-seven years old, full of the vigor and strength of early manhood. He brought rare gifts to the small congregation which had undertaken the building of a church. So confident was the vestry that success now would attend their efforts that they closed the church during the summer, a proceeding which was not entirely uncommon in New York at that time. The services were to be resumed after September 1, and the rector was to enter formally upon his duties on Sunday, September 12, 1847.

During the previous April, the vestry had again officially endorsed the idea of a free church. But by November of the same year, these resolutions were revoked, owing largely to the standing committee report. Parts of this report read as follows:

It was estimated that $7,500 was still needed to complete, furnish and provide the church with an organ. Toward this amount subscriptions had been made, and $1,750 realized. Attempts had been made to place another mortgage, but had been unsuccessful. . . . Already three mortgages had been placed; one of $2,000 to Trinity Church, and a second of $4,000 to Mr. Ray and a third of $4,000 to the builders, Messrs. Moses and Hunt,—a total of $10,000. . . .

One individual is willing to lend the sum required, $5,750, but unwilling to do so while the Church remains a Free Church. After reviewing the difficulties of the free-church system, even if they had the means, the vestry very reluctantly gave up the idea. The free-church system had ever been a cherished principle with a majority of its members, and it had been the object of their desires to erect a Free Church where all might worship God on a perfect equality in a worldly point of view.

Toward this end they had labored and toiled; for this they had given up the services of other churches to worship amid rude accommodations; for this their money had been expended, their time and abilities given for the three years, and all were willing to make these sacrifices in the hope of ultimately completing a free church. But the welfare and prosperity of the parish were at stake and so, putting aside personal considerations, and for the sake of completing the church and opening it under favorable auspices, they relinquished the object for which their efforts had so long been given.

. . . Your committee would strenuously object to any part of the Church being especially set apart as free seats, thus making an individual distinction between those who pay and those who do not. We object to the principle of sale of pews, if it could be avoided; but at all events, to the sale of any pews for more than five years, hoping that five years hence the Parish may be relieved from much of its present financial embarrassment.

The committee therefore took upon itself to assign rented pews in the new church to families who belonged to the parish, and to assign seats at reduced rates to such others who attended regularly. A number of pews in different parts of the church were free. Pew rentals were payable semi-annually, in October and April.

Among the list of the first pew-holders were the following: Walter Roome, William Borden, Robert Ray, Alonzo R. Cushman, John Smith, John P. Collord, Francis Many, James B. Glentworth, Walter H. Roome, Mrs. Woodriff, Tunis Bennett, Mrs. Brien, Joseph Nowill, Sr., David Tillotson, John A. King, Jr., J. D. Gill, C. Dixon Varley, M. D., Lewis Many, Orrin Terry, J. D. Ogden, M. D., James Blackhurst, Robert S. Howland, L. B. Terry, Mrs. Ogilby, John F. Fisher, Mrs. Kortwright.

An encouraging note was struck when the church was nearing completion in that the vestry of Trinity Church altered their terms of appropriation so as to give the vestry $2,000 cash, and gave their assurance that they would pay off, if necessary, the then existing mortgage of $4,000 to the builders when it became due in 1850. Mr. Robert Ray also aided by generously relinquishing the interest on the mortgage held by him.

The vestry of Holy Apostles gave up the lot purchased for a rectory, thus saving interest charges.

By January 1, 1848, the church was practically completed, and on Sunday morning, February 21 following, it was used for the first time for public worship. As originally constructed, it was without transepts or the present sanctuary, oblong in shape—its east line coinciding with a line along the edge of the present choir parapet. The organ and choir were in the gallery at the avenue end of the building. The exterior walls were of brick, trimmed with stone, as at present. The spire was built entirely of wood above the present brick work, topped by the cross.

There were several unusual features about this new Protestant Episcopal Church. It antedates the present Trinity and Grace churches, and while they present Gothic forms, characteristic Anglicanism, Holy Apostles bespeaks northern Italy and the slopes of the Alps. Its architectural form is Tuscan, an adaptation of the classic Doric, as are many of the New England Colonial churches; architecturally, therefore, Holy Apostles is often confused with the Colonial. Its spire is surmounted by a cross, not a weather vane. Its heavy, overhanging eaves and its lack of ornamentation about the tower below the spire all denote the Tuscan.

The interior is even more pronounced Tuscan, as illustrated by the groined clerestory windows and the severity of its columns without entablature, and without galleries. The altar of highly polished black marble stood out from the east wall, over which, high up, was placed a circular window. Thus things remained until 1854, when the church was enlarged by adding twenty-five feet eastward. It was still a parallelogram till the transepts were added in 1858. Under the circular window above the altar was placed the picture of the Ascension by the French artist, Thomas Rossiter, then a resident of New York. On either side of the picture were lettered tablets (removed in 1941). On the Gospel side, the tablet read: "The Word was made Flesh."

"And they crucified Him." On the Epistle side were the words: "He lifted up His hands and blessed them." "And was carried up into Heaven."

The fundamental doctrines—The Incarnation, The Crucifixion, His Living Presence to Bless, and His Power in Heaven, which the tablets expressed in words — the painting seeks to suggest. The Ascending Figure of Christ with the print of the nails, the hands uplifted to bless, and the glorified body rising from the earth serve to bring these deep mysteries always before the eyes. At the same time, the figure of our Blessed Lord in the act of benediction, just above the altar, seeks to impress the heart that at the Holy Altar the penitent will find the Presence of Christ to bless and strengthen him.

The sanctuary was raised three steps above the main floor to the altar, and was carpeted in deep red, as were the aisles throughout the church.

Stained glass, designed and executed by Mr. Bolton, of New Rochelle, N. Y., was placed in the windows. In each window, an angel supports scenes in roundels, representing scriptural incidents in the Life of our Blessed Lord and the Acts of the Holy Apostles, with explanatory scriptural texts under each medallion. These form a complete series, their centers in correct burnt sienna, after the coloring of Florentine windows.

EXAMPLES OF INTERIOR AND WINDOWS.

In later years, when the church was twice enlarged, the style and coloring of the original glass was duplicated in the newer parts of the church, so that today there is a harmony of design and coloring in all the windows.

A small organ stood in the rear gallery, built by Hall and Labagh of New York, to accompany a small voluntary choir. No person other than a member of the choir could occupy a seat in the organ gallery during services. The organ contained five Great Stops, three Swell Stops, and one octave in the pedal. It cost $1,200, and was pronounced very sweet in tone.

The church was quite complete at the opening service, and, with its pillars and arches, its clerestory windows, its stained glass, its marble altar, its raised chancel in red plush carpet, presented an unusual churchly appearance. It was then considered very "High Church" among the churches in New York. Besides, Dr. Howland wore a surplice and colored stoles, and was reported as elevating the chalice. The story has persisted that "the students of the Seminary were not urged to attend." In his teaching and practice, Dr. Howland was considered a "Puseyite" or "High Churchman." In one of his sermons he remarked: "I cannot concede the epithet 'Catholic' to the Church of Rome alone, and I cannot but consider it a serious error so to do, inconsistent with sound Protestanism."

At the opening service, February 27, 1848, the rector said Morning Prayer at 10:30 A.M., assisted in the lessons by the Rev. Mr. Houghton and in the Litany by the Rev. Mr. Preston. The Rev. Prof. Wilson of the Seminary said the Ante-Communion, and the Rev. Dr. Berrian read the Epistle. The sermon was preached by the rector. Other services took place on that day at 3 P.M. and at 7:30 P.M. There were to be three services on Sunday throughout the year, the Sunday School still meeting in Twenty-seventh Street at 9:30 A.M. During Lent of the same year, besides the Sunday services, daily week-day services were held at 9 A.M. and at 6:30 P.M., and after Lent one service daily was held at 9 A.M., with prayer and a lecture on Friday evenings at 7:30 P.M.*

The rector and vestry immediately appealed to the Bishop for the consecration of this new and beautiful edifice, although, at the time, there were three mortgages amounting to over $10,000. The Service of Consecration was arranged to take place

---

*"Historical Churches, Other Places of Worship and Religions in New York."—Clyde F. Rehring. Articles published 1941-1943. pp. 25.

on Monday, May 8, 1848, at 10:30 A.M. The Rt. Rev. William H. DeLancey, D.D., Bishop of Western New York, performed the Rite of Consecration. By this time, the interior walls of the Church had been stained to a remarkably chaste stone color, and one of the members of the parish had presented an altar frontal of crimson velvet with a fringe of deep and very rich bullion.

The vestry reports the Church was crowded to overflowing at the time and the service was exceedingly impressive. "The Procession, consisting of the Bishop, many of the Reverend Clergy and Vestrymen of several other churches, and students of the Seminary, formed in the line of march at the residence of John A. King, Jr., Esq., in West 28th Street. The Bishop was supported on either side by the Rev. Dr. Berrian and the Rev. Dr. Taylor and was received at the vestibule of the Church by the Wardens and Vestrymen of the Parish."

The following clergymen took seats in the chancel: The Rev. Drs. Berrian, Taylor, Muhlenberg, Forbes, Haight, Roosevelt Johnson; also, the Reverends L. Carter, Staunton, Carder, Marcus, Eigenbrodt, Parker, and the rector, R. S. Howland.

The following priests occupied seats prepared without the chancel, and knelt at the chancel rails: The Reverends Richard Cox, Southard, Walsh, Fish, D. Diller, Nichols, Walton, Embury, Hart, Van Rensselaer (of Western, N. Y.), Hall (of Maryland), and Washburn (of Mass.).

The Deacons were: The Reverends T. M. Peters, Duffie, Preston, McGee, Weston, and Shackelford (of Pa.).

All the foregoing were habited in surplices. The following clergy, not in surplices, were also present: The Reverends S. M. Haskins, Clapp, Loutrel, and Gordon.

The Instrument of Donation was presented by Mr. John Smith, Senior Warden, and read by the Rev. Mr. Eigenbrodt. The Sentence of Consecration was read by the Rector. Morning Prayer was said by the Rev. Dr. Forbes, assisted by the Rev.

Dr. Haight, who read the lessons. The Ante Communion was read by the Bishop; Dr. Taylor read the Epistle; and Dr. Berrian, the Holy Gospel. The sermon was preached by Rev. William Augustus Muhlenberg, Rector of the Church of the Holy Communion. The Offertory Sentences were read by the Rev. Dr. Johnson. The Holy Communion was administered by the Bishop, assisted by the Rector, Dr. Berrian and the Rev. Dr. Taylor.

The music was sweet and effective. Vhapek's Second Anthem was sung after the sermon, during the offerings of the congregation to the "Building Fund."

On the conclusion of the ceremonies, the Bishop said in part:

> After the embarrassment, under which this Parish has for some time labored, they are now enabled to give to God a structure in every way worthy of His service. God grant that within these sacred walls, many souls may be born anew in the waters of Holy Baptism, and often strengthened with Holy Food from the Altar, and refreshed with Common Prayer; and, edified by the reading and teaching from the Holy Scriptures, may rejoice here on earth, and inherit an eternal reward hereafter.

From this time onward the parish entered upon a period of usefulness and comparative prosperity. Many of the old families on the West Side attended its services, assisted in its music and engaged in its good works. At the first Confirmation in the new church, forty-nine received the "Laying on of Hands" by the Rt. Rev. Wm. R. Whittingham, Bishop of Maryland, who also signed, at this time, the testimonials of Mr. George L. Neide, Candidate for Holy Orders, and Messrs. Spencer, Williams, and Wagner, also candidates and communicants of the parish. The Rev. William Huntingdon had acted as Assistant Minister to the Rector from January, 1849, till April of the same year. He was succeeded by the Rev. William Everett in May of 1849, to supply while the Rector took a much needed rest because of ill health. Mr. Everett was Assistant Minister

from September, 1849, until September, 1851, when he left the
Church to join the Roman Communion.

The following March 30, 1850, the marble font, now in the
church, was presented to the vestry by the ladies of the parish,
who had procured it by subscriptions.

1849 and 1850 were years most trying to the rector and vestry. There
were the mortgages of $10,000 and a floating indebtedness of $2,801.89.
Then there were city improvements to meet, as well as the beautification of
the church yard, trouble in the choir, and a pestilence.

It is, indeed, pleasant to find on the records of the vestry
ample recognition of the thoroughness and zeal with which the
rector and his assistant devoted themselves to their laborious
duties. The congregation, for their part, manifested harmony,
good feeling, and attachment to their ministers. Daily as well
as Sunday services were well attended.

Comment by the Music Committee of the Vestry is interesting:

. . . There was no proficiency or system in the choir that they desired.
With a voluntary choir they realized that they could not enforce rules
without exciting feelings which they wished to avoid; and so they wished
to relinquish all control and oversight of the music, and all interest in its
success, except as individuals. They are aware of this strange censure, but
they wish to place it upon record—that they have done what they could
to enforce the rules of the vestry.

o   o   o   o

The grounds about the church had been filled in by now,
but the yard stood open to the public. It seemed imperative to
enclose the church yard with an iron fence on the street and
avenue sides, but the finances of the parish forbade further
expenditure. At this time, Mr. Robert Ray, realizing this need,
purchased a wooden rail fence, which was a part of the old
fence of the Army-Washington Parade Ground. As for the

floating indebtedness, this was monthly growing larger, and there appeared little prospect of reducing it.*

During the year 1850, thirty-nine communicants were added. There were sixty-three baptisms, twenty marriages, and seventy funerals. Services during the year numberd 498.

Early in 1850, a severe pestilence had caused many deaths in the district in which the church functioned. Not only parishioners, but also others in no way connected with the parish, made many sad demands upon the time and strength of the rector and his assistant. The standing committee of the vestry testify that all such demands were met promptly. In their yearly report, they say they "wish to take this opportunity to bear witness to the devotion of the clergy to their sacred duties in calling upon stricken families at all times, but especially during the period to which reference was made."

During the early summer of 1850, the room rented for the Sunday School on West Twenty-seventh Street was given up, and the school for a short time made use of the church. This arrangement was soon abandoned and the parish remained without a school for more than a year.

A fair was next planned by the ladies of the parish to help liquidate the indebtedness. It was held from December 20 to December 31, 1851, at the Cosmoranda Rosul, corner of Broadway, near Thirteenth Street, ending in January with a concert given at Stuyvesant Institution by graduates of the blind asylum. Unfortunately the labor and expenses were such that little profit was realized from these affairs—a mere $396.47. No similar attempt at fund-raising was made for many years.

In September, 1851, the rector, in consequence of poor health, obtained from the vestry "leave of absence for a year, or longer if his health should require." Dr. Howland sailed for Europe almost immediately afterwards. Previous to the rector's

*See Appendix K, Item 3.

departure, the Rev. Mr. Everett had severed his connection with the parish to join the Roman Communion. This step was deeply regretted by the congregation to whom Mr. Everett had endeared himself by his devotion to his duties and simplicity of life. But, reports the rector:

We are happy to say that not a single person of the parish followed his example. Although separated from us for some time before his secession, yet that event has had an unfavorable bearing upon the prospects of any in the parish following; as it did when the Rev. Mr. Huntingdon seceded, or upon the secession of the Rev. Mr. White, who had often officiated in our Church. While we have been severely tried by these successive departures from the true faith of the Church to the errors and corruptions of Rome, we cannot be too thankful to God for having preserved the laity unshaken in their attachment to that branch of the Catholic Church with which we are connected.

The rector's salary during his absence was to be used for clerical supply, the Rev. Christopher B. Wyatt supplying as "locum tenans," with the assistance during the following year of the Rev. Prof. Mahan. Hearing of the unsuccessful attempt of the ladies to raise funds, Dr. Howland wrote from Madeira of his willingness to give $1,000 toward the bonded indebtedness of the parish, provided the congregation subscribed a sum sufficient to pay off certain floating debts—namely, $1,700. The congregation responded nobly to this generous offer of the rector by raising more than the amount required.

Dr. Howland's letter to Francis Many read in part:

Madeira, January 3, 1852.

I am anxious to hear again to know the results of the Fair. I sincerely trust that the event was a success. An offer will be made to get rid of the Floating Debt. I shall gladly do my share, and hereby authorize you to make an offer in my name. If money is subscribed and collected to pay off the floating debt, so that by the tenth of May, all floating debts and salaries are paid (excluding that bill of Pollack & Cummings ($1,000) and those bonds due me, neither of which I suppose will ever be claimed); and this while still leaving the Treasurer with funds in hand or pew rents available to pay the July interest and the next quarters of the choir salary—if in other words the parish is entirely cleared from all debts but the mortgages, and placed in funds to meet the coming expenses, I will give a Thousand

Dollars toward the amount. I make my offer, however, conditional on the bona fide release of the Church from all its past petty embarrassments, and must withdraw it if on the tenth of May the money is not collected.

I think, however, with this lift there will be no difficulty—there certainly ought not to be any. I will only add that it gives me great pleasure to have this opportunity of assuring the Parish that my interest is undiminished.

Truly yours in Christ and in the Church,

R. S. HOWLAND.

The connection of the Rev. Mr. Wyatt with Holy Apostles dissolved with the return of the rector, October 1, 1852. The rector's salary upon his return was raised to $1,000 per annum. On the seventeenth of the same month, the Rev. George Jarvis Geer was called as Assistant Minister, with the understanding between the rector and vestry that the salary of the former should be appropriated to the support of the assistant.

Soon thereafter, the provisional Bishop, the Rt. Rev. Jonathan Mayhew Wainwright, who had been consecrated on November 10, 1852, made his first visit to the parish, February 20, 1853, and confirmed a class of twenty-three candidates prepared by the new assistant.

*   *   *   *

Since the founding of the parish a dozen years before, great changes had taken place in the neighborhood, and especially north and west as far as Central Park, which was named by an act of legislature in 1853. "The land now constituting Central Park," wrote an observer at this time, "was occupied by shanties, bone-boiling establishments, piggeries and pools of offensive stagnant water which rendered the neighborhood anything but park-like."

This description helps one to appreciate the vast amount of work, money, and artistic planning necessary to make the park the place of beauty and attractiveness that it is today.

It was already a straggling suburb when purchased by the city. . . . Upon it has been spent at least thirty million dollars since 1857.

when 300 dwellings were removed or demolished. A considerable number of the inhabitants were engaged in occupations which were a nuisance in the eyes of the law and forbidden to be carried on or near the growing city. It was freely predicted by opponents of the park that it would prove a white elephant on the hands of the city; never could be made into a decent-looking park, and would prove an unnecessary extravagance to the city.*

But Central Park was destined to play a more and more important part in metropolitan life and in attracting affluent people to its neighborhood. The paving of Fifth Avenue up to the park was completed in 1863. Previous to this, especially in wet weather, the approaches had been extremely bad. The paving of the avenue induced wealthy residents from the lower West and East Sides of the city to move uptown and toward the center of the island, and as time went on this trend became increasingly noticeable.

Other elements of growth and civic improvement came into play. Railroads, docks, and the "El" line on the West Side became dominant in shaping the life and prosperity of this parish. On the other hand, fashionable St. John's Chapel of Trinity Parish was adversely affected when the Hudson River Railroad (consolidated with the New York Central System in 1863-4 by Commodore Vanderbilt) placed its terminal at Thirtieth Street near Tenth Avenue and finally extended the line down along the West Side to St. John's Park. These variable factors were well understood by the vestry of Holy Apostles during Dr. Howland's rectorship, when they proposed that an endowment fund be started for the parish.

The population at this time (1852), north of the church to Central Park, was estimated at forty thousand, but was scattered over a large area. The people lived in wooden buildings of two or three stories. They were mainly of English and Protes-

*"Cradle Days of New York 1609-1825"—Hugh Macatamney—pp. 222.

tant Irish extraction. The district was partly served by a horse-car line along Eighth Avenue, completed in 1851.

Realizing the needs of this laboring class and the missionary character of the district, the Rev. James Cole Tracey, a young, devoted, and consecrated minister, began religious services in February, 1853, in a schoolhouse for the children of the locality. This mission was located at Fifty-first Street (beyond which the city had extended few improvements), just west of Eighth Avenue. Mr. Tracey called it St. Timothy's Mission, and at that time it was the only Episcopal mission north of the Church of the Holy Apostles, west of Seventh Avenue. In a very short time Mr. Tracey became the first rector of this church. His zeal and devotion in building the mission into a parish were such that he developed rapid consumption and died, June 6, 1855. For a time it looked as if this work would fail and his life had been spent in vain.

Bishop Horatio Potter in 1855, in his address to the Diocesan Convention, refers thus to the Rev. Mr. Tracey:

> Of the Rev. Mr. Tracey, so young, yet so able, so modest, so earnest and devout, so full of zeal and high principle in his endeavors to organize and build up a new parish, I need say that many an eye grew moist at the tidings of his departure, yet it was only those who knew him intimately that knew all his worth and all the promise of his character.

The shadow over St. Timothy's congregation was lifted by the rector of the Church of the Holy Apostles. He had watched with interest the beginnings of this work, and so now came to the rescue, aided by the valuable and untiring assistance of the Rev. Mr. Geer. A mutually satisfactory arrangement was entered into by which the assistant minister of this church would render whatever shepherding care to St. Timothy's congregation his other duties would allow. The Rev. Mr. Geer continued in these duties until April 30, 1866, when St. Timothy's Church had acquired enough strength to be able to call Mr. Geer as its rector, discontinuing the connection between the two parishes.

Meanwhile, Holy Apostles maintained a steady growth, as may be seen from the Annual Report of the Standing Committee of the Vestry, March 25, 1853:

> We are informed that all the pews but twelve are rented, and six are reserved for the poor of the parish. The church is becoming too small, and so a Sub-Committee was appointed to call upon Mr. Le Fevre, the architect, for information in respect to the advisability of extending the church edifice.

Before this extension was begun the following year, considerably more flagstones were laid in front of the church, the grounds were leveled off, and trees and shrubbery were planted. At this time, Dr. Howland purchased a church plot for $100 in the new St. Michael's Churchyard, Newtown, L. I., now St. Michael's Cemetery, Astoria.* The lot was forty feet by forty feet, and was purchased for the use of the parish for burials. Ten years later, August 15, 1863, the rector purchased a similar adjoining plot of the same size. Since the original purchase, more than one hundred and thirty bodies have been buried —many of them of little children. Surely that ground is "God's Acre."

The matter of the enlargement of the church was now seriously taken in hand. The architect reported that this twenty-five foot extension would give thirty-six additional pews, enough to satisfy the pressing demand for more space. An important consideration was that the yearly income of the church would be augmented by $1,350. There was also the fear that unless the church was enlarged, the population residing in this neighborhood and wishing to attach themselves to this parish might go elsewhere. These considerations induced the rector and the vestry to make the venture.

A meeting of the congregation was called by the rector for Tuesday evening, April 18, 1854, to consider this question. The rector presided and Mr. A. R. Cushman was appointed secre-

---

*See Appendix J.

tary. The progress thus far made was explained and (it was stated) that $4,000 had already been subscribed for the enlargement and that $6,000 was needed. Early in July the enlargement was commenced and the church reopened for services on Sunday, October 15, 1854. The total cost of the enlargement was $7,204—exceeding the estimates by $1,200.

The alterations consisted of extending the main building twenty-five feet to the east on a lot given by Mr. John A. King, Jr. This lot had formerly been earmarked by the church for a rectory. The design and furnishings remained unchanged, except that the small round window over the altar was eliminated. The sedilia (seats for the clergy) were placed in an enlarged chancel, and the robing room was enlarged, making it twelve by fifteen feet—one story high—with a fireplace. The vestry now used this room for vestry meetings, instead of gathering as formerly in a room over the vestibule, north of the organ gallery.

The enlargement called for other repairs to the church edifice. The exterior woodwork was repainted, with necessary scaffolding, and the entire spire was repainted and sanded. The roof was slated by Mr. John Brodie at a cost of $632. Mr. Clarke gilded the moulding of the picture over the altar. The firm of Sharp and Steel furnished four stained glass windows to correspond to those designed by Mr. Bolton. New gas fixtures, new pews, and a new carpet were purchased.

The rector's salary was increased to $1,500 per annum and the sexton was authorized to hire a helper to clean the church. An appeal was made to Trinity for a gift of $4,000, but this was unsuccessful.

At the vestry meeting, held on March 24, 1856, the Standing Committee observed that the "constant increase of our indebtedness is a source of much anxiety to the vestry, and in order to stop it a few individuals pledged themselves for $500, providing the annual financing should be raised by the offerings to meet the annual budget."*

On April 1, 1857, the vestry complained in these terms:

"Receipts did not meet . . . expenditures . . . every year adds more to the floating debt. . . . And notice that although the parish is favored with the services of two much esteemed clergy, only one receives compensation, the rector having for a long time generously appropriated his entire salary to the Assistant Minister."

The vestry also adds in a letter:

Three ways remain by which the deficiency may be met. First, by the increase of pew rentals, but this is a work of time. . . .
Secondly, by subscriptions, but this throws the burden upon a few.
Lastly, by the present course, that of quarterly collections, where all may contribute according to their ability. In May, 1857, the vestry recommended bonds to be issued, not to exceed $8,000 in all. Many of these were sold to the members.

Through the special collection made every three months and the selling of bonds, the church was able to purchase in 1858 the leasehold on a building in West Twenty-ninth Street —formerly used by the "23rd Street Baptist Church"—for $2,500. The lease had eleven years to run.

At first this building was used for the Sunday School, which now numbered over four hundred pupils and forty teachers, but which had held no sessions on Sunday mornings for the past two years. Afterward this same building was used as a mission chapel, under the name of "The Chapel of the Free Gospel."

By 1857, the enlargement debt had been reduced to $3,364, and early in 1858, the architect, Mr. R. Upjohn, was approached for plans to add transepts to the Church. The vestry accepted the plans at an estimated cost of $5,100. An appeal was made to Trinity Church to allow the vestry of the Holy

---

*See Appendix K, Item 4.

Apostles to give a mortgage of $10,000 to take precedence over their mortgage given at the time of the first building.

New York, March 5, 1858.

To the Vestry of Trinity Church
Gent:

The undersigned have been directed by the vestry of the Church of the Holy Apostles to apply to your honorable body for your consent to allow a mortgage for ten thousand dollars to take precedence of the one now held by you upon this church and grounds for six thousand dollars..

It is the desire of the vestry to enlarge their church at an estimated expense of ten thousand dollars which sum they can raise upon a first mortgage for five years and interest upon which for that time will be paid by a few members of the parish who have pledged themselves for this object. The present indebtedness of our parish is less than $8,000 and the proposed enlargement will double the number of sittings.

The undersigned trust that this application will meet with your favorable consideration as it will enable us to enlarge and strengthen our parish without any outlay on our part.

Resp'y yours,

WALTER ROOME
SAMUEL NEWBY   } Stand'g Comm.
FRANCIS MANY

There was no favorable response from Trinity. And finally, all the money needed for the second enlargement of north and south transepts was given by Dr. Howland—$8,900. By this addition, the Church was to reach its final development as a churchly building. The enlargement was to add sixty additional pews, with 240 sittings, and the church would be able to seat over 830 persons. While these alterations were in progress, the services were held in the Sunday School building in West Twenty-ninth Street, between Eighth and Ninth Avenues, where pews corresponding as nearly as possible to those in the church were assigned to the pew-holders.

The Church was closed for this final alteration on July 1. Chapin & Daymond did the masonry and carpentry work. The two rose windows and the other transept windows, as well as the clerestory windows, were finished by Sharp & Steel, which firm also altered other windows to harmonize in color and design. During the summer months an iron fence, with stone foundation, was built around the entire church property on the avenue and street sides, the work being done by M. A. Myers for the sum of $508. The addition of the transepts changed the whole interior appearance of the church, giving it a spaciousness and a dignity hardly excelled in the city up to that time, and even today not without charm and grandeur.

The Church was reopened Sunday, November 14, 1858, at 10:30 A.M. with an appropriate service of rededication by the Provisional Bishop, the Rt. Rev. Horatio Potter, D.D., who preached the sermon. The music was congregational throughout, with the exception of the "Te Deum" and the "Benedictus," which were rendered by Dr. R. F. Halstead, who presided at the organ. The Church was filled to overflowing as the Bishop and a large group of clergy entered in procession and took their places in the sanctuary and chancel. Two Canadian clergy assisted in the services—the Rev. Mr. Rollit, of the Diocese of Montreal, and the Rev. Mr. Burrage, of the Diocese of Quebec. The Rev. Dr. Howland and the Rev. Mr. Geer walked together at the end of the procession, before the Bishop.

Morning Prayer, to the creed, was said by Dr. Howland; the Litany and Prayers were read by the Rev. Dr. Van Kleeck; the lessons were read by the Rev. Mr. Ludlum and the Rev. Mr. Marshall. The Psalms and the lessons were from the Consecration Office. At the conclusion of Morning Prayer, a portion of the 86th Psalm was announced by Mr. Geer and sung by the choir and congregation. The Bishop then began the Ante-Communion, the Epistle being read by the Rev. Mr. Burrage and the Holy Gospel by the Rev. Mr. Rollit. The Rector made some announcements, among which he mentioned that the Offerings would be in behalf of the poor of the parish; and that, between two and nine o'clock, on the following Friday, the new pews of the enlarged church would be rented.

Bishop Potter, before preaching his sermon, heartily congratulated the congregation upon the event of the rededication of their church to the worship of Almighty God, after it had been enlarged so as to be more adequate to the demands created by the ministrations of their faithful pastors. The Bishop gave a very practical and timely discourse on the performance of outward religious duties, expressions of our Christian faith.

Hundreds made their communions, at which several of the

visiting clergy assisted. The Bishop closed the services with appropriate prayers from the Consecration Office and pronounced the Benediction.

In the afternoon at 3:30 there was another service at which the Rt. Rev. Henry John Whitehouse, D.D., Bishop of Illinois, preached, taking as his text Nehemiah II, part of the twentieth verse: "Then answered I them, The God of heaven, He will prosper us; therefore we His servants will arise and build."

In the evening of the same day at 7:30, a third service was held, at which the Rev. Dr. Muhlenberg, Rector of the Church of the Holy Communion, preached by request his sermon on "Congregational Music." Again the church was well filled. This was a "red-letter" day in the history of the church.*

At this time the clergy began to notice that they were rendering services to three times as many persons outside the parish as to those who were intimately connected with the parish church. Their ministerial acts showed in 1858 that while they had had twenty-nine baptisms of those whose families were connected with the parish, there had been seventy baptisms of those not definitely connected; of the funerals, forty-two in number, thirty were outside the parish; of the 250 Sunday School pupils, 200 were only loosely connected and were infrequent in attendance. In other words, they began to see that to the north and west of the parish, the neighborhood was destined to be filled with homes of the poor.

In the twenty years between 1841 and 1860, the total immigration into the United States was almost four and one-half millions. Some of the immigrants had made their homes north of Chelsea. During this time, immigrants represented 30 per cent of the total net increase in the nation's population and about 80 per cent came from Ireland, England, and Germany. Thousands of them, at least for a time, found homes on Manhattan Island. In fact, the mounting immigration from the

---

*See Appendix K, Item 5, for statistics bearing on this period.

northern countries of Europe during these two decades is noticeable in the rate of growth of the Episcopal Church in New
York. The rector and his assistant became conscious of the fact
that many of these immigrants (both church and non-con-
formist Englishmen) were not attending any services and were
not at home in a pew-holding church, such as Holy Apostles
had become. Dear to the hearts of both ministers was a "church
of all the people," in all conditions of life, but, as we have seen,
this ideal for Holy Apostles had to be given up. Financial
necessity had blacked out that dream. The situation pointed up
the fact that those who attend a given church give it a com-
plexion and character. Still, the realization that many of the
poorer classes in this neighborhood were not vitally connected
with the parish led Dr. Howland to attempt a Mission Chapel,
to be located in the building on West Twenty-ninth Street,
which the parish had acquired solely to house the Sunday School.

o   o   o   o

THE CHAPEL OF THE FREE GOSPEL

A free Episcopal Mission called "The Chapel of the Free
Gospel" was therefore established as a "poor man's church,"
where the poor man and his children might feel more at home
than in a church with rented pews. British and Irish Protestants
were used to free churches, which were mainly supported by
the government or endowments. On coming to America and
finding "class-churches," they had given up their church-going
habits. They therefore made themselves known only when a
birth, a marriage, or a death revived their sacred associations
and they felt induced to seek a Divine blessing upon themselves
or their loved ones in connection with the services of Christ's
ministers.

The services at the Chapel were under the direct care of the

Rev. George L. Neide, who took up his residence at 237 West Thirty-sixth Street with the title of Missioner. Plans were immediately made by the reverend clergy of the parish for a canvass of the whole neighborhood. In four months, in the heat of summer (the most unfavorable season for collecting a congregation), the Missionary and his lay assistants made over eighteen hundred visits, and eighty families and fifty-seven communicants came under his pastoral care. The first baptism in the chapel was on June 19, 1859, of Catherine Boyce, born in Manchester, England. During 1860-61, eighty-eight children were brought for baptism. The total number of baptisms during the chapel's work was 357, and the greatest number of communicants was about 250. The venture of the "Chapel of the Free Gospel" was a success.

On September 29, 1859, Bishop Horatio Potter made mention of this outstanding "mission to the poor" of our city. There were at that time only three other similar mission chapels in the Episcopal Church in the city—those connected with St. George's Church, Christ Church, and Trinity Parish.

To supply the financial needs of this work, the members of the Ladies' Sewing Association, begun in 1847, formed a "Woman's Missionary Association of the Church of the Holy Apostles" (1859) with two objectives: to provide for the expenses incurred in repairing the chapel and for missionary work in this neighborhood. That was thirteen years before the organization of the Woman's Auxiliary of the National Church in 1872. Each member of the parish—man, woman, and child—was asked to contribute a monthly offering. It was called "the mite," and was to be given willingly to Christ for this particular mission work of the parish.

Monthly mites were to be sent to the rector, to the Rev. Geo. J. Geer, to the Rev. Geo. L. Neide, and to Messrs. J. F. Seymour, J. B. Glentworth, W N. Hawkins, D. B. Whitlock, Orrin Terry, A. T. Colt, Wm. S. Town, Wm. H. Wells, John

T. Durkin, Edward Carter, Walter Roome, John Smith, Francis Many, Floyd Bailey, Robt. W. Nesbit, and Wm. Runk. Mr. James B. Glentworth, living at 333 West Twenty-third Street, who was much interested in the chapel work, offered a King James Bible, which is still in possession of the parish.

During the winter months of 1860, the rector, on leave of absence for a year, sent over from Paris on the good steamship "Vanderbilt" more than three hundred gifts to the children of the Sunday School. With these special gifts, Dr. Howland sent the children a letter dated December 4, 1859, which was read at the Christmas Festival by the Rev. Mr. Geer, who had just been made Associate Rector of the parish. The Christmas celebration at the Chapel was made even more joyous by the fact that a new organ had just been purchased for the Mission at a cost of $500, and used for the first time during the Christmas celebration. On the following New Year's Day, a further gift was made to the Chapel of a Communion Service, still in possession of the parish. The Rev. Mr. Neide was also remembered handsomely. Besides all this, to the surprise of the Rev. Mr. Geer, a purse of $200 in gold was placed in his hands on Christmas Day as a personal gift. This was not the first time that the Associate Rector had thus been surprised by his generous hearted people. Meanwhile, the annual subscription of nearly $2,000 for the City Mission Society was made, and the Ladies' Society, who met weekly with the Dorcas Society, were busily engaged in their work of providing garments and sewing for the poor women of the neighborhood.

However, in a few years, on account of the changes in the district, it became quite apparent that the Mission Chapel was situated too near the Mother Church and would therefore never become self-supporting. Efforts to locate the chapel and its congregation at some other point were made midway between the churches of the Holy Apostles and St. Timothy's Church in Fifty-fourth Street, but this plan proved impracticable. The vestry finally sold the property in 1866. Thus came to an end the venture of the parish in maintaining a Mission Chapel.*

The Civil War also supervened, and the neighborhood to the north began to show symptoms of a more settled and varied population. Just before the war, four ministers were connected with the Church of the Holy Apostles and its ministrations— the Rector, the Rev. Robert Shaw Howland, D.D.; the Co-Rector, the Rev. George J. Geer; the Missionary, the Rev. George L. Neide; and the Rev. Richard Clarence Hall, Assistant at St. Timothy's Church until 1860, when the Rev. William Tatlock became assistant at St. Timothy's.

At the vestry meeting on September 20, 1859, it was voted to grant the rector a year's leave of absence on account of the delicate state of Mrs. Howland's health. They sailed for Europe in November. During the rector's absence the Rev. Mr. Geer, with but little assistance, continued the services in every respect as before, at the same time keeping the oversight of St. Timothy's. On October 2, 1860, the rector's leave of absence was further extended till the spring of 1861.

Dr. Howland's return from Europe in the spring of 1861 found the parochial finances in an embarrassing condition, and he immediately relinquished $1,000 of his salary, trusting that the difficulties of the parish would be only temporary. The following Easter the floating debt was $9,060. It was noted that there had been a decrease of $463 in pew rents, and Trinity Church had withdrawn one-half of its annual gift of $300.

o   o   o   o

---

*While the Sunday School of Holy Apostles numbered about 500 pupils, nearly 500 more had been enrolled at the Mission and St. Timothy's Sunday School.

CIVIL WAR PERIOD—1861-1865

The Civil War was having its repercussions in church life, with its consequent financial disturbances. Although the Episcopal Church, probably because of its Episcopal Order of Church Government, was not divided into northern and southern groups, as a number of Protestant denominations were divided, men's hearts and minds were sorely tried and occupied by the distress of the times. This was reflected in church giving. The Church of the Holy Apostles was feeling this strain. Near the end of 1862, the total debt of the parish, after the expected income of the year was considered, would be something like $13,099. Meetings were called to meet this situation and to raise pew rents. The vestry at this time were Wardens John Smith and Walter Roome and Vestrymen C. Dixon Varley, M.D., Francis Many, John P. Collord, Samuel Newby, Anson T. Colt, Chauncey W. Winans, James B. Glentworth, and John F. Seymour.

It was noted that by August, 1862, enlistments were quite vigorous in New York City and in other parts of the State. City corporations and the State Government were acting with the greatest liberality toward enlisted men. The State offered a "bounty" of $50 for each volunteer, and equally large or even larger sums were offered by corporations, "the inducement being all-sufficient to those whose hearts were in the matter."

The vestry gave its consent to the Senior Warden, Mr. John Smith, to display the flag on the church spire on April 29, 1861, and to continue to fly the flag during the continuance of the war. Many men connected with the parish enlisted, but mention is made only of those who died with the exception of one, Samuel Malloy, who embarked as a member of the 12th Regiment of Volunteers for the defense of the Capitol. Before the end of the war, sixteen from this parish had given their lives for the Union.*

o   o   o   o

The abnormal conditions during the Civil War, with its heavy loss of life, interrupted both the rate of increase in the population of New York and the number of immigrants coming into the country. The Church of the Holy Apostles, however, maintained itself and its chapel, and even made a fair degree of progress. The debt had been reduced to $9,818. The Sunday School of the parish had forty-nine teachers and 495 scholars, with an average attendance of 325. Mr. Daniel B. Whitlock, who continued his work in the Sunday School for over twenty-five years, succeeded Mr. Greene as Superintendent.

The following year was a banner year in the parish, for with determined and persistent effort the indebtedness (except the mortgage to Trinity) was removed. A meeting of the parishioners was held at the home of Mr. Roome, 272 West Twentieth Street, at which fourteen were present. It was voted to try to raise $10,000 during the year, especially in view of the liberal offer from the rector and Mrs. Howland to give $1,000. At the meeting those present pledged $6,900 and by Easter Sunday, 1864, the object was accomplished.

For the first time in the twenty years of its existence, the parish was relieved from pressing debts, and, as the standing committee said, "A glorious Easter Festival was kept within the walls of our beloved church, now for the first time entirely consecrated to the worship of God."

It is difficult in our time to imagine the joy which must have been felt by those who for two decades had labored and hoped and prayed for this result. Great, indeed, must have been their satisfaction and deep their gratitude to Almighty God that

*See Appendix B for list of names.

COMMUNION SETT, 1845

CHURCH INTERIOR WITH WINDOWS, 1858

FONT AND GENERAL DESIGNS OF WINDOWS

He had at last given them their desire. In November of this same memorable year, Dr. Howland preached the anniversary sermon.*

At this time the committee, meeting together for the removal of the current indebtedness, also brought to the attention of the vestry the tendency of parishioners to remove to the upper part of the city and the probability that those now most able to contribute might in the not distant future no longer be attached to the parish. They reported the need of an Endowment Fund to be know as THE HOWLAND ENDOWMENT FUND. However, the endowment of the parish was not finally undertaken until 1894.

The stress of the long war period only helped to emphasize the fact, already noted, that the "Chapel of the Free Gospel" was located too near the Mother Church. Besides, there was the ensuing laxity that comes during the period of every war, and this made the upkeep of the chapel harder. Some of these free missions did ultimately grow into churches, but as time went on, the feeling grew that chapels for the poor were an abomination second only to churches for the rich. So, finding that the chapel no longer served a useful purpose, the rector and the vestry of Holy Apostles sold the property in 1866 for $4,000, and the Rev. Mr. Neide resigned to become the rector of Christ Church, Duanesburg, N. Y.

Immediately after the sale, the lot and dwelling at 296 Ninth Avenue, adjoining the church property to the south, were purchased for $10,000, and the money realized from the sale of the chapel was expended in part payment for this new property. It was the intention of the vestry to build on this newly acquired property a Mission House for daily religious services. Finally, the more general idea was evolved that the building could be used effectively for societies and especially to house the Sunday School. Thus the Church of the Holy Apostles

---

*See Appendix C.

became one of the first parishes in New York to have a Parish House.

The erection of this building on the rear portion of this lot, together with a part of a Twenty-seventh Street lot, bought for $1,000, was begun in October, 1866, and completed by the following March, 1867. This Mission Building stands today virtually the same as when it was built in 1866-7. It has given service during the years.

After the war, the parish introduced for the first time a boy choir. This made extensive alterations necessary in the arrangement of the chancel. These alterations were carried out by the firm of Chapin & Daymond, and at the same time a small organ, with a suitable organ chamber, was built to the right of the sanctuary. Thus for a time there were two separate organs in the church. Both were sold in the following year, and a new organ placed in the chancel.

In 1867 Mr. John Smith, who for over twenty-two years had served as Senior Warden, and Mr. Walter Roome, who for twenty years had been Junior Warden as well as Clerk of the Vestry, asked to be relieved from further service in the vestry.

The new vestry in 1867 included Wardens Samuel Newby and John F. Seymour and Vestrymen Christopher D. Varley, M.D., John P. Collord, Francis Many, Daniel B. Whitlock, William Borden, George Moore, Charles Hall, and Henry Griswold, M.D.

Another great loss was sustained by the parish in 1867 when the co-rector, Dr. Geer, beloved among the members of the congregation for his faithful and efficient work, resigned on April 30 to become the full-time rector of St. Timothy's Church. Dr. Geer had been chosen as rector of St. Timothy's in 1857, but continued in active service at the Church of the Holy Apostles until 1867.

The closing of the chapel on West Twenty-ninth Street, the progress of religious work in the northern parts of the city, Chelsea's loss of attractiveness for homes of the rich, and the paving of Fifth Avenue to Central Park, which made it "The Avenue"—these were among the many changes that effected the parish.

During its first twenty-two years (1844-1866) many well-known men of the Episcopal clergy preached at the Holy Apostles. Among these were Doctors Turner, Johnston, Berrian, Vinton, Schroder, Haight, Higby, Tuttle, Peters, Tatlock, Houghton, Muhlenberg, Hart, and Hopkins. Bishop Onderdonk had named this as his Parish Church.

Throughout these years, too, Holy Apostles was one of the few churches in the city that possessed a large marble altar, a religious painting over its altar, stained glass windows with scenes of religious subjects in them, and a lofty spire topped by a cross. The clergy wore cassocks, surplices, and colored stoles, and took the eastward position at the creed. During the early part of 1863, the Holy Communion was preceded by the Litany, with Morning Prayer said at an earlier hour. Undoubtedly, the general aspect of its services was one of dignity, reverence, and devotion.

For a time, after the resignation of Dr. Geer, the Rev. Thomas Seibt assisted in the parish, together with the Rev. Thomas K. Conrad. The latter had been rector of St. John's Church (1863-1866), Clifton, Staten Island; but for a short period, while he was non-parochial (1866), he had held services at the chapel of Rutgers Female Institute, then located at Fifth Avenue and Forty-second Street. Dr. Howland and Dr. Conrad at this time lived near each other in London Terrace. Dr. Howland had always delighted in new, aggressive mission work, and became interested in the new prospects at Rutgers Institute. From January of 1867, Dr. Howland, with the assistance of Dr. Conrad, shepherded this venture, which soon became an organized congregation, and in 1868 took the title of the "Church of the Heavenly Rest."

The services at the chapel became so well attended and the congregation so enthusiastic that lots were soon acquired on

Fifth Avenue for a future church. At the chapel, seats were free, although regular worshippers had their seats reserved for them until the hour of service. The inauguration of these free services in that part of the city and at that time was most attractive. Soon a free church was formed and incorporated into the Diocese.

It was not long before plans for a church were prepared and excavations made for a building to house this growing work. By October, 1868, the chancel part of a church was built and opened for Divine services. The Church of the Heavenly Rest then consisted of a "large antiphonal choir," similar to the one finally built. It was announced that "the parish will be supported by voluntary contributions, although the usual 'Free Church' system will be so far modified that regular worshippers will have assigned to them pews." During the summer of 1869 the church was closed to permit decorating the interior of the chancel, and in the fall of the same year, the Rev. Dr. Conrad, the assistant minister, held the re-opening services.

The new parish had been placed under the rectorship of Dr. Howland, and for more than eighteen months, Dr. Howland was rector both of the Church of the Holy Apostles and of the newly built Church of the Heavenly Rest. His assistant, Dr. Conrad, gave most of his time to the latter.

So rapid was the growth of this new parish that by 1869 the building was enlarged so as to have a seating capacity of seven hundred people. At the first anniversary service, January 22, 1870, Dr. Howland, the rector said:

> It will be remembered that this is not an old parish transplanted from another site, but as it were, a creation out of nothing. In nine and one-half months during which services have been held, eighty-six pews have been assigned, and $12,000 given by the congregation beyond its current expenses.

On November 16, 1869, Dr. Robert S. Howland tendered his resignation as Rector of the Church of the Holy Apostles in order to give his full time as Rector of the Church of the Heavenly Rest, which office he held until his death in 1887. On March 23 of the same year, the vestry of the Church of the Holy Apostles, through the advice of Dr. Howland, had called as an assistant the Rev. John P. Lundy, who succeeded him as rector of the parish on November 30, 1869.

The vestry reluctantly accepted Dr. Howland's resignation at their meeting on November 30, when the assistant was called to the rectorship. The following resolution was also adopted:

Whereas, Rev. Dr. Howland, for reasons which to him seem to render it desirable, has tendered his resignation to this vestry and has urged the acceptance of the same; therefore be it Resolved, That while we deeply regret the apparent necessity for this step on his part, we desire to acquiesce in what he thinks to be best and right under the circumstances, and therefore we accept the resignation of Rev. Robert S. Howland, D.D., from the position of Rector of this Parish. At the same time we desire to express to him our unanimous and hearty appreciation of the inestimable services rendered by him to the Parish in the long period during which he has been connected with it, and we assure him of the warm and unalterable love which we individually entertain for him personally, and we trust that this event may never work an actual separation between him and this Parish, so eminently under God the work of his hands, as we know it cannot separate him from the many hearts which hold him so dear.

Dr. Howland was then made Rector Emeritus in appreciation of the many services he had rendered to the parish as its rector.

Dr. Lundy preached his first sermon as rector on December 19, 1869. Dr. Howland, who was present, spoke a few words of gratitude to the congregation for their long continued kindness toward himself, and said that nothing could sever his "spiritual connection with the congregation and its work." He felt confident that "the Church, which had already learned to respect and admire his successor, would soon be bound to him by love and Christian affection."

Dr. Howland became the first and only Rector of the

Church of the Heavenly Rest until the time of his death. He died at Morristown, N. J., of an attack of paralysis, February 1, 1887. The funeral was held at the Church of the Heavenly Rest, New York, on Friday, February 4, 1887. The body arrived at the Church under the escort of the Rev. D. Parker Morgan, assistant minister of the parish; Mr. William Leavitt, a nephew of the deceased; and Mr. A. Davidson, the sexton of the Church.

The Church was crowded with friends and parishioners, many having come from the parish of the Holy Apostles to mourn the loss of their former rector and beloved counsellor. The hymns, "Hark, Hark, My Soul," and "Abide with Me," favorites of the deceased priest, were sung during the service.

At the following Diocesan Convention the same year, in his address to the Convention, Bishop Henry C. Potter said:

Dr. Howland has gone, after a long period of previous infirmity, leaving behind him the memory of his faithful work in earlier years, on the West side, in connection with the founding of the Church of the Holy Apostles and in his later struggles and sacrifices in connection with the building of the Church of the Heavenly Rest. His brethren will gratefully remember his kindly welcome and his willingness to bear his part in every good word and work.

GEORGE JARVIS GEER
Co-Rector—1858-1866

GEORGE JARVIS GEER MEMORIAL PLAQUE
In Church of the Holy Apostles

Chapter VI

THE REVEREND GEORGE JARVIS GEER—1852-1866

End of an Era

The Rev. George Jarvis Geer was born in Waterbury, Conn., on February 24, 1821. In his youth he studied at Cheshire Academy. He was graduated from Trinity College, Hartford, Conn. in 1842, and from the General Theological Seminary, New York, in 1845. Soon after being ordained to the ministry, he was called as rector of Christ Church, Ballston Spa, N. Y., where he remained for seven years doing effective work. On October 17, 1852, the Rev. Mr. Geer was called as assistant minister by the vestry at the suggestion of Dr. Howland, and in 1858 was made co-rector of the Church of the Holy Apostles.

Dr. Howland was so intent upon having the Rev. Mr. Geer associated with him that to relieve the parish of the additional financial burden of having to pay an extra salary, he volunteered to sacrifice his own remuneration. For fifteen years they were true yokefellows and ideal pastors of the parish. No wonder the church flourished under their pastoral care, for they supplemented one another in countless ways. The Rev. Mr. Geer lived at 229 West Twenty-seventh Street during his ministry here, and so was in intimate contact with the people of the neighborhood and the church's activities.

The acceptance letter of the Rev. Mr. Geer follows:

Ballston Spa, Saratoga Co., N. Y.,
Monday, Oct. 25, 1852.

My dear Sir:

Your esteemed favor of the 20th inst. did not reach me until Saturday evening. Having been addressed by the Rev. Mr. Howland a few days previous, relative to the purposed action of his vestry, I trust I have been able to give the subject of a change in my pastoral relations such careful deliberations as the proposal most surely deserves, knowing, as I do, many of the members of the vestry and congregation of the Church of the Holy Apostles and having been long favored with the much cherished friendship of your Rector. I have felt that in relinquishing my first and only charge, and in parting with a beloved people, I am in like manner again trusting myself and mine in the hands of true men and true friends as well as devout and earnest-minded churchmen.

Please communicate to the rector, wardens, and vestry of the Church of the Holy Apostles my acceptance of the call which they have extended to me and which I deem it an honor to have received. I trust that my usefulness among you, by God's blessing, will be equal to my hopes and wishes. I beg to acknowledge the kind terms in which you communicate the Resolutions of the Vestry, and that you will accept for yourself, personally, assurances of my sincere regard and esteem.

Most truly your friend and Servant in Christ,

GEORGE JARVIS GEER.

* * * *

George Jarvis Geer was peculiarly fitted for his work in the ministry by his large-heartedness and invincible spirit. He was a musician and had a good speaking voice. As he moved among the congregation and in the parish work, he showed an earnest spirit and a cheerful outlook. He admitted no failures, for he was persevering as well as practical. Dr. Howland said of him: "He always works harder than anyone else." His warmth and courage gave sincerity and force to all his undertakings.

As a preacher, the Rev. Mr. Geer was sound, logical, and persuasive. His good voice and his manner were most pleasing. He preached as if he felt his responsibility, and his tender though serious words went far to arouse his hearers to reflection. He sent his people home talking earnestly about Christian living, and comforted by the holy truths which he had expounded to them.

During the long, frequent absences of the rector from the parish, Mr. Geer carried the full burden of its ministerial work. He lived near the parish and was constantly in demand, often as pastor, choir leader, and precentor. Above all, he was the faithful friend, whose feet were never tired, and whose heart was never chilled. He was greatly beloved by all because he was so essentially lovable, and because no one ever left his presence without a sense of being better and braver for having been with him.

Dr. Howland leaned heavily upon his young assistant's youth and vigor. When in 1855 a quasi-union of the Church of the Holy Apostles and St. Timothy's Church took place (to be terminated at the pleasure of either parish), the Rev. Mr. Geer most of the time did double duty as pastor of both congregations. At the Diocesan Convention on October 28, 1855, when Bishop Potter spoke feelingly of the premature death of the Rev. Mr. Tracey, the Assistant Minister of Holy Apostles, fired with loving service, aroused its members to the ignominy of the lack of adequate support of their clergy.

Bishop Potter told of the uncertainty and anxiety resting over the bereaved parish of St. Timothy's. "Though there were sixty-two families connected with that parish," he observed, "still they had been really unable to give their rector adequate financial support." Then referring to the faithfulness of Mr. Tracey's ministry, the Bishop continued: ". . . Mr. Tracey had not received emoluments sufficient for his sustenance. He therefore broke down in his labors, disease came upon him, and he died."

Then the Rev. Mr. Geer "took the floor" and pleaded for better salaries for all the missionary clergy throughout the Diocese and State. He told how at a meeting of the clergy in northern New York, he had asked if the salaries they got supported them, and they had all unanimously replied, "NO!" Some of the better paid clergymen of New York City parishes inferred the old saying that if the "labourer" were worthy of his hire, he would get it. But from that day, the Convention of the Diocese of New York took more interest in their poorly paid brethren in the "up-state" mission fields. From that time, too, in the discussions in any Convention for helping the poorly paid clergy in their work, George Jarvis Geer took a leading part.

The mininstry of the Rev. Mr. Geer on the West Side of

the city was a remarkable one in that he assumed the dual office of rector of St. Timothy's Church and assistant minister at Holy Apostles. This ministry he continued to exercise until St. Timothy's acquired such a measure of strength and influence as to discontinue the connection between the two parishes (1867). On December 7, 1858, the vestry of Holy Apostles, wishing to express its respect and esteem for his faithful loyalty and sacrifical spirit, *by unanimous vote,* called him to the post of co-rector with the understanding that "nothing in 'said call' shall be so construed as to infringe upon any of the rights and privileges of the rector."

In 1862 the Rev. Mr. Geer received two honorary degrees: Doctor of Sacred Theology from Columbia University and Doctor of Divinity from Union College, Schenectady, N. Y.

By appointment of the House of Bishops he edited and published with Bishop Bedell and the Rev. Dr. Muhlenberg *The Tune Book* or *Hymnal* of the Protestant Episcopal Church (1858).

He also published in 1871 the book titled *The Conversion of St. Paul.* in 1874, he served as a Deputy from the Diocese of New York to the General Convention of the Protestant Episcopal Church, meeting in New York.

During the last part of his rectorship at St. Timothy's, he became threatened with the loss of vision. This affliction he bore patiently and concealed so successfully that none knew of it till shortly before the time when, for a season, he had to relinquish his duties. His partly restored vision did not last long—apparently his life's work in God's vineyard was fulfilled.

The Rev. Henry Mottet comments in his report of this period in the life of Dr. Geer: "On Sunday, March 15, 1885, the very first on which he felt that he could officiate alone, he conducted each of the services at St. Timothy's; was in his accustomed place in the Sunday School; gave his usual kindly greetings to his flock gathered about him—and, far uptown, read the Burial Service."

Poignant in this connection are the words of David Clarkson: "Your joy and his, God alone can know and understand. His whole expression of face and every word he uttered was the outpouring of a heart big with thought to make up for the months seemingly lost."

The last hymn at the evening on March 15 was "Abide With Me." The day after was his last here, and the beginning of the more blessed life beyond. For Monday morning, March 16, 1885, George Jarvis Geer, Priest and Doctor, Rector of St. Timothy's Church, and sometime Assistant and Co-rector of the Church of the Holy Apostles, entered into the Paradise of God.

It is startling to look back today upon those twenty-two years in the history of this parish, when Dr. Howland and Dr. Geer ministered here, and realize that the parish had reached the zenith of its affluence. With the death of Dr. Geer and the resignation of Dr. Howland in 1869, the parish ended an era. Later on, now and then, there would be a semblance of prosperity and advance, but never again a revival of the old-time splendor.

Had other Episcopal churches not been built to the north and east of Chelsea, the short-lived prosperity of Holy Apostles might have lasted longer. As it was, the church overbuilt itself; and in any case, South Irish immigrants had changed the neighborhood as an Episcopal field. The old, wealthy, American families had gone, and their disappearance was reflected in the social, financial, and general reorientation of the church.

The continuance of good work, loyally supported by newcomers, could not alter the fact that the need of a chapel had vanished; that there were now usually plenty of seats for those who wished to attend; and that the renting of pews was diminishing yearly. In two more decades even the thought of rented pews would perish. And year after year the parish was finding it increasingly difficult to balance its budget.

This was the situation that faced the next rector, Dr. Lundy—a scholarly man with no large means of his own except his salary. Dr. Lundy soon found himself unable to provide an adequate stipend for an assistant. What added to his difficulties and his relative unpopularity was the fact that his predecessors, the former rector and assistant rector, had established themselves not too far from the mother church. But the story of Dr. Lundy's short tenure of office belongs to the next chapter.

THE REVEREND JOHN PATTERSON LUNDY

1869-1875

Bishop of New York:

The Rt. Rev. Horatio Potter, D.D., 1861-1887

1869. Completion of the Transcontinental Railroad

1869. The Suez Canal Opened

1870. Doctrine of Papal Infallibility Adopted by the Roman
Church

1870. Franco-Prussian War

1873. Financial Panic in the United States

JOHN PATTERSON LUNDY
Rector, 1869-1875

Chapter VII
THE REVEREND JOHN PATTERSON LUNDY
1869-1875

Hard Times

The Rev. John P. Lundy came to the parish of Holy Apostles as rector in one of those unfortunate times when the Church had had an esteemed leader whose resignation the vestry received "with great reluctance." The new rector, a mature man of forty-six, did what he could for the welfare of the parish; but "the tide had turned." Many of the communicants of Holy Apostles were living in the vicinity of the charge of their former rectors, who, as we have noted, were active near the scene of their old work. What was worse for Dr. Lundy, more and more members of the parish were establishing homes farther uptown, and the changes in the neighborhood were becoming more rapid and recognizable by all.

John Patterson Lundy, the son of John and Mercy (Morrison) Lundy was born February 23, 1823, at Danville, Pa. He made a public profession of his faith at an early age. He was prepared for college at Danville, and was graduated in 1846 from the College of New Jersey (as Princeton University was called prior to 1896) with a Bachelor of Arts degree. Entering the seminary at Princeton the same year, he was licensed after two years by the Second Presbytery of New York. The following year (February 13, 1849) he was ordained and installed as pastor of the Mt. Pleasant Church at Sing Sing, N. Y. At this time he participated in the "Tractarian Movement," and because of his changed views, left the Presbyterian Church that he might enter the Protestant Episcopal Church and its ministry.

He was ordained Deacon in St. Paul's Church, Sing Sing, N. Y., on October 25, 1854, and was priested on October 28, 1855, in All Saints' Church, Philadelphia, Pa., by the Rt. Rev. Alonzo Potter. This latter church he served as rector from 1855 to 1857. Then he became the rector of Emmanuel Church, Homesburg, Pa. (1857-1865). The next two years he spent as Minister in Charge of St. Mark's and St. Stephen's, Philadelphia, Pa. And before coming to Holy Apostles, he was rector of Christ Church,

Reading, Pa., (1867-1869). In the same year (1869) he received the honorary degree of Doctor of Divinity from Andalusia College, Pa.*

It was while Dr. Lundy was rector of Christ Church, Reading, that Dr. Howland became acquainted with him through their mutual interest in the "Tractarian Movement," and induced him to come to New York as his assistant with a view toward being succeeded by him if the vestry approved.

Dr. Lundy was among the first members of the "American Church Union," a society of clergy and laymen for the advancement of the "Tractarian Movement" in the Episcopal Church. Its membership embraced in New York such outstanding rectors as Dr. Morgan Dix, Dr. J. S. B. Hodges, Dr. Ferdinand C. Ewer, and Dr. Isaac H. Tuttle. At one of their meetings on April 23, 1868, held at Trinity Church, New York, Dr. Lundy preached a sermon of an hour's length and held enchained to the end the attention of a large gathering. He set forth the principles and aims of the "Union," considered the main objections which had been made to its formation, and finally passed on to a full exposition of its real objectives as he understood them.

Dr. Lundy began his ministry in this parish on April 15, 1869, and the following November 16, Dr. Howland tendered his resignation. At the same meeting of the vestry at which the resignation was read, on November 30, 1869, Dr. Lundy was elected rector. The thought seems to have been that the shock to the parish of Dr. Howland's withdrawal would thereby be softened and the security of the parish assured. Dr. Lundy was well known as a man of high literary attainments and as an eloquent preacher.

On Sunday morning, December 19, 1869, the new rector preached his first sermon at Holy Apostles. Dr. Howland was present and spoke a few words of felicitation to the congregation and in praise of Dr. Lundy. The text for the initial sermon

---

*From Princeton University Records 1870.

was from the words of St. Paul to the Corinthians, I Cor. 2:16: "For who hath known the mind of the Lord that he may instruct him? But we have the mind of Christ." It was a splendid effort and seemed to inspire the congregation.

The rector's first Easter, April 24, 1870, was one of great rejoicing. The church was unusually beautiful with Easter lilies and other decorations. All present seemed bent upon showing their loyalty. Many made their communions during the day, and the evening service was exceedingly impressive, a marked feature being the singing of Easter carols led by a large double choir of men and boys. On the following Easter, the beautiful silver Alms Basin, designed by Mr. F. W. Cooper of Ammet and Son, N. Y., was presented to the rector by a communicant.

However, the finances of the parish were far from encouraging, with a deficiency of $3,356 and a floating debt of over $2,000.*

The church at this time had 167 pews and could easily accommodate 800 persons. Although the attendance upon the services was large and most of the pews were usually filled, not one-half of the pews had been rented for the last five years. The vestry undertook a thorough canvass of the neighborhood to find the reason for this situation, and found that the majority of people now living in the neighborhood were unable to contribute any appreciable sum toward the support of the church.

The report states in part:

Some of our communicants even obtain their scanty living by making shirts for Jews at 75 cents per dozen. Between 26th Street and 36th Street, from Eighth Avenue to the river, there live 4,500 persons and only 331 families are Episcopalians.

This report was signed by the Rector, Wardens John Smith and John P. Collord, and Vestrymen C. D. Varley, M.D., D. B. Whitlock, Geo. Moore, Wm. Borden, Robt. H. Goff, E. Chamberlin, B. W. Gibbs, and T. W. Marsh.

---

*See Appendix K, Item 6.

Then, too, the "Seventies" presented a less favorable picture for the growth of the church on the West Side of the city. The Ninth Avenue "El" Line had been extended from the Battery and Greenwich Street along Ninth Avenue to the Thirtieth Street station. After 1871, "dummies" (steam engines) were used. This line, running past the church, with its attendant smoke and noise, was especially disagreeable in summer when the church windows were open.

Other unfavorable factors characterized this period. The first "flathouse" (or "model house," as it was first called) was built in 1849. But by 1870, this type of house, in which two or more families lived, was displacing the "one-family" houses in Chelsea and to the north and west of the parish. The immigrants coming into the city at this time were about equally divided between the United Kingdom and continental Europe— a circumstance that did not help the growth of the Episcopal Church. The Civil War, also, had left behind it a laxity in spiritual matters. Then, soon after the beginning of the "Seventies," came the panic of 1873. Railroad building almost ceased, and the iron industry was prostrated. Business houses failed on every side. The following five years of drastic purgation imperiled the church's finances and prospects.

In 1870, the parish declared one-half of its pews free to all, the other half still to be rented. This was done, of course, in the hope of attracting new communicants and increasing the income of the parish. In 1871, a memorial, drawn up on behalf of the vestry by Mr. Whitlock, was presented to the vestry of Trinity Church, praying that body to allow the Church of the Holy Apostles a definite annual stipend.

In this memorial, reference was made to the great change which had occurred within the past few years in the nature of the population of this part of the city, whereby many of those who had mainly contributed to the support of the church had moved away from the parish limits and had ceased to be members of the congregation. "Their places in the neighborhood have been filled by those who lack either the ability or the inclination to assist in the Church's work.*

Understanding the real need of the parish, Trinity Church agreed to grant the Church of the Holy Apostles an annual stipend of $2,000. At this time of financial stress, there were about eighty distinct congregations of the Episcopal Church in the city, and of these, few were strong parishes financially. It was said that if Trinity with its helpfulness were suddenly removed, various congregations in many parts of the city would immediately go to pieces from sheer inability to meet their current expenses, even with the strictest economy on their part. And still there are persons in the church today, like those who do not favor missions, who say they do not believe in "endowed churches." It would be hard to visualize just what the Episcopal Church would be in New York today were it not for the "mothering" and generous gifts which Trinity Parish has made throughout the years of her existence.

A gift of $10,000 in 1871 from the estate of Maria Robins came at a most opportune time, and helped the parish meet its pressing obligations. The vestry, in commemoration of this munificent legacy, erected a tablet (let into the wall of the north transept) to her memory.

During the financial difficulties of this time, Mr. Daniel B. Whitlock assisted the rector, especially in the work of the Sunday School. Mr. Whitlock was one of the Vice Presidents of a large group in the diocese known as "The Protestant Episcopal Sunday School Association." The President was the Rev. Henry C. Potter, Rector of Grace Church; the Secretary was the Rev. Henry Mottet, Rector of the Church of the Holy Communion; and the Treasurer was Mr. Philip Oakley.

At one of the meetings in October, 1871, Mr. Whitlock expressed the view that "our religious life and service should

---

*See Appendix D.

have no vacations; also the Sunday Schools should have none, except in cases of absolute necessity."

However, Dr. Lundy, recognizing the correctness of the principle of vacations, thought "the faithful teachers needed a rest." But he added, "As matters now stand, perhaps a perpetual vacation might be a good thing. Our system of Sunday School teaching needs reorganizing. Might we not return to the old system of catechists, and, if necessary, pay them?"

The financial troubles of the parish grew more alarming during the "panic" years, and helped to cause disagreements between the rector and his vestry as to policy. The vestry felt unable to afford an assistant minister, but the rector asked the Rev. Mr. Lewis to assist him from December, 1870, to June, 1872, and then called in the Rev. Mr. Eugene L. Foy in 1873. Another source of friction was that many of the congregation were in disagreement with the rector's "high" churchmanship, his studious sermons, and his insistence on clerical help. These differences came to a head in 1875, the year in which the rector resigned.

Early in this year, one month's salary was due both to the rector and to his assistant of that time, with many other current expenses of the parish not met. The Rev. O. Valentine, the assistant, organized the "Young Peoples' Association" in a drive for funds to help meet the parish deficiencies, and 296 Ninth Avenue was rented to Mr. Samuel Hays, the sexton, to help finance the parish. The strained feeling between the rector and the vestry was now so acute that there was seldom a quorum at the vestry meetings, and whenever there was one, the rector excused himself.

At the October meeting, the rector informed the vestry that he had engaged temporarily the Rev. Thomas B. Newby to assist him. The vestry replied that the financial condition of the parish precluded this, and that they felt unable to add to the expenses of the parish. The rector then asked to be excused, and Col. William Borden, the senior warden, took the chair.

At the next meeting of the vestry, October 19, 1875, Dr. Lundy requested Mr. John P. Collord to take the chair, and left a paper to be read before he withdrew. The paper proved to be the rector's resignation, to take effect on November 30, next.

> 345 West 32nd Street, New York
> October 19th, 1875.

To the Wardens and Vestrymen of the Church of the Holy Apostles.
    Gentlemen,
        I had very much hoped that your body at its last meeting on the evening of the 5th inst. would have seen its way clear to have provided the means for an Assistant Minister of the Parish, as heretofore, especially as I had relinquished a considerable portion of my salary for that purpose.

    I deeply regret to be compelled to say that I am altogether unable to prosecute the work of this Parish alone; that the recent and protracted irregularity of my salary gives me a painful anxiety as to any future livelihood here; and that I am constrained by these considerations to cease my ministrations among you.

    From first to last I have loved my church and parish work here; and it grieves me to discontinue it. I herewith tender to the Vestry my resignation of the Rectorship of the Church of the Holy Apostles, and that I may not be unduly hasty in the matter, and that the Vestry may have time to deliberate as to a successor, I mention the 30th of November, Advent Season, as the time when I would like to have this resignation take effect.

    With best wishes and prayers for the future Spiritual and temporal welfare of the Parish, and for your own individual health and happiness, I am, Gentlemen, as ever

> Very truly yours,
>
> JOHN P. LUNDY, Rector.

*   *   *   *

At a meeting of the vestry on October 28, the vestry passed these resolutions:

Whereas, in response to the Rector's wish for an Assistant Minister, careful examination of the finances of the Parish [show that] the pew rentals which had been relied upon chiefly for support heretofore have for the last several years fallen off year by year, thus greatly restricting the means at the command of the Vestry, and

Whereas, the Vestry feels constrained to economy: Resolved, that the financial condition of the Parish precludes the Vestry from making any increased appropriation for clerical service at the present time, and

Whereas, at the last Vestry meeting, Dr. Lundy in a written communication tendered his resignation, declaring that he is "altogether unable to prosecute the work of this Parish alone," be it resolved:

That the Vestry see no alternative but to accept the resignation of the Rev. J. P. Lundy, D.D., as Rector of this Church and that such resignation be and hereby is accepted by the Vestry to take effect in accordance with his suggestion on November 30th, next.

Resolved, That while consenting to the dissolution of the relations which have for so long a time existed between the Rev. Dr. Lundy and this Church and around which clusters so many pleasant memories, the Vestry cannot refrain from expressing their regret at the circumstances which seem to render it necessary on his part to take such a step.

Resolved, That the Vestry one and all most sincerely hope and pray that Dr. Lundy's health may speedily be fully re-established and that his life may be spared for long years to come, and that health and unalloyed happiness may ever attend him and his, in whatever field of usefulness he may hereafter be engaged.

A motion was also recorded by the vestry requesting the rector to read the following notice from the chancel to the congregation on Sunday morning next, October 31.

The Vestry requests that all of the Rector's salary be paid up. The Vestry hopes that all pew-holders will promptly remit their indebtedness to the Treasurer, for they recognize that many have not done so during the long summer months.

On November 9th, 1875, a balance in the Treasury was $239.81.

Wardens:: COL. WILLIAM BORDEN, DANIEL B. WHITLOCK.

Vestrymen: JOHN P. COLLORD, ROBERT H. GOFF,
WILLIAM ORTON, HENRY IVEY,
CHARLES S. FISCHER JR., JOHN M. BUCKINGHAM,
ENOCH CHAMBERLAIN, ALBERT S. ROE.

* * * *

Whether Dr. Lundy read the foregoing we do not know. A letter from a vestryman is of interest in connection with this dispute:

519 West 33rd Street
December 20, 1875.

Gentlemen:

No one could have been more surprised than I was when informed of my election to the Vestry. . . . It was my intention not to accept the honor. I was constrained from a sense of duty, and the very kind and courteous attention shown me by the other members, to remain temporarily. I was also pained at the time to find already existing a breach between the Rector and the Vestry, and that my regular attendance was needed to make a quorum for the transaction of important business. Happily, those difficulties are now passed. . . .

Although it is known to you, I have felt all along that the Vestry was not quite right in the matter of not hiring an assistant after accepting the Rector's proposition to assist in providing the means for procuring one. With respect to accepting Dr. Lundy's resignation, ever since becoming a member of the Vestry, I have thought [that] would be for the best interest of the Church.

Sincerely your friend,

ALBERT S. ROE.

After Dr. Lundy's resignation (at the age of 52), he did not again officiate in this church, nor did he hold any other rectorship, although he resided in New York till late in 1877. In that year he removed to Philadelphia, Pa., spending most of his time in literary pursuits until his death, which was the result of a severe cold, on December 11, 1892, in his seventieth year.

At an early age, Dr. Lundy exhibited a strong taste for books, and became an omnivorous reader with a singularly retentive memory. He was an indefatigable student and writer. In his *Monumental Christianity* (1876) he has left an enduring and valuable legacy of his industry and learning. He published also in 1880 a treatise on *Forestry at Home and Abroad*. He was one of the founders of the American Forestry Association of Pennsylvania, and for two years its president. He was a member of the Masonic fraternity, of the Historical Society of Pennsylvania, and of the Numismatic and Antiquarian Society. At the time of his death he was engaged on a work on "Prehistoric Worship." He was a frequent and extensive traveler.

During the interim after Dr. Lundy's departure, the Rev. Thomas B. Newby was temporarily in charge of the parish at a weekly salary of $20. Dr. Howland showed his concern for the welfare of the church by officiating on the first Sunday in December. These clergy were asked to supply as preachers: the Rev. Mr. Sloan, the Rev. Mr. Jowett, the Rev. Mr. Houghton; and the Rev. Dr. Muhlenberg.

In the meantime the vestry were considering suitable candidates for the rectorship. Prominent among these, the Rev. Mr. Backus attracted attention by his ministry at St. Peter's Church while he was acting as assistant to the Rev. Dr. Beach, the rector.

On January 25, 1876, Messrs. Whitlock, Goff, and Orton were appointed as a committee to visit the Rev. Mr. Backus with a view toward asking him whether he would accept the rectorship of Holy Apostles. As an inducement, the salary was placed at $3,000 with an appropriation of $250 to cover the expense of his removal from Cooperstown, N. Y., to the city. At the vestry meeting on February 15, 1876, a communication was read from the Rev. Mr. Backus accepting the rectorship.

CHAPTER VIII

THE REVEREND BRADY ELECTUS BACKUS
1876-1901
Bishops of New York:

The Rt. Rev. Horatio Potter, 1861-1887

The Rt. Rev. Henry Codman Potter, 1887-1908

1876. Massacre of Custer and His Men by the Indians

1880. Rectory of the Church of the Holy Apostles Purchased

1880. Electric Lights Used for the First Time on Broadway

1883. Brooklyn Bridge Opened

1886. Statue of Liberty Dedicated

1888. "Great Blizzard"

1893. The World's Fair in Chicago (World's Columbian Exposition)

1893. Financial Panic

1893. First Gasoline "Buggy" Tested

1894. Endowment Fund Begun by the "Be Ready Ten"

1894. Motion Picture Industry Started

1898. Spanish American War

1898. Greater New York Becomes a Reality Under Mayor Robert A. Van Wyck

1900. World's Fair at Paris, France

1901. First Transmission by Marconi's Radio

BRADY ELECTUS BACKUS
Rector, 1876-1901

Chapter VIII

THE REVEREND BRADY ELECTUS BACKUS, 1876-1901

Ups and Downs

The financial panic of 1873 had about spent itself when the Rev. Mr. Backus became rector of the parish. The "Booming Eighties" were just ahead. During the last year of Dr. Lundy's rectorship, the vestry and congregation, sorely tried by financial worries and dissensions, awaited eagerly the coming of a new pastor. The Rev. Mr. Backus was adaptable to circumstances, cultured and dignified, intellectually able, and filled with determination. He awoke the congregation to their opportunities and obligations.

The late Seventies ushered in a period of general national prosperity. As one writer put it:

> Immigration from the United Kingdom reached its highest number in the decade ahead, and the Episcopal Church in general was pursuing a more aggressive missionary policy. The nation grew from about fifty million to sixty-two millions before 1890. Railroad building, interrupted by the panic of 1873, was resumed. The pine forests of Michigan, Wisconsin and Minnesota were ruthlessly exploited to the great cost of succeeding generations. The new iron mines at the head of Lake Superior commenced an extraordinary internal commerce along the whole length of the Great Lakes.*

Many factors in the growth and change of the city, such as the Hudson River and the Erie Canal, reflected themselves in the affairs of the parish. Particularly important from the standpoint of the church was the dockage placed along the Hudson River front at Chelsea. Flat buildings replaced private residences.

---

*"Immigration and Growth of the Episcopal Church"-1942-Walter H. Stowe

Business and manufacturing found a home in the immediate neighborhood, and the Ninth Avenue Elevated line was opened —incidentally spoiling the appearance of the avenue. In the wake of these changes, the parish was fast becoming a church of the small-income laboring class and of those possessing only moderate means.

It was the time for the beginning of "institutional" churches, that is, churches which gave over their plants to various religious and humanitarian activities during week days. The Church of the Holy Apostles was already equipped with a mission building which was easily converted into a Parish House.

The vestry realized the financial implications of these changing neighborhood conditions, and made urgent appeals to the magnanimity of Trinity Parish. However, when the new rector came to the parish he was fortunate to find all the bills paid and a balance of $502 in the hands of the treasurer.

Brady Electus Backus was born in Troy, N. Y., in 1839, and was the grandson of Col. Electus Backus, who was killed at the battle of Sackett's Harbor in 1813. He received his early education at Troy and at Grand Rapids, Michigan, where his family had moved in 1854. After graduation, he was for two years a teacher in the public schools of Grand Rapids, but in 1859 he took up the study of law. Mr. Backus was admitted to the Supreme Court of Michigan, and practiced his profession in Detroit. He continued his legal practice until 1866, when he decided to enter the Episcopal ministry. Subsequently, he entered Trinity College, Hartford, Conn., and was graduated in 1870. While at college, Mr. Backus became a member of the Beta Beta Chapter of the Psi Upsilon fraternity. In the same year he was admitted to the General Theological Seminary, and was graduated from the seminary in the class of 1873. Mr. Backus was ordained Deacon by Bishop Horatio Potter, and was appointed assistant to the Rector of St. Peter's Church, New York. In 1874 he was ordained to the priesthood and was elected Rector of Christ Church, Cooperstown, N. Y., where he remained until the spring of 1876 before entering upon his duties as Rector of the Church of the Holy Apostles.

A letter from Col. Wm. Borden, Senior Warden, to Mr. Daniel B. Whitlock, Junior Warden, reads as follows:

February, 12, 1876.

Dear Sir,

I have just rec'd communication dated Cooperstown, Feb'y 11, 1876:
To the Gentlemen, Wardens and Vestrymen of the Church of the Holy Apostles, New York.

I hereby communicate to you my acceptance of the Call to the Rectorship of your Parish and in the term as extended to me in your resolution bearing date Feb'y 4, 1876. I hope to enter, God willing, upon my duties with you by March 19, prox.

(Signed) BRADY E. BACKUS.

*   *   *   *

Just before coming to Holy Apostles, while rector at Cooperstown, the Rev. Mr. Backus married Miss Annie Taylor, whom he had known in his seminary days. Dr. Cornelius B. Smith, a personal friend and Rector of St. James' Church, performed the wedding on June 9, 1875. At the beginning of his ministry here the rector and his young bride made their home at 354 West Twenty-eighth Street. Three children were born to them: Cordelia Mann, (born Feb. 14, 1878, died July 16, 1937); Helen Amanda, (born May 6, 1881, died Jan. 6, 1888); and Electus Taylor, (born Oct. 8, 1888, died March 10, 1938).

At the first Annual Meeting and Election of Vestrymen, held on Monday in Easter Week, April 16, 1876, immediately after a morning service, at which the Rector presided, Messrs. William Borden and Daniel B. Whitlock were elected as Wardens, and Messrs. Robert G. Goff, John P. Collord, E. Chamberlin, Henry Ivey, J. M. Buckingham, William Orton, Chas. S. Fischer, Jr., and A. S. Roe were elected as Vestrymen.

By the spring of 1877, the energetic and determined young rector had so rallied the congregation and church societies behind him that he felt able to lay before the vestry the necessity and desirability of extensive repairs to the Church and the Mission House building. The interior of the church was to be redecorated, the exterior walls and the steeple were to be painted, and alterations were to be made on the upper floor of the mission building. The vestry acceded, with the stipulation that the repairs were to cost no more than $3,000. The sexton was now to occupy 296 Ninth Avenue, with a yearly stipend of $500.

Soon the societies and congregation were infused with the spirit of renewed enthusiasm. The church work now embraced a wide and varied character, especially beyond Thirty-fourth Street. Social groups, led by the rector and aided by those of wealth, interested their members in social service among the less fortunate. The traditional Sunday School library of 1846 was enlarged and faithfully served by Mr. John P. Collord and later on by Miss Helen Jean Aitken.

The Young People's Missionary Association, begun in 1874, was a great help in all the new endeavors, especially as visiting groups. During the year they reported having made nearly two hundred visits to the sick and needy, providing clothing, food, fuel, and medicine, at a total expense of over $400. Their leader was the young and energetic assistant minister, the Rev. Mr. Valentine. They had divided the neighborhood into four districts, each to be covered by its own appointees.

One of the most important works of this society during 1877 was to awaken the whole parish to the necessity of putting the Mission Building in thorough repair, so as to render it neat and attractive to the children of the Sunday School. This they accomplished with enthusiasm and dispatch. It is interesting to peruse the history of this most helpful group of young people, so much like other young peoples' groups and yet so different in their outlook.

Of course it was probably too much to expect this high pitch of devotion to be sustained. After the repairs to the Mission Building were completed, a letdown was perhaps inevitable. To stimulate lagging interest, meetings were called at the homes of individual members. About this time (October, 1880), the organization became known as the "Young People's Association." One of their objectives was described as getting the attention of the absent "John Kellys," who were rebuked by at least one individual as "spoiled children—when asked to do anything, or show what they know, they fail even to respond."

But the pith and point of the association were lost when they gave up their vital practice of missionary visiting. At their June meeting in 1881, Dr. Backus and Dr. Lyman, who were present, pleaded with them to continue their "good work." Apparently this appeal had little effect, for the society went the way of many another young people's group. Once a bright shooting star, it now faded into the night. There was no meeting in the fall.

During the summer of 1877, the church was closed until September for repairs and repainting. The exterior of the church was thoroughly repaired, and the interior decorated and refurnished. The method of lighting the edifice was greatly improved. A handsome stained glass window, contributed by the Sunday School and its friends, was placed in the front of the church over the organ gallery. At the same time the Sunday School building was refitted with new seats. The upper floor, which had been used by various sextons for dwelling purposes, was converted into Bible class and Guild rooms, and the first floor was arranged for use as a chapel. The amount expended improving the property and beautifying the church was not far from $10,000.

At the reopening of the church for services on September 23, 1877, the rector took for his text Psalm 27:4:

One thing have I desired of the Lord, that will I seek after; that I may dwell in the house of the Lord all the days of my life, to behold the beauty of the Lord, and to inquire in his temple.

A year after the reopening of the church, the balance in the treasury was $15.91 with which to meet $2,000 and a floating debt of over $1,000. There also remained the Trinity mortgages of 1847, which at this time were forcefully brought to the attention of the vestry in the following letter:

187 Fulton Street, New York.
14 Oct., 1878.

Rev. and dear Sirs,

I am requested to make application to you in relation of two mortgages held by Trinity Church upon the property of the Church of the Holy Apostles. As for a long period no interest has been demanded or paid upon these mortgages, their continuing validity is liable to be questioned, and it is therefore desired to have a confirmatory instrument executed.

(I refer to) the mortgage for four thousand dollars, dated February 18th, 1847, executed by your corporation to William S. Hunt and Lorenzo Moses, and the mortgage for two thousand dollars, dated September 16, 1847, executed by your corporation to that of Trinity Church. . . .

I am, Rev. and dear Sirs, Very truly yours,

G. M. Ogden.

These mortgages were subsequently renewed.

To increase the income of the parish, Mr. Benoni Lockwood, a vestryman, moved a revision of pew rents. A "Memoranda of Points" was printed and given out to the congregation. In it the pewholders were reminded that rents were payable semi-annually in advance and that bills would be presented in accordance with this rule. They were also reminded that the Easter offerings—$1,236.26—were less than half of what was asked for and needed. "Let every pewholder resolve that his weekly contribution shall be at least half as much as his pew rent. It is believed that those who attend here regularly, but pay no pew rent, are able to rent pews or single sittings. Let us hope that a sense of duty will prompt all to do their duty, from the occupant of $150 pews to the pewholder for whom ten cents per week is as much in the eye of God, if in giving this he gives according to his or her means." The results, as usual, were almost nil.

The feasibility of purchasing the dwelling at 360 West

INTERIOR OF CHURCH, EASTER 1880

IN MEMORIAM

MARIA ROBINS

A Communicant and Benefactress of this Church,
WHO WENT TO GOD SEPTEMBER 14TH, 1871.
"She Hath Wrought a Good Work."
Erected by the Vestry.

INTERIOR OF CHURCH, 1895

Twenty-eighth Street for a rectory was investigated by Messrs. Fischer, Goff, and Whitlock. In March, 1880, at the request of the vestry, the house was purchased from Ann E. Caleb, the owner, for $13,000. Of this amount $5,000 were subscribed by members and the remainder of the amount secured by mortgage. The rector's salary was reduced by $500 annually, and his vacation to six weeks in the summer.

In 1883 the rector and vestry sent an urgent appeal to Trinity Church to grant an additional sum of $1,000 annually for the support of Holy Apostles, but especially for an assistant or missionary to work in the neighborhood and parish.* The petition was not granted. In 1884 another request was made to Trinity, and later on in 1889 another plea was sent through the Bishop of the Diocese. Meanwhile the treasurer of the parish had found it necessary to borrow $2,000 for current expenses during the summer months. Finally in 1890 the rector and vestry were much encouraged when they received on January 21, 1891, the following communication from the Corporation of Trinity Church:

> I have the pleasure of enclosing herewith an extract from the Vestry of Trinity Church increasing the annual allowance to the Church of the Holy Apostles. "Resolved, that the annual allowance to the Church of the Holy Apostles be increased from $2,000 to $3,000 per annum from November 1, 1890."
>
> R. P. NASH, Clerk of Trinity Church.

This gift from Trinity continued to be given annually until 1916. The matter of meeting the expense of clerical help was always a serious problem since the time when Dr. Howland gave his salary toward the stipend of the assistant minister. There has been no assistant at Holy Apostles since 1916, and possibly the work of the parish has suffered thereby in this ever-changing neighborhood.

----

*See Appendix E.
See Appendix K. Item 6½.

After the purchase of the rectory in 1880, the rector gave himself without stint to the parish work and its organizations. The "Eighties" became noted for extensive alterations and improvements in the sanctuary and chancel. Many memorials were given during these years. A beautiful brass lectern, for example, was presented to the church at Easter, 1883, by Mrs. N. E. Baylies, in memory of her daughter Ruth. At this time, too, a further effort was made to reduce the mortgage of $8,000 on the rectory. In March, 1886, permission was given to Mrs. Baylies and Mr. Robert Ray Hamilton to erect a memorial tablet in the south transept to the memory of the donors of the church property.

The inscription reads:

To the Glory of God and in Memory of
ROBERT RAY
AND CORNELIA, HIS WIFE
Who Gave to the Parish the Greater Part of the Land
Upon Which This Church Stands

R. R., 1794-1879　　✠　　C. R., 1800-1874.

After Easter, 1887, the rector, conscious of having greatly overworked, was granted a three months' leave of absence. He and Mrs. Backus sailed for Europe on June 7, spending most of their time in England. During their absence, the Rev. Arthur H. Judge was Minister-in-Charge. In October of the same year, Mr. Judge was called to the parish as Curate. He became greatly beloved by the congregation and a lifelong friend of this parish and people.

One change followed swiftly upon the heels of another. The surface tracks of the horse-drawn street-car line on Twenty-eighth and Twenty-ninth Streets were laid in front of the church property in 1888 with the consent of the vestry. The company granted the church $10,000 in stock, but by 1898 this stock had become worthless. In 1917 the car line was discontinued.

Ninth Avenue prior to the building of the Elevated Railroad was a pleasant street of modest homes. It had been restricted for the most part by covenants for the erection of private dwellings. The Ray home opposite the church was probably the finest of the private houses along the avenue. There were six churches along Ninth Avenue between Fourteenth and Fifty-ninth Streets, while on Eighth Avenue only one had been built, *viz.*, "The Tabernacle" at Forty-fourth Street.

In 1869-1870 a single elevated structure of iron girders supported by iron columns was erected upon the westerly side of the avenue. The property and franchises of the "El" were acquired by the New York Elevated Railroad Company in 1870; and the latter then proceeded to erect a double-track structure. By 1873, the "El" was extended to Thirty-fourth Street, with a station at Thirtieth Street and Ninth Avenue. The noise of the passing trains had much to do with destroying the value of the avenue for better residential purposes and also with the deterioration of the character of the whole neighborhood.

Dr. Backus and the vestry fully realized the damage being done to the prosperity of the parish. Accordingly, on June 4, 1889, Mr. Edmund L. Baylies employed an attorney, Mr. James B. Ludlow, and prepared to commence action against the Elevated Railroad Company for injury to the property of the church. The rector and members of the vestry maintained that there had been a "gradual change in the character of the congregation; the wealthier going, and the poorer people coming in their stead." This had been going on for some years past, "but more particularly and more rapidly during the past ten years, because of increased traffic on the line." The action was divided into two cases: the church property and 296 Ninth Avenue. In 1893 the church was allowed the sum of $1,000 for damages to 296 Ninth Avenue, of which net to the church after trial was a meagre $136.75. The case for the church continued in

court till 1900, when a decision for the church was made for
$6,000—the church realizing but $4,000.

Operations of the Ninth Avenue "El" were ended at midnight June 11, 1940, and it was razed during the following
months of 1940-41. The city placed a removal assessment on
the church property of $2,205, but this was subsequently re-
mitted.

The parish suffered a great loss on April 10, 1888, through
the death of its Senior Warden, Daniel B. Whitlock. He had
been connected with the church for over thirty years, and was
superintendent of the Sunday School for twenty-five years. He
was greatly admired as an outstanding Christian gentleman,
sincere, with a quiet and calm judgment, earnest in purpose,
amiable in disposition, kind and affectionate.*

About this time (1888), the "Be Ready Ten" of the King's
Daughters became most helpful in furthering the material interests of the parish. Composed of married ladies for the most
part, this society met one Friday afternoon of each month at
the residence of one of its members. It contributed largely to
the "Fresh Air Fund" and charities outside the parish, but above
all, it acted as an Altar Guild, providing for the furnishings,
decorations, and care of the altar. In 1894 the "Ten" sponsored
the beginnings of the "Endowment Fund" for the parish and
were the leading spirits in its furtherance and accomplishment.

The "Gay Nineties" were not so "gay" for the church. Even
with the increased yearly grant from Trinity Parish, the rector
and vestry saw the "writing on the wall." The residential part
of the city about the church was constantly shrinking through
the encroachment of business, and was becoming from Sixth
Avenue westward a foreign and unchurched district. Twenty-
eighth Street at Sixth Avenue turned into a little "red light"
district.

---

*See Appendix F (Memorial Resolution by the Vestry).

Mr. Edmund L. Baylies won a judgment against encroachments of business on West Twenty-eighth Street, and was instrumental in having Twenty-eighth, Twenty-ninth, and Thirtieth Streets, between Eighth and Ninth Avenues, zoned for residential purposes. Twenty-seventh Street was left open for business till some years later, when this street also was placed, among the zoned streets. The territory north and west of the parish, between Thirty-fifth and Forty-first Streets, along Tenth Avenue, was to become known as "Hell's Kitchen." Even the northern part of Chelsea, at one time or another, was loosely included in this designation.

Since many respectable families have always lived in that part of town, the reader may wonder how such a slurring name originated. It seems that "Hell's Kitchen" became associated with this somewhat vaguely defined district because of a restaurant at Eleventh Avenue and Thirty-ninth Street. Into this restaurant came hard-boiled drovers from New Jersey who brought sheep and cattle into the New York market. Frequently these men had heated altercations with local "tough guys," which often ended in more violent manifestations of disagreement than words. When things got out of hand in this restaurant, the proprietor would call up the local police station with the admonition that "hell's broke loose in the kitchen." Newspaper men caught onto the phrase and began to apply it generally to the neighborhood. So the legend grew. It is only as the phrase has lapsed into tradition that it has been applied to a large section of the West Side of New York.

By the end of the last century many of the old families had long before departed from the vicinity of the church, although they kept up their interest in the parish and were instrumental in beginning the Endowment Fund in 1894. But what was most noticeable from 1890 to 1900 in Holy Apostles, as well as in many a downtown church, was the increasing influx of foreigners from continental Europe.

After 1890, the rate of the growth of the Episcopal Church throughout the United States dropped like a plummet. The decennial increase in communicants declined from 55.8 per cent in 1890 to 39.7 per cent in 1900. Before 1890, it had taken fifty years for fourteen-and-a-half million immigrants to enter this country. In only forty years after 1890, twenty-two million immigrants, mostly now from southern and eastern Europe, had come.*

Not many persons living today can grasp the paralyzing effect that this unrestricted immigration had upon our large city parishes until comparatively recent years.

The Episcopal Church makes its strongest appeal to the native born among the unchurched population. When immigration was from north Europe and especially from the British Isles, the usefulness of our city's churches was decidedly enhanced. Now the reverse was true, and many Protestant churches moved to fairer fields uptown, merged, or ceased to exist. ||[1]

During the last five years of Dr. Backus' life as rector, removals caused him many heartaches, as only those most intimate with him knew. Mrs. Backus' feelings (if not often expressed) were: "Lord, you keep 'em humble, and we'll keep 'em poor."

Early in the "Nineties" the rector and vestry began to make an earnest effort to raise a suitable and permanent Endowment Fund. It will be remembered that thirty years previously (1864) the Standing Committee of the Vestry had recommended that steps be taken for the establishment of a fund to be known as the "Howland Endowment Fund." But for various reasons, nothing was done at that time. Again in 1892, Dr. Backus, by public and private appeals and by articles in *The Parish Trumpet,* urged the growing importance of such a program, but again action was postponed. In January, 1894, the "Be Ready Ten" (the parish circle of the King's Daughters) decided to take steps toward the realization of a plan, to which they gave tangible

---

*Appendix K, Item 7. "Immigration and Growth of the Episcopal Church." 1942—Walter Herbert Stowe.
||[1] op. cit.

form by subscribing $100 from their treasury. ||²

Their resolutions reads as follows:

New York, February 15th, 1894.

In view of the fact that for causes beyond the control of the congregation or the vestry of the church, its revenue has been steadily diminishing for several years past, and as some action seems advisable toward securing
an income for the future, thereby enabling the church to continue its great
and necessary work in this immediate neighborhood:
We the undersigned hereby agree to pay the sum set opposite our names
toward the establishment of an Endowment Fund, which shall be for the
use and benefit of the Church of the Holy Apostles in the City of New
York; the interest of said fund not to be available for the use of the church
until the principal has reached an amount not less than $10,000.

*   *   *   *

A meeting was called on March 6, 1894, by the "Be Ready
Ten" at the residence of Mrs. Daniel B. Whitlock, 356 Twenty-
eighth Street. Most of the meetings were held there for twenty
years. An organization was formed and a committee appointed
to carry out the "Be Ready Ten" program.

At this meeting, James Pedersen, M.D., was elected Chairman and Mr. Clement S. Parsons, Jr., Secretary. Others present
at this meeting were Miss Ella B. Whitlock, Miss M. E.
Ferguson, Mrs. C. S. Parsons, Jr., and Mr. William J. McDonald.
The group elected Miss Whitlock, Miss Ferguson, and Mr.
McDonald as Trustees of any funds raised toward their object.
In recognition of the "Ten's" efforts, a committee was appointed
during the March vestry meeting to represent the vestry in the
furtherance of the fund.

By the middle of May, 1894, the "Trustees" of the "Ten"
had deposited funds in a number of saving banks. Their objective was $10,000, and they planned "to use and apply the in-
terest and income arising therefrom to . . . purposes of the
Church of the Holy Apostles so long as the edifice of said
Church wherein Divine Services are held shall be located at the

||² See Appendix F (Endowment Fund).

southeast corner of Ninth Avenue and Twenty-eighth Street in the City of New York."

Soon after this, the organization was to be known as "The Endowment Fund Association." Meetings in the future were to be called at the discretion of the chairman, James Pedersen, M.D., but an annual meeting was to be held in January of each year, at which time the election of officers for the ensuing year was to take place. The rector, upon being asked to set aside a Sunday for the observance of the Endowment Fund,* designated the last Sunday in November, 1895.

The Rev. Cornelius B. Smith, Rector of St. James' Church, was the first "outside" pastor to champion the fund, and he was followed by the Rev. William J. Seabury, S.T.D., in November, 1896, and the Rev. Henry Mottet, Rector of the Church of the Holy Communion, in 1897. The rector and the vestry of Holy Apostles now approved a circular letter explaining the need for the fund, the progress made, and the objective. "One Hundred Tithe Gleaners" (mite boxes) used by the "Be Ready Ten" were given away. Definite "Endowment Fund Sundays" (the next to be set aside was the fourth Sunday in January, 1897) and the mite boxes helped to keep the fund in the minds of all.

Through a report by Mr. Andrew H. Kellogg of his call upon Mr. Wm. Watts Sherman, treasurer of the Diocesan Committee, which was incorporated and consisted of Bishop Henry C. Potter, Mr. Cornelius Vanderbilt, Mr. J. Pierpont Morgan, Mr. Henry Lewis Morris, Mr. Wm. Alexander Smith, and Mr. Wm. Watts Sherman, the information was received that there were "just such funds as that of the Church of the Holy Apostles in care of the Diocesan Fund Committee."

By March 2, 1900, the Fund had reached a sum of over $15,000, and was then placed in the hands of the Diocesan Fund Committee (now known as "The Trustees of the Estate and Property of the Diocese of New York") to invest.

---

*See Appendix F (Endowment Fund).

In 1901, at the meeting of the "Trustees of the Fund," it was decided that the interest and gifts obtained be added until the Fund become $20,000, which goal was reached December, 1904.

In the following year the first "indenture" was signed with "The Trustees of the Estate and Property of the Diocesan Convention of New York," in which it was stated that if *the parish of the Holy Apostles went out of existence, the funds would be given to Trinity parish, the income to be used at their discretion for the support of a downtown church.*

It now becomes necessary to return to the eventful year of the beginnings of the Endowment Fund, without which it is doubtful whether the parish could have withstood the constant changes in this neighborhood during the last fifty years. As one looks back, upon this time one wonders how any rector—with the constant turnover in workers and curates and the mountains of labor—could have remained a well man for twenty-five years.

In the first eighteen years of his ministry up to 1894, Dr. Backus personally baptized over 1,500 children and adults; presented 600 persons for confirmation; performed 700 marriages; officiated at 800 burials; and gave what remained of his energy and attention to finances, repairs, and missionary and charitable objects. On Saturday nights, he worked on his sermons, which he wrote out in longhand, literally burning the midnight oil. Deaf to the remonstrances of his worried family, he toiled indefatigably all year around except for six weeks in the summer, which he spent resting at his summer home at Ridgefield, Conn.

During the year 1894, an "Historical Sketch of the Parish" was compiled by Charles Knapp, Ph.D., on behalf of the Brotherhood of St. Andrew, to be sold for the benefit of the Endowment Fund. In recognition of Dr. Knapp's efforts, the vestry passed a resolution of thanks to him "for his painstaking

---

*See Appendix F (Endowment Fund).

and scholarly labors in editing and directing the publication of this sketch of forty-six pages of the church's history."

All during this time, various adjuncts of the church kept playing important roles. The Sunday School had three departments, the infant class, the intermediate class, and the Bible class, each occupying its own floor in the mission building. There were five Bible classes, numbering fifty members. The Lay Superintendent was Mr. Charles Knapp, Ph.D., who was aided by two secretaries, Mr. Albert G. Carnienke and Mr. Eugene M. Willard. Nineteen teachers composed the teaching staff: Miss Josephine Harrison, Miss Gertrude V. Stephenson, Miss Lucy D. Pearce, Miss Jenny V. R. Page, Miss Gusta Hatch, Miss Theresa Phyllis Braham, Miss J. Warden, Miss W. B. Cookman, Miss Anna J. Vermile, Miss Clara L. Hyde, Miss Alma Jackson, Mrs. Charles Knapp, Mrs. F. M. Collins, and Mr. Frederick M. Collins.

The library had a real function in the school inasmuch as free public libraries were not yet plentiful. At this time the librarian was Mr. Philip Riess, whose four assistants were Messrs. John Custons, Charles Hays, George Chapman, and David Brown.

The choir consisted of twenty-five boys, ten women, and eight men. The music was under the able direction of Mr. Sheldon W. Ball; the organist was Mr. H. S. Church.

Numerous special activities highlighted this period. During the nights of the week there were meetings of many guilds and societies which demanded the rector's attention. The Women's Missionary Society met quarterly in the choir room. The Parish Guild held two meetings a month, which Dr. Backus usually attended. Then, two afternoons a week, St. Martha's Society and the Dorcas Society (or Mothers' Meeting), engaged in sewing. The Industrial School, composed of 125 young girls, met on Saturday afternons, The Girls' Friendly Society and the Knitting Class met on Mondays. On Tuesday nights the hall was used by the Young Crusaders, fifty strong, complete with band and military drill. The "Be Ready Ten" of the King's Daughters engaged in the Altar work and preparations for the summer "fresh air vacations." The Brotherhood of St. Andrew edited the monthly paper of the parish—*The Parish Trumpet*. The rector and his assistants were indeed busy people in 1894!

A word about the spire may be interpolated here. People in the neighborhood today, gazing at the lofty spire terminating in a large Latin cross, little realize what anxiety this structure has always caused. Like many others of its kind, it has been a source of worry and expense during every rectorship. While built of wood, it required attention every few years. In 1894 the vestry entertained a plan for its removal down to the belfry, but the objections voiced by the congregation "won the day." The spire was then covered with slate and copper trimmings.

Again in 1908, during the rectorship of Dr. Grannis, extensive repairs were made rather than remove the spire. At that time it was strengthened, and the base and belfry completely covered with copper. Bishop Paddock and the Rev. Mr. Edelblute also have had to repair the spire and give it much attention.

An incident now occurred that illustrated the adage about the ill wind. The trend of business and the changes in the neighborhood about the Church of the Annunciation on West Fourteenth Street between Sixth and Seventh Avenues, together with that church's nearness to Grace Church and the Church of the Ascension, caused the rector and vestry of Annunciation to feel its usefulness there was at an end. A Committee of the Vestry and the Rector, Dr. William J. Seabury, therefore formally offered their organ and bell to Holy Apostles, which gratefully accepted these gifts. Extensive repairs had to be made for an enlarged organ chamber, and new braces and joints were added throughout the spire to support a swinging bell. The work was done by Mr. W. H. Burnherd at a cost of $550.

The following are the Latin inscriptions on the bell, rehung in the belfry of the Church of the Holy Apostles, on Tuesday, April 23, 1895. (The parenthetical translations do not, of course, appear on the bell.)

ANNUNCIATION
(Church of the Annunciation)

✠

IN GLORIAM DEI
(To the glory of God)
DIE FESTI PENTECOSTES A.D. MDCCCLXXV
(On the festival day of Pentecost of the year 1875)
IN LOCUM CAMPANAE A.D.
MDCCCXLVII ELEVATAE—SUCCESSI
(I have succeeded to the place of the bell of the year 1847)
A.D. MDCCCLXXIV FRACTAE
(which was broken in the year 1874)
OMNIS SPIRITUS LAUDET DOMINUM. AMEN
(Let all souls praise the Lord. Amen)

✠

I.N.D.P.F. et SS. AMEN
(In the Name of God—Father, Son and Holy Spirit. Amen)
BENEDICAM DOMINUM IN OMNI TEMPORE
(I will praise the Lord at all time)
SEMPER LAUS EJUS IN ORE MEO
(Praise is always in my mouth)
ALLELUIA
(Hallelujah)

As for the organ, three conditions accompanied this gift: (a) Removal was to be at the expense of the recipient; (b)

Mr. A. A. Wild, the organist, was to accompany the organ and become the organist of the Church of the Holy Apostles; (c) An appropriate brass plate was to be placed on the organ case, recording the gift and the twenty-two years of Mr. Wild's services at the Church of the Annunciation.

The second condition, despite the fact that Mr. Albert Alexander Wild was considered one of the most distinguished organists in the city (a number of his hymn tunes were used in the Church Hymnal) did not add to the harmony in the choir of Holy Apostles or remedy the hurt feelings and unhappy position of Mr. Sheldon W. Ball, who for the past five years had served the church efficiently. Admittedly this was a difficult situation, but Mr. Wild, too, had a just claim that could not be ignored.

The old organ was sold for $300, and the new three-manual instrument put in its place. Removal of the old organ and its replacement by the new were handled by W. H. Davis and Son. While the old organ was pumped by hand, the new one was powered by a gas engine. The gift organ was first used in its new setting on Thursday evening, October 3, 1895, at which time a choral evensong took place, followed by an organ recital.

Other expenses were incurred at this time (1895-6). On either side of the chancel the floor was extended, a door was built leading into the vestry room, and new carpets were laid in the chancel and baptistry. On the second floor of the rectory, a door was cut leading to a space in the clerestory, forming a room from which the rector's invalid daughter, Cordelia, could hear the church services.

These alterations and improvements did not betoken solvency. In fact, the financial strain in 1895-6 became so acute that several of the vestrymen resigned. Still to be paid were the mortgages ($6,000) to Trinity Church, notes of over $2,000 and the mortgage on the rectory. The treasury showed a deficit of $2,330.20. The pew-renting system had almost ceased.*

---

*Appendix K, Item 8.

The rector made special appeals by letter to the congregation during the month of November, to increase their pledges to the church and to the Improvement Fund. Four hundred envelopes were sent out, and about two hundred persons responded with pledges amounting to about $1,500 annually.

Appeals were again made to Trinity, stressing the need of additional clerical help. Trinity responded December 31, 1897, by canceling the two mortgages held by that parish.

A campaign was deemed advisable to increase the interest in the parish and its work by appointing additional visiting clergy. Dr. Isaac C. Sturges was approached, but politely refused:

> Mt. Vernon, N. Y
> February 11, 1896.
>
> Mr. Clement S. Parsons:
> Dear Sir:—
> I beg leave to acknowledge your favor of Jan. 15 on behalf of the Rector, Wardens and Vestry of the Church of the Holy Apostles inviting me to become Curate and Missionary of said Chuch under the stipulation that after one year's service the connection may at any time be dissolved by a three (3) month's notice given by either party.
> I beg leave to express my thanks for the honor of the invitation.
> The stipulation renders it impossible for me to accept an invitation to a regular assistantship or curacy such as I now hold, such as any other clergymen who are regular assistants to ministers or curates of their parishes hold. You do not all of you, I am sure, realize how precarious and uncertain a clergyman's position might be under such a call. It would summon me from a much more secure position to one most insecure. I could not and would not accept the invitation under any such stipulation. You not only ask me to take a salary much less than I now receive, but you also ask me to change a secure position for one most insecure. The stipulation is strange and unusual. . .
> Wishing every success to your parish, I am
> Yours most respectfully,
> (Signed) I. C. STURGES.

* * * *

At the vestry meeting called November 1, 1898, a long discussion was opened as to the finances of the parish—its future means of support and the necessity of increasing the Endowment Fund. While it was generally agreed that there was no immediate need for action, it was also held that in the near future it would be necessary to make some radical change, and adopt plans other than those now pursued; *viz.*, it would be vital to raise an endowment that would be sufficient for all foreseeable contingencies. Victor C. Pedersen, M.D., advocated the advisability of inducing Trinity Church to assume full control of the parish. He suggested that the church and all other related properties be transferred to Trinity, with the understanding that the Church of the Holy Apostles be maintained in its present location. This plan seemed to meet with general favor, but no action was taken.

During the spring and early summer of 1899, the treasurer often showed a balance of only $30 as against bills and outstanding notes of over $2,000. The Music Committee of the Vestry were often in conference with the organist, Mr. Wild, who informed them that he was expending some $300 of his salary in various ways, leaving him only $700 for his personal use.

The twentieth century opened more brightly with a letter from Mr. Edmund L. Baylies, informing the vestry of the settlement of the suit (pending since 1889) for damages against the Ninth Avenue "El" line, whereby the church was awarded $6,000, or about $4,500 net after all expenses had been met. So in the following June, 1900, the treasurer could report, "All notes were paid and there is a balance in the treasury of $2,198.90, of which $2,000 has been allocated to reduce the mortgage on the rectory."

Some of the representative ladies of the parish on February 21, 1900, had already formed a committee for the celebration of the twenty-fifth anniversary of the coming of the rector to the, parish. A plan was also formulated to raise funds at this time for the cancellation of all indebtedness. Mrs. N. E. Baylies was made chairman, and associated with her were Mrs. Joseph S. Pedersen and Mrs. Victoria Pedersen. Officers and subcommittees were appointed in different representative organizations of the parish that "each and all might take part in this work." It was hoped "that the gentlemen of the vestry would give their hearty approval and strenuous efforts in co-operation in the good cause." The fund was named the "Quarter-Centennial Fund Association." Members of the vestry responded on February 28, 1900 in the following note:

> Your letter was read at the vestry, and I have been requested to convey to you and the ladies of your committee our thorough appreciation of your undertaking and assurance of our co-operation and support.
>
> John F. Bush, Sec'y.

The work of this committee was wound up in October, 1901, through the generosity of Mrs. Baylies, who paid the last sum necessary for the cancellation of the mortgage on the rectory. The church also came into a small legacy from the estate of the late Abigail W. Lyman.

Meanwhile, the preparations for the rector's Twenty-fifth Anniversary Service were progressing. Invitations were sent out early in the year to all members of the parish and their friends. Few knew what a strain the rector was undergoing, as it was not generally known in the congregation that he was suffering from cancer. On the vestry, at this time, were five men of medicine: Drs. James Pedersen, Charles E. Hubbard, Victor C. Pedersen, J. Walter Lyman, and John E. Smith. Dr. Backus was comforted by their understanding and sympathy. The Rev. William M. Mix had been engaged to assist him.

At the Anniversary Service, it was planned that the rector give a resume of his work, of present conditions, and of his expectations and hopes for the future. A silver cup containing $500 was presented to him.

On the day of the festival, March 17, 1901, the church was filled by a devoted and loving people. Dr. Backus bore himself with remarkable fortitude and courage, but those who knew his condition were truly anxious and apprehensive, especially his dear wife and children. His health seemed to fail rapidly toward the summer. Dr. Backus was too ill to attend the April meeting of the vestry, and the Senior Warden presided. After their meeting, the wardens went to the rectory to confer with him about a prolonged vacation, and to urge him to "continued [it] to his pleasure."

Dr. Backus' last service in the church was on Easter, April 6, 1901, when he expressed a wish in his sermon that all present had "as many lovely flowers in their hearts as [he saw] on the hats before him." His last official act took place in a most unusual way, an incident both startling and pathetic. From the celerestory window of the room above the chancel organ, he gave the Blessing at the occasion of the wedding of Mr. Henry Harrison Suplee to Miss Catherine Elizabeth Colwell, April 24, 1901, which Dr. Judge (then Rector of St. Matthew's Church) had been called to solemnize. Dr. Backus sounded like a voice from the grave—a ghostly voice—as few saw him or knew whence the utterance came.

A letter follows, written from his sick bed:

Rectory, Holy Trinity Sunday.

To the members of the Parish Guild:

I received your very sweet, cordial and encouraging communication some weeks ago, but have been too weak to reply before. It came to me with the freshness and glow of faith which characterized the Epistles of the Early Christians. . . .

Particularly do I wish to thank our dear sister Josephine Harrison for that lovely, fragrant bunch of May flowers which accompanied or preceded your note of greeting. Of all the grand bouquets of flowers I received, none are more beautiful and attractive to me than this little group of children from Plymouth Woods.

All the Saints salute you, especially those of this household. How dear the Parish Guild is to me! It is a Home in which we have done the Master's work and passed many pleasant hours together. It has realized some of our ideals and we have all been benefited. May God continue to prosper it and send His Holy Spirit to make us wise and fruitful in the spread of Christ's Kingdom in the world. We have much to thank Him for, but most of all for warm, devoted and prayerful hearts—His bright little circle of our consecrated friendships. We are brothers and sisters. We shall remain so to the last and forever. This is my first letter written since my sickness. I am discouraged some days, yet God is able to raise me up and restore me to health and to my dear friends of the Church, to the Parish Guild. God bless you all and keep you safely through the summer.

Your affectionate Pastor,

BRADY E. BACKUS.

Soon after writing this letter, Dr. Backus and his family left New York for his summer home at Ridgefield, Conn., where he died on Friday, August 2, 1901, in his sixty-second year. The funeral services were held at the Church of the Holy Apostles on Tuesday, August 6, at 11 A. M., attended by many of his fellow clergymen, who were in the city.

A Memorial Service for the late rector was arranged for Sunday morning November 10, 1901, so that the Bishop of the Diocese, the Rt. Rev. Henry Codman Potter, could be present. The Rev. Dr. Cornelius B. Smith, Rector of St. James' Church, gave the eulogy.

Members of the Churchman's Association placed the following Memorial Minute before its members:

The Bishop and Clergy of the Diocese of New York express their heartfelt sorrow at the untimely death of our dear brother, who fell asleep in Jesus at Ridgefield, Conn. In 1876 he became Rector of the Church of the Holy Apostles, in which position he continued for more than a quarter of a century until his lamented death. The church during this period went through a transition from an independent parish with a secured income to a missionary church on the borders of one of the most difficult fields of labor in the city.

But its zealous pastor never faltered in his decision to make the best of circumstances, and though many proposals were made for the removal of the church to a more wealthy part of the city, he determined to hold on to the Gospel plough in that field to which he felt he had been especially called, never looking back.

He won the esteem and respect of the people of the district as well as of the bishop and clergy of the Diocese. Dr. Backus was singularly well equipped, both as a scholar and a theologian, for the high office to which he had devoted his life. His humility was remarkable. This, combined with great steadfastness of purpose and determination of character, won for him the affection and esteem not only of his own people but of his brother clergymen.

Dr. Backus was a member of the Beta Beta Chapter of the Psi Upsilon fraternity, and for two successive years was elected President of the Alumni

Association of Trinity College..He was a member of the Mayflower Society. He was also a member of the New England Society of Colonial Wars, Sons of the Revolution, the Society of the War of 1812, the Society of Colonial Governors, the Bible and Prayer Book Committee, and the Churchman's Association.

The Bishop and Clergy of the Diocese desire to convey to his surviving widow and her family the assurance of the deepest sympathy.

(For the Clergy)

THOMAS P. HUGHES,
AUGUST ULMANN,
GUSTAV A. CARSTENSEN.

The rector's salary was continued to his widow till January 1, 1902, with the privilege of her occupying the rectory until the appointment of the new rector. At their August meeting, the vestry invited the Rev. Mr. Mix, the assistant, to assume temporary responsibility for the parish with the aid of Mr. Frederick A. Coleman, a student at the Seminary. On November 29, 1901, the Rev. Robert L. Paddock, Vicar of the Pro-Cathedral in Stanton Street, N. Y., was called as rector, and on December 17 Mr. Paddock wrote a letter of acceptance. The vestry forthwith requested the Rev. Mr. Paddock to assume the duties of rector on or about January 15, 1902. Notice of his acceptance was sent to the Bishop of the Diocese, the Rt. Rev. Henry Codman Potter, D.D.

THE REVEREND ROBERT LEWIS PADDOCK
1901 - 1907

―――――

Bishop of New York:

The Rt. Rev. Henry Codman Potter, D.D., 1887-1908

1903. First Successful Airplane Flight Near Kitty Hawk, N. C., by the Wright Brothers.

1905. Work Started on the Panama Canal.

1905. President Theodore Roosevelt's Campaign Against "The Trusts."

1907. All the Properties for Chelsea Park Asquired by the City.

1908. Federal Council of Churches of Christ in America Organized.

ROBERT LEWIS PADDOCK
Rector 1901 - 1907

ROBERT AND JEAN PADDOCK
Don in farm attire at Williamstown, Mass.

Chapter IX

THE REVEREND ROBERT LEWIS PADDOCK
1901 - 1907

The Social Gospel

The Rev. Robert Lewis Paddock was born in Brooklyn, New York, December 24, 1869, the son of John Adams and Fannie Chester (Fanning) Paddock. His father was then Rector of St. Peter's Church, Brooklyn, and his father's younger brother, Benjamin Henry Paddock, became Bishop of Massachusetts in 1873. At a meeting of the General Convention in New York in 1880 Robert's father was elected the first Missionary Bishop of the State of Washington, and in 1892 he became the Bishop of Olympia, the western part of the state.

As a lad, Robert attended the Polytechnic Institute of Brooklyn. When twelve years old he accompanied his family to their new home at Tacoma, Washington, early in 1881. On the trip west, his mother contracted pneumonia and died at Portland, Oregon. His sister Fannie took up the duties of home-making. The family, traveling by the Central Pacific Railroad, took eleven days to reach their destination. Many new and varied sights met the boy's eyes: Indians and Indian ponies, the covered wagon and stage coaches, and the great open prairies.

In 1888, young Paddock came east to attend St. Paul's School, Concord, N. H. At twenty he entered Trinity College, Hartford, Conn., and was graduated in 1894 with the degree of B.A., with honors in history and politics. He then attended Berkeley Divinity School (1894-7), Middletown, Conn. Upon graduation from Berkeley, he received a Master of Arts degree from Trinity College. In 1910, he was given the honorary degree of S.T.D. from Hobart College.

In 1897, Robert Lewis Paddock was ordained Deacon by the Rt. Rev. William Woodruff Niles, Bishop of New Hampshire, and ordained a Priest in 1898 by Bishop William Andrew

Leonard of the Diocese of Ohio. His first ministry was at St. Paul's Church in Southington, Conn. After his ordination to the Priesthood he became Assistant Rector of St. Paul's Church, Cleveland, Ohio, and while there was made the General Secretary of the Church Students' Missionary Association. From Cleveland he was called to New York as Vicar of the Stanton Street Mission, known as the Pro-Cathedral, under the Bishop of New York. His associates in this work were the Rev. George F. Nelson, D.D., the Rev. William Axford B. Homes, and the Rev. Frank Landon Humphreys, D.D. In that work Mr. Paddock remained until called as Rector of the Church of the Holy Apostles to succeed the late Dr. Backus.

While Vicar at the Pro-Cathedral, he threw himself into civic and social reform movements as a member of the "Committee of Fifteen," and actively associated himself with the "Reform Campaign" in the city which resulted in the election of Mayor Seth Low in 1901

After the long rectorship of Dr. Backus, the Church of the Holy Apostles felt the need of a young enthusiastic missioner on the changing West Side. The call was extended to him in November, 1901, in these words:

New York, N. Y., November 30, 1901.
My dear Sir:
    I have the great pleasure of advising you that at a meeting of the Vestry of the Church of the Holy Apostles, held last evening, you were unanimously elected Rector of the above named Church, to succeed the late Brady E. Backus, D.D., deceased; and I beg to quote from the minutes of the meeting above mentioned:
    "Moved and seconded that the Clerk be authorized, on behalf of the Vestry, to write to the Rev'd Robert L. Paddock, of the Pro-Cathedral, 130 Stanton St., extending to him a call to the Rectorship of the Church of the Holy Apostles, and requesting him to advise the Vestry through the Clerk of his intentions, it being understood that the yearly salary to be paid is $3,000.—Adopted."
    Awaiting the favor of your reply in response to the request of the Vestry, I am, dear Sir,
                    Yours faithfully,
            John F. Bush, Clerk, 453 West 21st St., New York.
                        *   *   *   *

The reply to Mr. Bush came on December 7, 1901:

My dear Sir:

I wish first to express my appreciation at receiving your unanimous call to the Rectorship of so noble a Parish.

I have weighed the matter carefully and prayerfully, and have decided to accept.

At your urgent request, I [shall] take office Jan. 1st, next.

May I ask for your prayers that God may give me the wisdom to fulfill so great a responsibility.

Commending you all to His keeping, I remain

Faithfully yours,

ROBT. L. PADDOCK.

*   *   *   *

A few days later in December, after his acceptance, the Rev. Mr. Paddock wrote the vestry asking them to defer his coming to the parish until the middle of January, 1902, "for a much needed rest." The Vestry acceded to this postponement to the fifteenth of the month and notified the Rev. Mr. Mix and the Lay Reader, Mr. Frederick A. Coleman, that their services would no longer be required after that date.

In a final letter to the vestry, the Rev. Mr. Paddock said in part:

I shall take up my residence in that part of town on the 15th of Jan. 1902. Before that time I will see Mr. Mix and talk with him of the work he has been doing. On the 15th when I move in I shall be ready to assume every duty. Bishop Potter will try to arrange to institute me on the morning of Tuesday, January 19th. If he cannot do so he will ask Bishop Worthington to represent him. I am looking forward with the greatest satisfaction. I am daily praying that priest and people may be greatly blessed, and that God may enable us to do "great things" for His glory and the good of our fellowmen. Kindly present my most cordial Christmas greetings to the congregation.

The first quarter of the twentieth century saw another great influx of foreigners to our shores. Over one million immigrants were now coming in each year. Many of them stayed, at least for a time, in and about New York. They crowded the East Side of the City, and numbers were to be found on the lower West

Side. It was the beginning of the day of the "social Gospel," in the forefront of which was the new rector of Holy Apostles. Like David, he had no fear of Goliath, the "Sachem" of Tammany Hall and his Philistines; he was ready to sponsor both honest government and the poor man's cause, and to give freely of his time and means.

The Christian social clergy were often feared as "Socialists." "Bob" Paddock, at thirty-three, was unafraid. He had shown his mettle in his leadership at the Pro-Cathedral in Stanton Street. His early New England training had left him with a deep-rooted conviction that truly Christ-like men acted like brothers. The Rev. Mr. Paddock believed in the Social Gospel in action, with it spower for good in any district of our city. He saw the weakness and inconsistency of training youth in religious habits and moral rectitude only to have them stained and degraded by contact with flagrant social evils which they were meeting in every walk of life and at every turn. While he was intent upon building up Christian character, he fought the satanic forces (ward heelers) that were making money by tearing down youthful integrity and uprightness. So he set himself to rectify these conditions.

One of the bitterest fights in which "Bob" Paddock had engaged was on the East Side of the city when he had campaigned to drive organized vice from the Stanton Street neighborhood. He had put the vice ring on the spot; now, located not far from the disorderly district about Sixth Avenue and Twenty-eighth Street, he was feared, his very life was threatened. The opposition, engineered by persons in high authority, was powerful and determined, but he never wavered in his purpose. With courage and fortitude, he gave himself for social betterment in his Master's name.

At a barbecue, held in a vacant lot at Tenth Avenue and Twenty-ninth Street, "Big Bill" Devery (Chief William Stephen Devery) paid his respects to his critics including "Dr." Paddock,

a preacher who had called him a "demagogue." Devery was no
master of the king's English, but he certainly knew what today
is called "mob psychology."

"I class Dr. Paddock, not me, with the demagogues," said Big Bill, his
face purple with rage and his hands trembling. "I claim the reverend Doctor
sowed seeds of a riot in the East Side in the red-light district. I claim that
he prostituted his cloth in the Eleventh District in driving prostitutes among
respectable folks. He can't say a word against me as Chief of Police, but I
can say this of him that in the trial of Capt. Herlihy, the reverend Doctor
swore that he had been in a house of prostitution for six hours. Perhaps his
watch stopped. Let Paddock go back to his red-light district job, as he calls
it. Mayor Low says that Commissioner Partridge can handle the vice problem
in New York City. Well, no one knows the East Side better than Paddock.
He spent six hours in one house of prostitutes—how many hours in other
houses? Why, the red-light district is worse now than it was ever before.
He once said that anyone who went on strike ought to be in jail. He is an
Englishman, y'know! He came from no one knows where. I doubt if he can
tell where he was born or how old he is. Coming over on the boat he lost
his character."*

The Rev. Mr. Paddock's influence was not confined to this
parish while he was its rector. He was known and admired by
many liberals in the city, for his personal convictions of what
he thought his Master's will. By the same token, as we have
seen, he often aroused violent oppositions, which was largely responsible for breaks in his health. He was often sought for meetings, addresses, and sermons, and always had something worth-
while to say. Through his leadership and personality many individuals and families were attracted to this church. The old, staid
Holy Apostles took on new life.

He who "came from no one knows where" set to work to
reorganize the parish. He formed new social groups and revital-
ized others. Though he may have overshot the mark occasionally,
his efforts on the whole were singularly successful. He started a
"Sewing School" and a "Good Will Boys' Club." Under his
guidance the "Dorcas" became the "Mothers' Club and Helping

---

*Dock Walloper, 1933. Richard J. Butler and Joseph Driscoll.
By courtesy of G. P. Putnam's Sons.

Hand." He formed the "Men's Neighborhood Club," open to all faiths, which grew in numbers and political influence until it was housed in its own building. He changed the typical city rectory into a staff-training home, in which he used but one room for himself. The books of the various societies were merged into one general library. The congregation became conscious of the neighborhood needs and even of the world-wide mission of the church. Soon the parish was to have its own missionary in Mexico.

So democratic became the atmosphere about the church that a wealthy lady who taught in the Sunday School, disliking to appear ostentatious, dismissed her coachman and carriage every Sunday a few blocks away from the church and walked the rest of the way. The rector's programs for advancement never ceased. When any objective was realized, "Bob" always came forward with a new one.

The Rev. Mr. Paddock was a convincing preacher. Always interesting, he carried his social and missionary message into the pulpit with zest and inspiration. He was intense in manner, speaking from few notes and often with his eyes closed. The whole life of the parish was quickened despite the uptown removal of parishioners. He was instrumental in creating a civic consciousness in the neighborhood, so much so that Chelsea Park came into existence largely through his influence.

The vestry interposed no objection to his program. It was composed at the time (1902) of Wardens, Robert H. Goff and George W. Ferguson and Vestrymen, James Pedersen, M.D., John F. Bush, J. Walter Lyman, M.D., Louis Ferguson, William N. Wilmer, Andrew H. Kellogg, John E. Smith, M.D., Charles E Hubbard, M.D., and George W. Ferguson, Jr. Early in the spring of 1902, upon the urging of the rector, the vestry passed the following resolution:

Resolved, that the Rector in establishing his "Forward Movement" be authorized to use the rectory for that purpose, and to engage an Assistant

Minister, two Deaconesses and a House-mother, all of whom shall be absolutely under his direction and control, at an expense not to exceed $2,500 per annum, the rector wishing it noted that he is giving $500 per annum as his share from his salary of $3,000.*

Before the end of the year, Mr. Paddock had expended $1,250 from his salary. Of course, there was the usual grumbling and opposition. The sexton, after thirty years of service, was much surprised to find that he had new duties assigned to him: the care of the rectory's furnace, cleaning the sidewalks, and any other chores required by the rector. But no matter, the work about the rectory or community house was not to be halted.

Early in 1902, the rector began work among the Chinese, remarking how "earnest and intelligent they are in learning our language and religion. Foreign missions are right here at our very doors." An earnest appeal was made for teachers. Also, in the fall of 1902, he announced that he expected to open a Sunday School for the Armenians and hold services in their language.

The rector's program for his first Lent was "Religious Conditions in the City of New York" and the work being done among different nationalities. Workers from various groups were to make addresses. He often said, "I wish the Church of the Holy Apostles to fulfill its mission to the West Side—To be a 'Seven-day-a-week Church!'" He hoped soon to have a new parish house and a settlement house connected with the church. He felt that societies of the church seemed a little selfish, insofar as they tended to assist and help only their own members. Members of societies, he believed, should call upon new parishioners and help all sorts of men and women to build up the church. He suggested that church organizations take up the study of different ethnic groups: "Germans, Italians, Swedes, Armenians, Hungarians, Jews, Indians, Negroes, the Oysterman along the Connecticut coast, Seamen, etc." In view of the work to be done, he questioned if it were not better for ten men to work

---

*Appendix K, Item 9.

and help rather than for the rector to endeavor to do the work of ten men. "The rector should be Director and Priest, and the people should cooperate to be successful."

The theme for his first Palm Sunday sermon was the "Forward Movement and Plans to Extend the Work of the Parish." He early announced that he intended to engage several workers who would live in the rectory as a Community House. At the Easter Monday election to the vestry (1903), there was some opposition, but the rector's recommendations won.

The first Memorial Service for the late rector, Dr. Backus, was held on March 22, 1903. The rector preached the sermon and spoke of the appreciation that was felt by all for the splendid work done in the past, and of the new day dawning for the Twentieth Century Christian Social Service. A fund was started to refinish the vestibule of the church and erect there a tablet to Dr. Backus' memory.

The inscription on the Memorial Tablet follows:

REV. BRADY ELECTUS BACKUS, D.D.
Beloved Rector of this Parish for Twenty-five years
1876 - 1901
"Be thou Faithful unto death and
I will give thee a Crown of Life."

His Devoted Friends and Parishioners have Erected this Tablet
and Beautified this Entrance in his Memory.
A. D. 1903.

By the early summer, Mr. Paddock had so given himself to the work that the vestry deemed it advisable that he take a two months' vacation—"at his own convenience."

Upon his return to the city, the rector found that the steeple had been badly damaged by a severe wind storm. A Special Meeting of the Vestry was called for the express purpose of consultation with an architect, Mr. Hill, who suggested a tile steeple to cost $1,000. The matter of tiling the entire church roof was also discussed, the whole work to cost about $3,000. Taking down the steeple and supplying a small belfry tower was suggested by the rector. Mr. Hill listed three possibilities: (a) tiling the steeple and the entire roof of the church; (b) tiling the steeple with necessary repairs; (c) taking down the steeple and finishing off the brickwork into a small tower.

The Treasurer's report, however, halted all ideas of immediate improvements when it showed a balance of only $143.19 in the treasury, with outstanding notes of over $1,000. It was then decided that the steeple be temporarily repaired with board sheeting until funds could be raised. The rector seemed to favor taking down the steeple, and asked at a gathering of seventy-five persons "whether it would not be better to take down the steeple and put the money into a club house for young women living in boarding houses and in hall bed-rooms, often without fire in the winter."

However, the majority present professed their great affection for the steeple and did not like to see it destroyed; though quite willing to help and comfort young girls as a part of their season's work. By May the following year sufficient funds were in the hands of the treasurer, and the actual work of repair was entrusted to a Mr. Richter.*

In February, the vestry complied with the new bylaws of 1895 governing the number and election of vestrymen. Three vestrymen were now to be elected each year for three years, and wardens alternately for two years. The rector announced that through the generosity of two friends, he had acquired the property of 365 West Twenty-seventh Street to further the plan of settlement house work. Early in the fall of 1907, he made known the donors, Mrs. Joseph Tuckerman, who had given $5,000, and Mrs. James Herman Aldrich, who was to provide $5,500 in her will. This building therefore became an integral part of the church properties. Unfortunately, however,

---

*See Appendix K. Item 10, 1904.

the latter sum was never forthcoming, leaving a mortgage of $5,500.

The summer of 1904 was spent in Europe by the rector. In October, after his return, he gave short accounts of his trip, mentioning the different cities visited. He told of the Mamertine Prison in Rome, where St. Peter and St. Paul were imprisoned, and the rings in the wall and floor to which prisoners were chained. The City of Venice held a charm for him. Then he spoke of the Chinatown Mission, which was close to his heart.

The general repairs during the summer of 1904 depleted the finances of the parish and left a deficit of $151.54. But at the December meeting the rector was able to announce the good news that Miss Helen Jean Aitken had promised $1,000 as a gift for the benefit of the Sunday School, available in February, 1915. This became an annual gift by Miss Aitken, donated for many years.*

The early fall was one of great eagerness to finish the redecoration of the interior of the church and other repair work in time for the Sixtieth Anniversary of the Incorporation of the Parish, to be held on November 6, 1904. Invitations were sent to all the members over the name of the rector. The notice recalled the date of the Incorporation, All Saints' Day, November 1, 1844, and stated in part:

A splendid history has been her portion, for God hath greatly blessed this parish work. To Him be all the glory. Let us crowd the dear old church hallowed by sacred memories of those gone before, and ready now to do a greater work than ever.

At the Holy Communion service at 10:45 A. M., the Rev. Cornelius B. Smith, Rector Emeritus of St. James' Church, was the special preacher. At the evening service at 7:45, the sermon was preached by the Rev. Dr. Mottet, Rector of the Church of the Holy Communion. The offerings on "Founder's Day" were

---

*Appendix K, Item 10.

for the expense incurred in redecorating the interior of the church in the light tint of Caen stone. On Thursday evening of the same week, a reception was held in the Parish Hall. Dr. Smith's sermon is quoted fully because of its intimate references to past rectors and their work.*

Meanwhile the Endowment Fund, under the able leadership of Dr. James Pedersen and Miss Minnie B. Ferguson, had reached its first objective of $20,000. The following January it was planned to hold special services to increase interest for a second fund of $30,000. The special preachers invited were the Rev. Lawrence T. Cole, Ph.D., Rector of Trinity School; the Rev. D. Parker Morgan of the Church of the Heavenly Rest; the Rev. Arthur H. Judge of St. Matthew's; Dr. William M. Grosvenor of the Church of the Incarnation; and the Rev. Howard C. Robbins.

In reference to the final disposition of this second fund, should the Church of the Holy Apostles cease to exist, three main opinions were voiced (a) The rector favored the transfer of the fund to the Church House Foundation of the Diocese; others believed that (b) the Bishop should be appointed a sole trustee, with the request that the income be expended in the missionary work in this locality; (c) the third view was that Trinity Church receive the income for the same purpose.

The final decision, as placed in the indenture, was that the Church House Foundation, if functioning, receive the income for missionary work in the Diocese; if not, Trinity Church was to receive it for work in this part of the city.

Again extensive and necessary repairs had to be made. Mr. Hill reported to the vestry that the second floor of the Parish House was unstable, even dangerous when overcrowded. Early in April, 1905, the rector announced to all societies using the Hall that the middle floor could not be used for dancing, basketball, or violent forms of exercise. He immediately set the

---

*See Appendix G.

parish in motion for the necessary funds to correct this situation.

Iron pillars and beams were suitably placed for additional support to the second floor, and a fire escape was added. The exterior was painted. At a cost of $1,980, the interior of the church was redecorated in light caen-stone color by Teschka-Muller Decorating Co., giving it a warmth it had not had for years. The organ was also thoroughly repaired and a new carpet placed in the choir and sanctuary. This work, begun in the spring, continued to occupy the attention of the vestry and the interest of the congregation through the year.

In January, 1906, the treasurer announced that all improvements had meant an outlay of $4,087.67. Thus the winter and spring of the New Year (1906) saw the Church of the Holy Apostles with its fabric thoroughly repaired and brightened in color. The whole spirit of the church was quickened in a way it had never equaled since. Besides the material improvements, the rector began to realize his dream of community service.

Great activity was in evidence—"Our Missionary in Mexico" —had returned to the city as assistant to the Rev. Mr. Paddock. Deaconnesses Edith C. Smith, Alice J. Knight, and Pauline M. Neidhardt were in residence. Mr. Louis E. Schwab and Horace E. Clute were active as lay workers. Mrs. Buckingham, as house mother, had taken over the duties at the rectory.

The rector suggested the advisability of increasing the official staff by another male and female worker, making 365 West Twenty-seventh Street a Deaconess Home and a shelter for young working girls. As examples were cited the work done for young girls in Chinatown and the rescue mission on Doyer Street, where special work was being done by maintaining reading rooms and a tea room.

The rector rejoiced that so much was being accomplished for the sake of the cause, not merely to please any particular person. "We are hitching our ideals to a star, aiming high, even if we do not always reach the heights."

No one appreciated more the unanimity in the parish and the improvements made to its fabric than the rector. Soon after the fire escape was in place on the Parish Hall, the rector apologized for mentioning such a depressing subject, whereupon one of the ladies present suggested that it be called a "veranda." The rector thoroughly enjoyed the remark, and laughingly invited all present to step out and enjoy their new veranda.

Early in 1906, the Twenty-seventh Street house was definitely turned into a Settlement House. The top floors were occupied by female workers of the staff, and the parlor floor was used as a club room for the Men's Neighborhood gatherings, open every evening and Sunday afternoons, with Mr. Edward Schoch as caretaker. At this time an iron-covered passageway was built between this Twenty-seventh Street building and the Parish House. For a year or more, the meetings of the vestry were held at the home of the Senior Warden, Robert H. Goff, because of his poor health.

For various reasons, this year of 1907 was an eventful time for the parish and its rector. For one thing, it was the year of the Rector's Fifth Anniversary celebration. Incidentally, the rector was becoming exhausted, and a six month leave of absence was granted to him in 1907 for rest and relaxation. Outstanding in this year, too, was the Rector's election by the House of Bishops as the first Missionary Bishop of Eastern Oregon.

The rector's Fifth Anniversary celebration was held on Sunday morning, January 20, with much rejoicing and thanksgiving for God's blessings vouchsafed to all. The Junior Warden, Dr. James Pedersen, expressed the sentiments of the congregation at the service in the following words:

Let us not be ashamed of, but rather rejoice in, the fact that we are attempting the humanly impossible. We are definitely undertaking a great deal more than we have either the time, strength, money, or talents to accomplish. But we are in no worldly business.

A letter was then read from the Senior Warden, who was too ill to attend:

> I can never thank sufficiently the good people who have honored me with their confidence, who have encouraged and inspired my life with no less a resolve than to give myself, body, mind, and soul, and all that I have, for God's children, wherever they may live, of whatever color or condition, however indifferent or hostile. Looking for no praise, no honor, not even expecting to be understood, but wanting to give myself in the spirit of the Master for saving of humanity.
>
> Think of it, nobody else can take our place. We have a definite niche to fill. If we do not do our work, it will be left undone. Brother, sister, shall we do it for His sake and for the sake of those for whom He has made us responsible?

A reception was held at the rectory on Thursday, January 24, and a parish dinner followed in the Hall on Friday with refreshments furnished by the ladies of the Parish Guild and the Dorcas Society. It made a happy week of rejoicing and a tribute of affection and loyalty to the rector.

The death of the Senior Warden, Robert Henry Goff, in his eighty-fifth year, February 28, 1907, was deeply felt by the whole parish. The funeral service was held at the church on Saturday, March 2.

Mr. Goff was an intense and active member of the parish since his early boyhood. He was always to be found in his pew, on the left side of the church with his family, until the year before his death. He was greatly loved by all—an upright, conscientious gentleman. His children possessed the same characteristics and, when living at home, were active in the work of the church. One son, Freeman Goff, was the first secretary of the Parish Guild begun in 1877, and Miss A. Zenaide Goff was an active member of the Women's Auxiliary and on the Committee of the Endowment Fund of the Parish.

The work in the parish had not all been "easy sledding" for the rector, even with an appreciative congregation and a helpful vestry behind him. His energy and nervous force were near exhaustion. The vestry, sitting as a whole at the April meeting (1907), carefully considered this fact, as well as the use he made of his salary, and passed the following resolution:

Whereas, it has come to the knowledge of the vestry that the rector has generously expended a large sum, probably $3,500 within the last year alone for expenses in connection with the parish work; therefore, be it resolved that the treasurer be authorized to pay him at once the sum of $1,200 in partial payment of the same, and that the rector furnish memoranda of such expenditures of vouchers he has at hand.

The vestry continued:

Further, Your Committee also finds that the rector by reason of overwork is in need of a more extended vacation than usual and that he is desirous of visiting the Holy Land and therefore it recommends the passage of the following motion: "Moved and seconded, that the rector be granted a vacation commencing May 1, for a period not exceeding six months, that he may visit the Holy Land and get a needed rest."

The rector returned in October, much refreshed. Shortly after his return, he announced his acceptance of the call by the House of Bishops, meeting at Richmond, Virginia, to become the first Missionary Bishop of Eastern Oregon. It was a difficult decision for the rector and a blow to the congregation.

Many memorials were sent to the rector by individuals and societies of the parish, as well as by the vestry, voicing their "earnest prayer for his guidance and ours that, standing together in the bonds of fellowship, all may be governed by what God would have us to do."

On November 3, 1907, at a Special Meeting called at the Rectory before the morning service, the Rev. Mr. Paddock stated to the vestry his decision. He considered it his duty to accept, and no argument could alter his determination, which had been arrived at "after prayer and thought."

Later on, when he spoke of his coming consecration, he said that his wish was to have only the friends personally interested in him present. He also spoke of the "confidence in and love for him manifested by the vestry during his rectorship, and the mutual affectionate relationship existing between them. He could not recall the day when the rector and the vestry had not been unanimous."

The Rev. Mr. Paddock, on November 14, 1907, then tendered his resignation as rector to take effect at the time of his consecration as Bishop. Thereupon his resignation was accepted "with profound regrets." The vestry added, "that they hoped he would remain at the rectory until his successor was in charge of the parish, or until he departed for Eastern Oregon."

The Consecration took place in the Church of the Holy Apostles on December 18, 1907. Admission was by card. The Consecrator was the Presiding Bishop, the Rt. Rev. Daniel Sylvester Tuttle. He was assisted by Bishop Henry Codman Potter and the Bishop of Washington, D. C., the Rt. Rev. Henry Yates Satterlee. The Rt. Rev. David Hummell Greer, Bishop Coadjutor of New York, was the preacher. His theme was "The Voice and the Presence, or Duty and Religion." The text was from St. John 1:23—"I am the voice of one crying in the wilderness, and The next day John seeth Jesus coming."*

Late in January, 1908, Bishop Robt. L. Paddock left New York for his new field of labors. His rectorship would have had a lasting effect on the parish, and there might have been no sudden let-down after his departure, if the neighborhood had been growing from American or North European stock. But this was not the case. Tides of population in our large cities have had more to do with the stability of parishes than the personalities of religious leaders.

Visiting the Parish Guild of the church during his leave-taking, he said he hoped that they would bestow a thought upon him, now and then, when he was far away and lonely, going among people who really did not want him to come, "and to pray for him also."

---

*See Appendix G. (Consecration Service).

Two years later he wrote the Guild:

The more I think of the Guild, the more I believe I love its members. Though my desire to accomplish great things along many lines kept me from giving the time to the Guild I would have liked, yet I always enjoyed looking in on the meetings, saying a word and having a little prayer. Please tell the good women that I can still pray for them, though absent in the body, and that I hope they will sometimes pray for their Bishop in Eastern Oregon.

Shortly after Bishop Paddock's departure to take up his arduous duties in the new field to which the church had called him, a number of his former parishioners and friends met and banded themselves into a society called the "League of Eastern Oregon." The members pledged themselves to pray for the success of Bishop Paddock in the work that God had given him to do, and to assist him in such ways as seemed best. By December, 1908, the League had been able to promise Bishop Paddock $600 a year to use at his discretion; in addition, it had paid all of the traveling expenses of Deaconess Knight from New York to her new place of residence in Baker City, Oregon, where she had gone to assist him.

Bishop Paddock began his new work "by spending a week in each of the principal places wherein the church had been organized, and conducting what practically amounted to a mission in several of these places." In Baker City, where he arrived on the evening of Friday, February 28, he met with a hearty reception. During the week, besides holding many services, he addressed various societies and laid the cornerstone of a new parish house. From Baker City he went to La Grande and gave afternoon addresses on Baptism, Confirmation, Holy Communion, and Prayer, and in the evenings spoke on the subject, "The One Holy, Catholic and Apostolic Church." The people of La Grande that year built a new rectory, planned a parish house, and refurnished their church. Bishop Paddock's next stop was at Pendleton, where on Sunday, March 8, he confirmed a class of twenty-five and preached to large congregations. The Dalles was the next town to which the Bishop went. There were many others, and from one of these towns, Cove, he sent an Easter greeting to the Church of the Holy Apostles which read as follows:

'Christ is Risen! Rejoice! Eastern Oregon greets Holy Apostles, Love.

During the spring and early summer, the Bishop visited the southern part of his district, stopping at towns off the railroad which had to be reached by stage or horseback.

From an article in "The Living Church" of this period:

Bishop Paddock blew in on me last evening as if he had been traveling by cyclone. A dusty slouched hat, flannel shirt, leather belt, sack coat and any old trousers formed his equipment. What with an unshaven face and several pounds of alkali dust, he would have driven the Archbishop of Canterbury over into Methodism, or drink! After a bath and a shave, and also an exchange of clothes, he again looked like the fine, attractive fellow he is. He had been staging it nearly constantly for several months. His last trip was especially trying. In many places he could get neither milk nor butter, and finally the potatoes gave out. He is, however, full of good spirits. To my mind he is making an ideal Western Bishop, notwithstanding the fact he comes from the East! Some of our clerical friends seem to think that "where a man lives" is of more importance than "what he can do," so far as the Episcopate is concerned, Paddock is a living example of their folly.

Bishop Paddock developed four self-supporting parishes and twenty-five missions and preaching stations. He conducted services in Baptist, Presbyterian, and Methodist churches, traveling by stage, on horseback, and often on foot with a pack on his back. In percentage of confirmations his record was the highest of any Missionary Bishop in the Church during his Episcopate. He declined the "Apportionment"—money allocated from the Domestic Board for Missions—except his salary, the largest portion of which was spent in his work. "We are a self-respecting people in Eastern Oregon," he remarked. "We haven't much, but we'll pay for our religion as we do for anything else."

Unfortunately, itinerant ministers frequently leave little outwardly to show for their efforts. Bishop Paddock's great ideals and sacrifices often yielded no commensurate results for the Episcopal Church in Eastern Oregon.

At the Fourth Convocation of Eastern Oregon, May 7, 1911, Bishop Paddock said:

> Since becoming Bishop, I have visited 110 towns and settlements. . . . Most of the towns are overchurched and oversupplied with ministers. For us to build another church and have another local pastor would seem to me to be a mistake, if not a crime or a sin. I found men constantly disgusted with duplication, diversity and fighting in the name of religion. . . . One town of 1,000 inhabitants has five churches and five ministers, where one could do the work and do it better, while the large opportunity would appeal to a large man, who would be able to employ assistants who would help him in the work.

He thought it might be possible to reconcile existing differences if in a united church an apostolically ordained minister were to hold a Communion service at night, another in the early morning according to our liturgy, and a third service of the Congregational and Presbyterian type at eleven. Another service of the Methodist type might be held in the evening, which would attract the Baptists and Disciples. He himself would be willing to attempt such a ministry. Not that these various types were necessarily the ultimate ways of worship, but a united church would effect at least a reduction of ill feeling, and perhaps there ought always to be more than one mode of worship. "God did not make us all alike. Unity is limited." He ended his address with an aspiration for the essentials of Christian unity.

As years passed by, he was severely criticized in some quarters for his "unorthodox methods." He wrote to Mrs. George W. Ferguson, a member of the Church of the Holy Apostles as follows:

P. O. Hood River, Oregon.
January 26, 1912.

I am still absorbed in this missionary field and problems. Many of the people are asleep or dead, and want to stay so. They rather resent my intrusion in wanting to disturb them and shake them out of their carelessness, indifference, selfishness and sin.

One of the greatest difficulties I know is to knock them, not so much senseless as into some sense, and yet to do it so lovingly and tactfully that they will get up and thank you for it.

We are making progress slowly, but surely on some unique lines, and we are strengthening our own members and winning many who have not been helping the Master definitely heretofore. Perhaps best of all, we are bringing the Christians of all names together, and are going some day to have unity in Eastern Oregon, and then may have something to give to you people way back in New York.

* * * *

In writing to Mrs. Ferguson's son Louis on December 5, 1912, the Bishop holds out a sporting hero's chance:

P. O. Hood River, Oregon.

My dear Louis:

Some day before the railroads have come to change things, I hope that you may pay me a visit and roam around with me. It might be a sort of Moody and Sankey combination; I doing the preaching, you the singing. Another part of your duty would be to arrange for a place of meeting, sweep out the hall, make a fire, and try and find some benches or planks for seats. Then with an iron triangle or dinner bell, to call the people to meeting.

If that formal announcement did not bring you, you would be expected, of course, to make the rounds of the stores and saloons and hypnotize those whom you found loafing on the street corners to come around. When we got them inside, though, some might be in rather bad condition, others hostile and others absolutely indifferent, almost defying us to rouse their interest; yet we would have to so interest them that they would have to like us personally, and give us a chance later, as we could talk with them to show them the importance of the better life and the way in which they could attain it.

For this rather difficult job, I could offer you about the wages that we pay to the man who digs dirt or breaks stone or chops wood. Along with it, I might promise a broken heart and the misunderstanding of most of the people amongst whom you go, for some would think you a fool and others a knave. You would be accused of doing the work for graft, and would meet with very little appreciation, for they would rather resent your wakening them out of their sleep, and in many cases would tell you that as they were dead, they preferred to stay dead, and wished, blankety-blank, you would leave them alone.

After this tempting offer with its rewards, I shall expect to receive a telegram saying that you accept at once, and for a life term.

* * * *

But it was in an earlier letter that the Bishop best summed up his feeling about the meaning of the work in Eastern Oregon:

From Baker City, Oregon.
November 30, 1908.

To the Vestry of Holy Apostles:

The outlook now is hopeful. That which I sought to accomplish, I feel I have attained, at least in a reasonable measure. Hereafter, I shall be able to live more normally. I have been almost a general missionary. I mean now to be more of an administrator. I have been reconnoitering and studying the problem and evolving a plan of campaign. Now, I believe we are ready to move forward. You, where the Church is strong, have the source of supplies. I am thankful that you feel the responsibility for keeping the outposts manned and provisioned. We missionaries are glad to help save, but we depend on you to hold the ropes. Miss Knight, your other representative here, is doing splendid service and has already won her way into the hearts of the people.

* * * *

If Bishop Paddock could have divided himself into as many parts as there were towns in Eastern Oregon, his work would have been astonishingly successful. But where were the helpers! However, no one can gainsay that Bishop Paddock put into his work in his Diocese a great spirit of self-sacrifice and largeness of heart. His was the Spirit of the Master: to be a shepherd in the Church of God among a widely scattered people.

After the American Expeditionary Forces embarked for France in 1917, Bishop Paddock also went overseas, serving first as Associate General Secretary of the Y.M.C.A. at its headquarters in Paris, and later being assigned to duty at the front. For a few years after his return from France, he resumed his work in Oregon; but criticism, together with the strain of his work and his war service, continued to undermine his health, and on pressing advice, he submitted his resignation as Bishop of Eastern Oregon to the General Convention of 1922, then meeting at Portland, Oregon. When it was accepted, Bishop Paddock was ill in New York.

A year later (Jan. 9, 1923) he married Miss Helen Jean Aitken in St. Columba's Chapel of the Cathedral of St. John

the Divine, the Rt. Rev. Arthur Selden Lloyd, Suffragan Bishop
of New York, performing the ceremony. For almost two years
Bishop and Mrs. Paddock traveled and visited many mission fields
in all parts of the world. It was hoped that he would regain his
health, but such was not to be and so he retired in New York,
giving himself to the advancement of church, social, civic, and
international causes. Because of his ill health, he seldom officiated
at church services.

Mrs. Paddock died January 31, 1937, and the funeral was
held at the Church of the Holy Apostles. The last rites were said
by Bishop Charles K. Gilbert and the rector. In 1938 Bishop
Paddock entered St. Luke's Hospital, requesting that he be placed
in a ward bed in a corner between a colored boy and a young
Italian. They formed a trio of Prayer and Praise. One of the
young men wrote the following letter to the Bishop and Convocation of Eastern Oregon:

April 25th,, 1939.

This is a message from Robert, to you personally and to all at Convocation who know him; yes, and to those who have "come after"—because
he feels that you and he and they all, belong to the one indivisble Eastern
Oregon family.

As he lay on his hospital bed on Easter morning, your message came to
him' I think a bolt was suddenly shot back in his mind and a door opened
into that country your letter describes as "right now in its loveliest dress—
the hills and plains covered with wild flowers—wish you could see it."

I believe it filled him with a deep yearning and when you added, "And
then get again the touch of the friendly people"—something else happened
within him which I feel certain became a surging wave, mighty like "home-
sickness."

Then he opened his eyes and looked about him. The sun was shining in
all the many windows of the ward and from just across the way the lights
and shadows from the Cathedral of St. John the Divine shot a tracery of
terrets and angel wings over the walls of the ward, and there were Easter
flowers everywhere. . .

The twenty beds in "Ward III" are occupied for the most part by men
of hoary heads, with a sprinkling of the blonds and brunets of youth; but
"everyman" of whatever color or faith partook of the Holy Communion at
the Easter Services on Easter Day, as Brothers and Children of One Father.

Next to Robert's bed, on one side, is a little colored boy, who has lain
there for six months, with a very bad heart and a very big smile! He is the

pet of the Ward—everybody loves "Porgie." He tells me that he and the Bishop have organized a "Club" at their end of the Ward.

"Tony," an Italian chap, occupied the bed on the other side for fourteen months with rheumatic fever. His real name is Anthony Glinbuzzi. "Tony" was able to go home for Easter and the members of the Club were thrilled to have a postal from him addressed to "Rev. Paddock." It said: "Hello Rev. I dropping you a line in hope it find you improved with all the rest of the boys who are in that corner! I hope you are teaching 'Porgie' his lessons so he can come for those ham and eggs you were talking about. . . . I am feeling well these days. I have nothing to do but rest and watch the world go by. Well, regards to your sister and all the folks around you. Regards, Tony."

P. S. I wonder if the "Ward Club" may join the Eastern Oregon Family for a moment and everybody close his eyes while "The Rev." raises his hands and voice in Benediction, as in the old days, asking a blessing on all the Eastern Oregon Family, and then join hands in singing, "Blest be the tie that binds our hearts."

* * * *

Bishop Paddock was able to leave St. Luke's Hospital for a few weeks. In his fatal illness, the Bishop was confined to St. John's Hospital, Brooklyn, where he died May 17, 1939, at the age of sixty-nine. The funeral took place at the Church of the Holy Apostles on Friday, May 19. The Rt. Rev. Charles K. Gilbert, Suffragan Bishop of New York officiated, assisted by the rector; also in the sanctuary was the Suffragan Bishop of the Diocese of Long Island, the Rt. Rev. John Blair Larned.

At the close of the funeral service, Bishop Gilbert read a special message:

Our departed brother arranged his own funeral long ago. He asked that his body be placed in the cheapest and simplest pine box and covered with a church pall which anyone can borrow. After the service his body will be cremated and his ashes scattered to the four winds in the harbor.

He believed Jesus would have us Christians follow His example in spirit, in life and death. He hoped his poorest friends and perhaps some of the richest, and those in between, would find it easier on principle to live on the least in order to share the more with those in need.

His message requests also that there be "no procession, no reserved seats, no ushers, no professional pallbearers." All his friends belong to one family in the sight of God.

May his soul rest in peace, through the mercies of God,
and may light perpetual shine upon him. Amen.

THE REVEREND APPLETON GRANNIS

1908 - 1910

Bishops of New York:

The Rt. Rev. Henry Codman Potter, D.D., 1887-1908

The Rt. Rev. David Hummell Greer, D.D., 1908-1919

1910. World Missionary Conference in Edinburgh.

APPLETON GRANNIS
Rector, 1908 - 1910

Chapter X

THE REVEREND APPLETON GRANNIS
1908 - 1910

Carrying On

Though the loss of "Bob" Paddock was next to irreparable, the vestry, in consultation with Bishop Greer, obtained a young, energetic, and forceful young man whose worth had been manifested in the church—the Rev. Appleton Grannis. It is no reflection on him to say that few men, if any, could have continued the former rector's policies, maintained the numerous contacts and friendships outside the parish, or obtained the publicity which had followed "Bob" from his Stanton Street days. Then there was the new-born "Eastern Oregon League" which focused attention on Bishop Paddock's new field of activity, his frequent letters, and his anticipated visits to New York. Above all was the fact that "their Bishop Paddock" was trying to do a new thing in a new field. In the nature of things, no successor could hope to pick up where Bishop Paddock had left off.

When the Rev. Mr. Grannis took up his ministry here, he found an absurdly overstaffed church for the demands of the neighborhood. There were two curates living in the rectory and four women workers in the Twenty-seventh Street Settlement House, all taking their meals at the rectory.

Within a year, the Rev. Horace E. Clute became a curate at Grace Chapel and the Rev. George Seymour Adriance Moore, curate at St. Chrysostom's Chapel. Deaconess Knight left for Eastern Oregon to work with Bishop Paddock. Deaconess Smith stayed on for a little over a year, Miss Loomis and Mrs. Darricott soon found engagements elsewhere. The lay assistants Messrs. Edward Schoch, superintendent of the Neighborhood House, and Louis E. Schwab continued with the new rector. Mr. Schwab became a member of the vestry in 1914 and Senior Warden in 1915, which post he occupied with great helpfulness until his death in 1935.

The Rev. Appleton Grannis was born at Manlius, N. Y., on April 9, 1871, the son of Charles Kelsey and Annie (Appleton) Grannis. He attended school at Utica, N. Y., and was confirmed at Grace Church, Utica, in 1884. Mr. Grannis was graduated with an A.B. degree from Columbia University in 1893. A year later he was graduated from the General Theological Seminary, then given a Master of Arts degree by Columbia in 1897. In June of 1896 he was ordained a Deacon in Grace Church, Orange, N. J., by the Rt. Rev. Thomas Alfred Starkey, Bishop of Newark, and the following year he was ordained to the priesthood by the same Bishop.

His first charge was at St. Peter's Church, Essex Fells, N. J., 1896-1902. While there he became acquainted with the Rev. Henry K. Denlinger, pastor of the Presbyterian Church, in Caldwell, N. J.—two miles distant.

The Rev. Mr. Grannis soon was called from Essex Fells to assist the Rev. Dr. Peters at St. Michael's Church, New York, 1902-1905; and from there to Trinity Church, Boston, Mass., where he remained until he accepted the Rectorship of the Church of the Holy Apostles in 1908. Mr. Grannis received the honorary degree of Doctor of Divinity in 1941 from International College, Springfield, Mass.

The Senior Warden, Dr. James Pedersen, conveyed the notice to Mr. Grannis of his election as Rector of the Church of the Holy Apostles. In his reply, the Rev. Mr. Grannis wrote:

I have received your formal notice of my call to the Rectorship of the Church of the Holy Apostles, and I am enclosing in this letter a formal acceptance addressed to the Wardens and Vestry of the Church. I appreciate your confidence in me, and I shall hope with your cordial cooperation to further the splendid work that Bishop Paddock has inaugurated. It is my intention to be with you the first Sunday in March.

*   *   *   *

The letter of acceptance read:

> Trinity Church, Boston, Mass.
> January 27, 1908.
> To the Wardens and Vestrymen of the Church of the Holy Apostles:
>   It will be my pleasure to accept the call to the Rectorship of the Church of the Holy Apostles with which you have honored me, and I shall hope to take up my new duties the first of March. I trust that under God's providence our mutual labors may be blessed, I am, your sincerely,
>   APPLETON GRANNIS.

Upon the receipt of the Rev. Mr. Grannis' acceptance, the vestry, at their regular meeting in February, entered into a frank and prolonged discussion lasting two hours on the affairs of the parish. The talk covered a wide range of subjects, such as the possibilities of improvement in the work, the staff system, the church's present opportunities, a prearranged and systematized plan of distribution of the church's offerings, its own missionary fund, and other kindred topics. But owing to the fact that the new rector had signified his intention of taking up his post on March 1, it was the consensus of opinion that no action be taken of any kind in his absence, nor until he had familiarized himself with the work and indicated his wishes. The vestry expressed itself as ready to extend the same support and sympathy to him and his views as had been given to the late rector.*

At the following March meeting, with the rector present, it was regularly moved and seconded that "the rector have every privilege to make such arrangements for the present and future as he deems wise and expedient." The balance in the treasury stood at $111.01, with outstanding bills of $300, and a loan of $500.

At the Sunday morning service, November 29, the Rev. Mr. Grannis was officially made rector according to the forms used in the "Office of Institution of Ministers" as printed in the Prayer Book. At an impressive service, Bishop Greer preached the sermon, and acted as Institutor. The church was filled to bid the new rector welcome and to show their good will.

On April 20, 1908, the date of the Easter Monday election

---

*Appenix K, Item 11.

to the vestry, that body was still headed by Wardens James Pedersen, M.D., and J. Walter Lyman, M.D. Mr. John B. Duncan was elected vestryman to fill the vacancy left by the death of Mr. William H. Wilmer. The other vestrymen at this time were Messrs. John A. Custons, Louis Ferguson, John C. Wolf, Courtney Hyde, Matthew Kennedy, Charles E. Hubbard, M.D., Oscar W. Ehrhorn, and Ross C. Van Bokkelen.

Tribute to the memory of Mr. Wilmer was paid by the vestry in the form of this memorial minute:

Resolved, that the vestry as individuals and as representatives of the parish bear witness to the strong personality of the late William N. Wilmer, a conscientious and painstaking public servant of the church, a generous and faithful communicant.

The son of a Bishop of the Church, he was by birth an aristocrat in the true sense of the term, yet ever preached and practised the democracy of Christ. A lawyer of high standing, amid manifold and professional and public obligations, he yet found some time each day to devote to this parish. Mindful of its needs, he stinted neither of his time nor of his talents and means, of which he gave without measure. His life and activities were as living sermons on the brotherhood of man, for of him it could be said: "He was one of Nature's noblemen."

The rector soon took hold of the complicated affairs of the parish with forcefulness and decision. He called as his assistant minister the Rev. Royal Ransom Miller, and as women workers, Miss Hermione A. Baldwin and Mrs. Florence E. Dunn—though he felt only one was needed.

The societies of the parish were well provided with leadership among their own members. Groups for women and girls now comprised the Woman's Auxiliary, the Altar Guild, the Dorcas Society, the Rector's Aid, the Helping Hand, the Junior and Senior Girls' Friendly Society, the Sewing School, the Parish Guild, and the Church Choirs. Those for men and boys included the Cadet Corps, the Senior and Junior Brotherhood of St. Andrew, the Electus Junior Club, the Paddock Club, and the Men's Neighborhood Club.

For the moment, the Sunday School was in a flourishing condition, with morning and afternoon sessions and about four hundred children on enrollment, but was soon to feel the effects of the changes in the neighborhood. In the fall of 1909, one morning session of the school seemed ample. Still, all the floors in the Parish House were used for classes, as well as the vestry room and the choir room. The faithful corps of teachers were seldom absent and brought into the school a spirit of earnestness and devotion. A good reference library for the teachers and interesting books for the pupils were available as of old. The offerings of the school were given to missions. Mr. Louis E. Schwab often cheered the hearts of the pupils and sick members of the school by sending down from Sharon, Connecticut, bunches of flowers from his gardens. This gracious kindness he continued for many years.

The afternoon session of the school was maintained for Chinese men under the able leadership of Mrs. Frank Eely, assisted by Mr. Albert Gong Poy, interpreter. Most of these eight or ten Orientals came to learn English; a few embraced Christianity and were baptized. Since the beginning of this school by Bishop Paddock in 1903, seven had embraced the Christian faith. Before the summer of 1909, Mrs. Eely became ill, and Mr. Gong Poy left for his native China. The Chinese Sunday School did not reopen in the fall. Mrs. Eely received the following letter from "Albert":

I will try to say a few remarks and do the best I can. I have been with you only five years, so my English is not very good. These few words will be a good-bye to you all. You have been very kind to me and I want to thank you for all your kindness. I will tell you what you have done for me.

Once I was blind, but now I can see. It is salvation for mind and soul. I hope to come back next year and see you all again, but am not sure because our life is given from God. We cannot tell from this morning till the night, but I know that if we do not meet on earth, we will meet in heaven. When I reach China, I shall try my best to tell the good tidings to my countrymen, and with the help of God I hope to turn them to believe in Christ as their Saviour.

*See Appendix K. Item 11, Report of the Treasurer, December, 1908.

I want to ask you to do me a favor—it is to pray for me—to ask God to give me more strength that I may be a good Christian in China. I hope God will bless you all.

ALBERT GONG POY.

* * * *

Early in April, 1909, the rector brought before the vestry and congregation the necessity of tiling the sanctuary and chancel, thus doing away with all badly worn carpets. This task was accomplished at a cost of nearly $3,000. Hardly had this work been undertaken when a near calamity placed an additional strain on the finances of the parish. A heavy windstorm during the summer blew off a large section of the paneling from the base of the belfry. This accident necessitated the construction of scaffolding from the ground upwards encircling the whole spire. Just what damage and how much work was to be done could not at once be easily determined. While the repair work in no way interfered with the regular services, the added financial strain was felt by the congregation and at the wrong time. Removing the rotten wood, covering the belfry entirely with copper, and rebuilding the drum of the spire cost $2,500.

From the Parish News, October, 1909, we take this item:

How proud and self-respecting the new copper-covered spire looks! After undergoing a long surgical operation it stands forth strong and sound. How it seems to put to shame poor little Chelsea Park in its desolate state of litter and confusion. But we have faith that some day Chelsea Park will be swept and garnished and that the lofty spire with its beautiful cross will look down upon a clean and lovely breathing place, where people of all ages may find rest and refreshment.

North of the church at this time, the neighborhood had been gutted by the excavations for the approach and station of the Pennsylvania Railroad. Along Ninth Avenue between Thirtieth and Thirty-third Streets, the avenue had its causeway and boardwalk. A number of parishioners had to find new homes, which usually were not to be found in this immediate neighborhood.

But bright spots also appeared. The vestry were called in a Special Meeting, April 26, 1910, to consider a letter from the Corporation of Trinity Church, dated January 14, which stated that "on November 8, 1909, the Vestry of Trinity duly resolved and were given power to cancel any mortgages held by the Corporation of Trinity Church on the property of other churches without payment provided."

In recognition of this gracious consideration by Trinity, the vestry of the church notes in their minutes:

> Whereas it is desirable to take advantage of the generous action and offer of the Vestry of Trinity Church: Be it resolved, That the Vestry of the Church of the Holy Apostles respectfully requests the cancellation without payment of the two mortgages; and the Vestry is authorized to sign receipts for the bonds and mortgages and to take all necessary steps for the effectual carrying out of the purposes of this resolution.

The nervous strain of his first two years as rector, plus the flooding of the rectory with gas fumes for a year or more because of the laying of gas mains in Twenty-eighth Street, affected the rector's health. Upon advice, he asked the vestry for a leave of absence to extend to such a date as his advisors considered it proper for him to return to the city. Other changes were at hand through the death of the sexton, Mr. Samuel Hays, who had served the church in that capacity since 1875. Mr. Hays had filled his place with an honorable record. He was a man respected by all who knew him and he performed faithfully and conscientiously the duties of his office, which he dignified by his consistent conduct. His son, Charles Hays, succeeded his father as sexton, occupying 296 Ninth Avenue.

Before the rector left for Colorado, he called in the Rev. Dr. Denlinger to assist the curate, the Rev. Mr. Miller. Dr. Denlinger was an able preacher, and was planning at the time to take Orders in the Episcopal Church. The rector knew him slightly while he was rector at Essex Fells, New Jersey, and wished now to assist Dr. Denlinger in his change of ministries. At this time, Dr. Denlinger had resigned his position as pastor of the High

Street Presbyterian Church in Newark, N. J. Fate destined him to become the next rector of the parish.

During January, 1910, he proved his ability to the congregation in his addresses on Wednesday evenings on the subject of the "Four Types of Brotherhood"—a series of addresses he had recently delivered in Newark, and which had met with a wide and popular response. By June, 1910, Dr. Denlinger was invited by the vestry, shortly after he was ordained to the Deaconate, to cooperate with the Standing Committee of the Vestry and to make such suggestions as he considered to be necessary for the best interests of the Parish. The Rev. Mr. Miller, the assistant, had resigned early in the spring of 1910.

The absence of the rector and the resignation of the assistant left a void in the parish, which was especially felt among the congregation and the vestry. By May it seemed necessary for the Standing Committee of the Vestry and the Officers of the Sunday School to form a special Supervisory Committee with power to regulate the use of the Parish Hall and other Church buildings and the conduct of the organizations using the buildings.

By October, 1910, the affairs of the parish and its work had so deteriorated that the vestry felt compelled to send the following resolution to the rector:

Resolved, that it is the sense of the vestry that the best interest of the parish will be conserved by having the work directed entirely by a Minister-in-charge, residing in the parish, and the vestry requests Mr. Grannis that he direct the Rev. Dr. Denlinger to take full charge of the parish work under the supervision of and until further action of the vestry, and it is further Resolved: That the salary as Rector cease from October 1, last, until further action of the vestry.

To this the rector replied:

Hotel Grand View, Manitou Springs, Colo.
October 29, 1910.
Mr. Courtney Hyde, Clerk of the Church of the Holy Apostles,
My dear Mr. Hyde:
As it seems advisable for me not to attempt to continue my duties as Rector of the Church of the Holy Apostles, I hereby formally tender my

resignation to take effect November 30, 1910. It is with the deepest regret that I have decided to take this step, and with a high appreciation of all the kindnesses that have been shown me. I believe that there is a great field for the Church of the Holy Apostles and I trust that my successor may do effectively the work that I had hoped to accomplish.

Praying every blessing on the work and the workers, I am, faithfully yours,

APPLETON GRANNIS.

*   *   *   *

The resignation of the Rev. Appleton Grannis as rector of the parish took effect November 30, 1910, and was accepted with sincere regret. The Clerk of the Vestry was instructed to write Mr. Grannis in comformity with a resolution expressing good wishes.

A farewell letter from the Rev. Mr. Grannis to the congregation follows:

Manitou Springs, Colo.
November 30, 1910.

My dear Friends:

It is with the deepest regret that I am writing to tell you of my resignation as Rector of the Church of the Holy Apostles. I had hoped that I might continue to be your Leader for many years to come, and that I might grow old in your service.

But it seems otherwise ordered. Gradually I have become convinced that it will be wisest for me not to settle again, for the present at least, in New York City, but to re-establish myself in a new location somewhere in the East, under somewhat different conditions.

At the same time I rejoice to say that the trouble which necessitated my enforced vacation has disappeared and that I am in better health than for years. I am planning to be in New York after Easter when I trust that I may have the pleasure of seeing you all. In the meantime I am temporarily in charge of St. Andrew's Church, Manitou, Colorado.

I shall always cherish the happiest memories of my association with the Church of the Holy Apostles and of the friends whom I have made there. It was both a pleasure and privilege to have known and worked among you.

I cannot speak too appreciatively of the willing and hearty support and encouragement that you gave to every good cause. No parish has more loyal or earnest workers. And I know full well that you will give the same cordial and hearty support to whomsoever, under the providence of God, is chosen as my successor.

I am, faithfully and sincerely yours,

APPLETON GRANNIS.

The Rev. Appleton Grannis remained in charge of St. Andrew's Church, Manitou Springs, Colo., for eighteen months, until the fall of 1911. He had by this time fully recovered his health, and on February 1, 1912, accepted the rectorship of St. Anne's Church, Lowell, Mass., where he remained for twenty-seven years; and then for a year took charge of St. Paul's American Church in Rome, Italy. Since his retirement, he has supplied as locum tenens in a number of churches.

As of the winter of 1949, the Rev. Appleton Grannis, D.D., is the only former rector of the Church of the Holy Apostles still living.

God grant him continued health and a long life of useful service.

THE REVEREND HENRY K. DENLINGER

1911 - 1917

Bishops of New York:

The Rt. Rev. David Hummell Greer, D.D., 1908-1919

The Rt. Rev. Charles Sumner Burch, D.D., 1911-1919
(Suffragan Bishop)

1914. World War I started.

1917. Entry of the United States into the War.

HENRY K. DENLINGER
Rector 1911 - 1917

DR. HENRY K. DENLINGER
1916

Chapter XI

THE REVEREND HENRY K. DENLINGER
1911 - 1917

Storm and Stress

The esprit de corps of the parish had been deeply affected by the loss of Bishop Paddock and the short rectorship of Mr. Grannis. Changes in the neighborhood and removals of parishioners did not help matters. The parish was hardly ready to realize that its main support now came from members no longer resident in the neighborhood. Already it was becoming somewhat difficult to retain a competent group of leaders and teachers in the Sunday School. The determined and tenacious qualities of the new rector were of no avail. On May, 1913, members of the vestry met with Dr. Mottet, Rector of the Church of the Holy Communion, "to discuss the future of the parish, or if there be any, how to avail itself for future usefulness." Later in the same year, two members of the vestry were appointed "to confer with the Bishop of the Diocese in regard to the future prospects of the parish."

By February 9, 1911, a Special Committee of the Vestry for the selection of a new rector reported the name of the Rev. Henry K. Denlinger, D.D. as their unanimous choice. The entire vestry, without a dissenting voice, then recommended that "Dr. Denlinger be called as the next rector of the church." A committee of four was appointed by the Senior Warden, Dr. James Pedersen, to wait upon Dr. Denlinger, Minister-in-Charge, now living in the rectory and to present to him the call in person.

The vestry has recorded this call as follows:

The Committee in the name of the Vestry and Church of the Holy Apostles extends to you a call to become its rector, feeling that you appreciate that in so doing, besides being the spiritual leader of the parish, you

173

also become the Presiding Officer of the Vestry with an equal voice with each of the other eleven members.

As by law the vestry as a body is charged with the temporalities of the church, it necessarily reserves the right to employ or call any assistants or other workers, to fix their compensation, and to prescribe their duties where necessary. The relations between the vestry and the rector of the parish have in the past always been pleasant and based on mutual consideration of one to the other. In the matter of compensation, the vestry has ever sought to be equitable and fixed the same from time to time, having in mind both the needs and welfare of the rector and the ability of the parish. While your compensation as Minister-in-Charge has been $2,100 per year, the vestry feels justified, in the event of your accepting the call, in increasing that amount from February 1, 1911, to $2,500 per year, in addition to the use of the rectory—rent and coal free.

Dr. Denlinger courteously replied that he would notify the vestry of his decision within a fortnight. This was his answer:

> Hotel Strand, Atlantic City, N. J.
> February 17, 1911.

My dear Dr. Pedersen:

I have decided definitely to accept the call to become Rector of the Church of the Holy Apostles. Will you then prepare a statement to be read by you for the vestry at the Sunday morning service? I will also have a statement to make at that time.

Should you wish to consult me about this in any way, I expect to be back in the city by Saturday noon. In the thought of many kindnesses,

> Faithfully yours,
> Henry K. Denlinger.

*   *   *   *

A report of the vestry's action was sent to the congregation and read by Dr. Pedersen, Senior Warden, at the morning service.

The new rector of the church was forty-five years old, of decided opinions, and rather impulsive. These qualities helped make this period in the history of the parish dramatic, if not always constructive.

*   *   *   *

Henry K. Denlinger was born September 25, 1866, of Swiss-Quaker ancestry, the son of Emmanuel and Sarah Denlinger.

His early life was spent in Lancaster County, Pa., and he was received into the Presbyterian Church upon profession of faith in 1882. As a youth he attended the country school at Sardonville, Pa. He entered Princeton Universtiy at twenty and was graduated from that University in 1890. In 1892 he received a Master of Arts degree, and in 1895 he was graduated from Princeton Theological Seminary with the degree of Bachelor of Divinity. In 1904 the Seminary awarded him the honorary degree of Doctor of Divinity.

His first ministry was as Pastor of the Presbyterian Church in Caldwell, N. J., 1895-1899. It was a large church for a youngster and built in anticipation of an influx of New York commuters.

"Fortunately," he says, "during my time, the commuters did not come. The congregation was largely rural. The salary was $2,000 a year and a parsonage with about two acres of ground. I loved it! The Manse of the Church was the home in which Grover Cleveland was born, his father having been pastor of that church for many years. The Manse is today set aside as a memorial to him."

Dr. Denlinger adds: "I stirred up resentment at Caldwell by inviting to my church an outspoken Socialist, the somewhat famous Bolton Hall, who was much like Norman Thomas today."

While at Caldwell, Dr. Denlinger struck up a friendship with the Rev. Appleton Grannis, the Rector of St. Peter's Episcopal Church, Essex Fells, N. J., and whom he was to succeed as rector of the Church of the Holy Apostles.

In 1899, Dr. Denlinger was called from Caldwell to a church at Bloomington, Ill., the largest Presbyterian Church in the State outside of Chicago. He says, "There I experienced a kind of landed aristocracy and a mingling of the two cultures—New England and the South, especially Kentucky and Virginia. In a sense, it completed my education."

While at Bloomington, he was instrumental in financing an

old ladies' home left without endowment, and in making possible a very much needed second hospital for that city.

Dr. Denlinger's next pastorate of consequence began in 1906 at the High Street Presbyterian Church of Newark, New Jersey. Perhaps the one outstanding note in his pastorate there was the fact that he became recognized as the leading preacher in Newark. He had a taste for literature and was a clever speaker. In spite of his success at Newark, and the prospects of a call to one of the largest Presbyterian churches in New York in the offing, he burned his bridges behind him to enter the Episcopal ministry at the age of forty-three.

Certain heartaches, brain beats, and questionings cannot be summed up in words. Dr. Denlinger was himself seeking a haven for a troubled soul. He knew that his ministry fell far short of God's Grace, but felt nevertheless that he must obey the call to declare that grace and glory. He turned to the Episcopal Prayer Book, Sacraments, and Ritual. Bishop Lines of Newark received him as a postulant, making his change of ministry as easy and rapid as possible under the canons. The Rev. Mr. Grannis aided by appointing him as Rector's Assistant at Holy Apostles. When in December, 1909, Mr. Grannis had to leave New York for Colorado, the assistant, the Rev. Mr. Miller, did the pastoral work and Dr. Denlinger supplied as special preacher. In June the vestry tendered a reception in his honor.

The Rev. Mr. Miller terminated his connection with the parish in June. Dr. Denlinger was ordained Deacon by Bishop Greer on Sunday, June 26, 1910. By his eloquence and ability and his affectionate nature, he quickly won a place for himself with the vestry, and for the most part with the congregation.

The brief incumbency of the Rev. Mr. Grannis had somewhat broken the spell of the congregation's "hero worship" for Bishop Paddock. Dr. Denlinger's comment in this connection is of interest:

While Bishop Paddock's two or three returns to the parish were marked by an unreasoning adulation that goes with "hero worship," I came to know him only slightly, and was not among them who admired him greatly.

They were, of course, miles apart in temperament and spiritual makeup. Dr. Denlinger's ambition, his relative disregard for the opinions of others, and his decided tenacity made his seven years as rector of the parish a kind of spiritual struggle that marked his whole career and destiny. There were constant changes of lay workers, sextons, curates, and vestry. Changes were frequently made in policies.

A few of the assisting ministers during this period were the Rev. Messrs. Maurice Kain, George M. Geisel, John H. Heady, Kenneth S. Guthrie, Freeman Daughters, Van Rensselaer Gibson, and Donald J. MacDonald.

In 1915, nearly a complete change-over had taken place in the personnel of the vestry to "men of the neighborhood"; although many of the former vestrymen retained their interest in the welfare of the parish. The yearly receipts were drying up, and the floating indebtedness increased from year to year.

One of Dr. Denlinger's first ventures during his rectorship was to turn the Twenty-seventh Street house into a Men's Community House for Christian men to live there with the assistant minister, the superintendent, and the organist. The first floor was to be open every night for the use of the Men's Club of the church.

The church was to be opened daily for rest and prayers, and the churchyard for refreshment. The rector stimulated interest in these objectives by addressing church groups on gardening and fresh air work, saying he wanted to have a pleasant lawn and benches in the yard around the church where mothers and babies who wished to avoid the crowds in Chelsea Park could sit and have the benefit of fresh air.

Dr. Denlinger successfully celebrated the seventy-fifth anniversary of the beginnings of the Sunday School in 1836. He connected this celebration with an endeavor to increase the Endowment Fund—now $77,500. A third objective was to rebuild and enlarge the Parish House at a cost of $40,000 by adding nine feet to the Ninth Avenue property on the church side, thus securing a thirty-five foot front on the avenue including 296 Ninth Avenue. This new addition to the hall running back from Ninth Avenue and connecting it with the present Parish House.

By May, 1912, on motion of the vestry, the committee of five on this enlarged Parish House idea was discharged, "having reported that in their judgment the project was inadvisable at the present time." By the fall of 1913, the two upper floors of the Men's Community House were rented and the Club removed to the second floor of 296 Ninth Avenue. It was also found impractible to keep the church and its yard open to the public without proper supervision.

During the anniversary week beginning Sunday, November 26, many gathered at the church and in the parish hall, Bishop Greer came and preached, confirming those presented. Addresses at various gatherings were made by Judge Robert Carey, the Hon. William Fellows, the Hon. James Faulkner, Mr. Dudley T. Upjohn of the "All Night Mission," Dr. Wm. Parker Morgan, the Rev. Arthur H. Judge, Dr. W. M. Geer, and Dr. William T. Manning, then Rector of Trinity Parish.

The Endowment Fund, now about $90,000, had been going on its momentum, increased largely through legacies and the leadership of the men and women long devoted to its furtherance. Three years hence, the Fund was to be increased by a legacy of $10,000 from the estate of the late Natalie E. Baylies.

Early in Dr. Denlinger's rectorship, on February 20, 1912, the Men's Neighborhood Club of Bishop Paddock's time was reorganized. The new men's club, though taking the name of its predecessor, was mainly parochial in spirit and membership. It became a lively organization in parish affairs and quite forceful in shaping parish policies. One of its first acts was to appoint a committee to investigate the affairs of the old neighborhood club. It criticised the few uptown, absentee vestrymen, and by

1914 challenged their election to the vestry. For a few years, the club had the "go-ahead signal" of the rector. Some of its members were vociferous at its meetings, although not always well informed.

Their first attack, which stirred the parish, was upon the sexton and the performance of his duties. Mr. Charles A. Hays, son of the former sexton, was forced to resign and vacate his place of business at 296 Ninth Avenue, which was now intended for the parish offices. According to the rector, "the first floor had become a sort of loafing place with use for an occasional corpse, Funeral Homes having sprung up all about. The sexton's brother-in-law had his office there and mulcted the settlement and the church in furnishing coal.

However, it should be emphasized that for the majority of the members of the men's club, their place of meeting, whether at the Twenty-seventh Street House or at Ninth Avenue, provided social benefits and recreation and was generally helpful in furthering the interests of the parish.

The voice of the club was first forcefully heard at the Annual Parish Meeting and Election on April 13, 1914. The church was now popularly known as "Chelsea's Old Home Church," a name first applied to it by the rector. The annual election date was changed to Easter Monday Night at seven o'clock. Heretofore, three to six men had usually made up the Annual Meeting; now, large gatherings were assembled who could be swayed by the orators of the occasion.

At the meeting in 1916, it was moved and passed that the right of women's suffrage be extended to the women of the parish, and that the Annual Parish Meeting be held on the first Monday in Advent at 8 P. M. In 1914, when changes began to happen, two men newly elected to the vestry were appointed to represent the Parish as Delegates to the Diocesan Convention. The Convention of 1916 was given a merry shock when Mr. Jens Nelson, one of the delegates, offered this resolution: Resolved: "that the rectors of parishes in the diocese give to their vestries an accounting of how they spend their time."

Another effort of Dr. Denlinger in 1914 was to bring the Endowment Fund of the Parish to its full objective—$100,000. The interest of the Third Fund, now $38,700, was necessarily added to the principal until it became $50,000. Members of the "Rector's Men's League" appeared before the Vestry in February with a larger scheme for an ultimate goal of $200,000, and explained to the vestry how easily this could be accomplished. No doubt there will always be some individuals who delight in devising visionary schemes that invariably work out better on paper than in real life.

In the meantime, the rector called together the associates of the Endowment Fund and asked their aid. After he described to them the status of the Rector's Men's League, the associates agreed that they would remain in office and help.*

The campaign began April 1, 1914, in the form of a "Letter of Appeal" commemorating the twentieth anniversary of the Endowment Fund, begun in 1894. This letter was sent to all members and former members of the parish and also to wealthy individuals of New York. It made the following interesting points:

1. Year by year the parish has become more and more a "downtown" parish.
2. It has felt the usual neighborhood changes incidental to the expansion of the city.
3. The income from sources within the parish have become reduced in consequence.
4. The demands upon the resources of the parish have increased and the character of the work to be done have become more exacting.
5. The city needs the downtown churches and parishes. In their locality they make for all that is implied in good citizenship.
6. The area covered by our parish is large; it extends from Twenty-third Street to Thirty-fourth Street and Sixth Avenue to the Hudson River.

---

*See Appendix F (Members of the Endowment Fund Association in 1914).

The largest sum received during this campaign was $1,000 from the Otis Elevator Company. Dr. Denlinger had spoken frequently to men at noon in the factories of the neighborhood under the auspices of the "McBurney"—Twenty-third Street Y.M.C.A. At the Otis Elevator Company each Wednesday during the winter season he had given a five-to-seven minute address, playing a portable organ. The company in May, 1915, presented the church with its check for the above amount. Dr. Denlinger goes on to say:

The voluntary attendants in the various shops and factories formed a Christian Labor Movement for which I wrote a Manifesto and helped frame a Constitution. At one of the meetings, I remember one of the laborers saying, "What bothers me is, I can't stand these"—Well,—something that sounded like "Pessimists."

Another year passed, and the sum visualized as necessary by Dr. Backus became a reality. Small gifts from individuals and parish societies, a year's interest, and a large gift of $3,000 from the Senior Warden, Mr. Louis E. Schwab, completed the fund—$100,000. The rector made an announcement to that effect at a parish dinner in the Parish Hall, February 29, 1916. All present then sang the Doxology.

At a last meeting of the Parish Guild before the summer, the rector was asked to say a few words:

I appreciate your calling upon me at this time. Mr. Dunn has just been singing one of the popular songs of the day, "Good-bye, Good luck, God bless you."

It brought to my mind the only use of the word "luck" in the Bible; found in the 129th Psalm. It is used there in a negative way. The Psalmist has been using the figure suggested by growing grain on the corners of the housetops, that never comes to a harvest. The flat, low-roofed houses in Palestine lent themselves to dust gathering in the corners, where now and again seeds would come and lodge themselves and grow; but of course soon withered. Then the Psalmist goes on to compare certain people to this grain, saying "Let them be as the grain upon the housetops, which withereth afore it groweth up; Wherewith the mover filleth not his hand, nor he that bindeth sheaves, his bosom. Neither do they that go by say, 'The blessing of the Lord be upon you: good luck in the name of the Lord.'"

I am glad that for this Parish Guild I can use this illustration in the positive sense. All who work for the Master, all groups who strive to do something in His Spirit, belong to those spiritual fields upon which we can wish blessing and luck. I congratulate you on your history. I can and do wish you "good luck in the name of the Lord." And then, as this is your closing night, and Mr. Dunn has sung a song that has in it "Good-bye," I will give you a farewell in the words of a little poem by George McDonald:

"Thou goest thine and I go mine;
Many ways we wend.
Many ways and many days
Ending in one end.

"Many a wrong and its curing song;
Many a road and many an inn.
Room to roam, but only one Home
For all the world to win."

The death of Mr. Herbert McCallion during the summer of 1916 came as a great shock to his many friends in the parish. He died saving others when a rowboat upset on a small lake in which were two of his Sunday School boys. Herbert McCallion was an ardent churchman, and as lay reader established the Mission of the Good Shepherd, Wakefield. In the "Parish News" of March, 1909, he wrote, "Much of the best missionary work in New York City is done by laymen. This is particularly true of the pioneer work in establishing missions in the Bronx and elsewhere."

Mr. McCallion saw children without a shepherd in the sparsely settled district of the upper Bronx just south of Mt. Vernon. He began to gather these children together, much as were gathered the young men and women who in 1836 formed the Eighth Avenue Sunday School. Possibly this prototype was part of his inspiration. For a time classes met at the homes of the people interested. Soon a Sunday School emerged, which held its sessions in an unused barn. The stable was soon transformed into a place of worship. A congregation gathered through the interest of the parents in their children, and it became known as the Good Shepherd Mission. A lot, valued at $7,000, was given by the De Peyster family, on which a cornerstone for a Chapel was laid in 1915 and completed at a cost of $5,000.

After the tragic death of Herbert McCallion, Dr. Denlinger in September, 1916, began a fund for a memorial. He asked the children of the Sunday School of Holy Apostles and others to send ten cents or more to the rector as a memorial gift to "this noble young man, who grew up among us into worthy living. Death came to him in noble guise and found him, as those who knew him would have expected, not unready but answering, 'Here am I. Greater love that no man than this, that he lay down his life for his friends.' "

The inscription (all in capital letters) on the tablet erected in the Church of the Good Shepherd reads:

HERBERT McCALLION
Born February 19, 1886—Died July 27, 1916
The first lay reader of this Chapel
Through whose efforts
The parish was established
He died while strong
To rescue two boys from drowning.

———

Greater love hath no man than this
That he lay down his life
For his friend.

*   *   *   *

During the one hundred years of the history of this parish, the rectors and one member have been instrumental in organizing or maintaining four mission churches, three of which are still integral members of the family of churches which compose the Diocese of New York. The last mission to be formed (in 1909) was the Chapel of the Good Shepherd, at Matilda Avenue and 238th Street, New York. It has now an independent Parish of 418 communicants, with the Rev. Herbert R. Stevenson as the present rector.

The organized churches which sprung from or were maintained through the efforts of rectors or members of the Church of the Holy Apostles are The Chapel of the Free Gospel (1859-1865), St. Timothy's Church (1856-1867), the Church of the Heavenly Rest (1868-1869), and the Church of the Good Shepherd (1909-1916).

* * * *

In the Church of the Holy Apostles, the year 1915 was like a lull before the storm of 1916-17, which would have wrecked the parish had not the Endowment Funds been completed by March, 1916.

One of the ventures of the rector in 1916 was the placing of an Art Room on the street floor of 296 Ninth Avenue. The second floor of the same building now housed the Men's Neighborhood Club, which was now displaced by Church Offices. At a Special Meeting of the Vestry on April 6, the change and action of the rector was approved. The rector now wrote in the "Chelsea Church Chronicle" (parish paper) that "Religion and Art are closely related at the roots. A love and appreciation of the beautiful is an element in all true refinement. It is a privilege given us as a church to grant this opportunity to the neighborhood and to relate ourselves in this way more closely to the community life." The opening of the Art Room took place in May, and was in charge of the rector.

Clouds were gathering! On July 13, 1916, following a motion made by the rector, the vestry passed the following resolution:

Resolved, that for the purpose of making necessary repairs and improvements to the church buildings and property owned by the church, for which no funds are available, that this church borrow $12,000 on bond and mortgage for three years with interest at the rate of 4½ per cent per annum on the property of 296 Ninth Avenue, and the rectory 360 West Twenty-eighth Street, with the buildings thereon. That the said sum is to be applied to general repairs to the church edifice and parish house and the other real estate of the Corporation including among other things a new heating plant to replace the present one, which is worn out, and also electric lighting plant to replace the gas now used in the church edifice.

The question of the necessity of the Art Room and the fact that the rector and the vestry had borrowed $12,000 were now lively questions among the congregation, to be followed up at the next Annual Meeting of the Parish.

A large gathering came to the Annual Meeting. Much criticism and apprehension had taken hold of members of the parish. Divisions of opinion had intensified as months had passed. Little had been done to allay anxiety. The unity and stability of the parish were threatened.

On the appointed night of the Annual Meeting and Elections to the Vestry, April 9, 1917, two rival factions and tickets held the field. The "Ballot of the Congregation" and the "Ballot of the Church." The ballot of the congregation nominated for Warden Mr. William J. Ballard, and for Vestrymen Messrs. James W. Patterson, William H. Hookey, and Andrew Thompson. Mr. Walter Hays was to fill the place of the late Sergeant Oliver Tims. The ballot of the church put up for Warden George B. Covington, and for Vestrymen Messrs. Frank L. Garrison, George A. Cripps, and George B. Kiely. Mr. Franklin Johnson was nominated on this ticket to replace Sergeant Oliver Tims, deceased.

The Rector opened this Annual Meeting with prayer and then read the laws governing the qualifications of voters at church elections. Soon the two factions declared themselves. Mr. James W. Patterson raised a point of order on the clause which refers to qualifications based on "membership since the parish was organized." He spoke to the point.

The Rector explained that this clause concerned parishes established within the year of election. It was ruled by a two-thirds vote of the congregation to proceed to the vestry room for balloting. The rector wrote:

Nothing just like a fight took place. The brother-in-law of the sexton, Mr. James W. Patterson, seeing defeat, came running up to me as my warden and I were taking the ballot box to the vestry room for the count, and shaking his fist with horrible profanity, dropped dead at my feet. It raised a stink, but I got the Art Room.

The "Ballot of the Church" won. In a hush of awe, the Rector announced the results of the election:

We came here tonight on God's business. It is the season of Calvary and Resurrection, and in the freedom of that purchase you have exercised your franchise. In the presence of the event that adds solemnity to the occasion, I announce the election overwhelmingly of Mr. George B. Covington, Warden; Mr. Franklin Johnson, Vestryman for two years; and Messrs. Frank L. Garrison, George A. Cripps and George B. Kiely, Vestryman for three years.

The meeting then adjourned, but the pent-up emotions of the parish were in no wise relieved.

The parish received another shock in 1916. In a letter dated March 22, 1916, the rector and parish were notified by Trinity Church that "the Vestry of Trinity Parish have decided that they must consider seriously whether they are justified in continuing the gift of $3,000 each year to the Church of the Holy Apostles."

Dr. Denlinger replied the following day:

My dear Dr. Manning:
    It would certainly be a severe blow to the cause of Christ on this West Side of the city, at this crucial moment, if the $3,000 which Trinity has been giving annually to the work of the Church of the Holy Apostles should be taken from it. I am glad that before such action is taken, as Rector of the Church, I may have opportunity to meet the Committee and talk the matter over with them, as your letter suggests.

Dr. Denlinger met with the Committee of the Vestry of Trinity on April 6, with the result that the allowance was continued for one year from May 1, 1916, and from that date, the sum of $1,500 till January, 1918, when the allowance would cease.

On January 20, 1917, Dr. Denlinger wrote the Rector of Trinity:

Holy Apostles is shaping and adjusting its finances to meet the discontinuance of aid on the part of Trinity Corporation. I beg, however, that you will consider that the adjustment to the withdrawal of so large a sum is not easy. . . . On the other hand, if Trinity will continue the gift of $3,000 to Holy Apostles for another year, from May 1st, 1917, to May 1st, 1918, such is the progress of the readjustment that the Rector and Vestrymen are making that I can guarantee for myself and for them that we will not again ask for any of this aid whatsoever.

To the foregoing letter, Dr. Manning replied on January 24 1917:

. . . Presented your letter at the meeting of our Vestry last Monday night and said the best word of it that I could. I am sorry to say, however, that the Vestry feel unable to change the arrangement which they have already made and which is incorporated in the budget for the current year.

The arrangement is that the allowance to the Church of the Holy Apostles will be continued at the rate of $3,000 per annum until May 1, 1917; and that from May 1, 1917 to January 1, 1918, the allowance will be at the rate of $1,500 per annum.

After the late date mentioned, the allowance was discontinued altogether.

* * * *

Dissensions and financial troubles now multiplied. The rector seemed to feel that members of the Men's Club were the chief culprits. He appeared at one of their gatherings, notified them of the necessity of moving the church offices into their quarters above the Art Room and told them to move into the Parish House. Protests were made against this displacement, and one of the Vice-Presidents asked whether it was "worth the men's time and trouble, without the support of the church, to carry on the club?"

The Rector was accused of false statements and misrepresentations. The club took possession of the Parish House for a meeting, but the rector persisted in refusing rooms to them, and towards the end of June, 1917, disbanded the Club as a church organization.

One of the rifts in the clouds of 1916-7 was the securing of a new organ through the Carnegie Organ Fund. Dr. Denlinger described this transaction thus:

> I owed this to a meeting with Archer Gibson, at that time the private organist of Mr. Charles M. Schwab.
>
> I met Mr. Gibson at a wedding in our church, the second marriage of a Whitney . . . and for the wedding, Archer Gibson had been lured to play our rattle-bang organ. Gibson took a fancy to me, and at the wedding breakfast complained of the organ.
>
> Through him we picked the lock of the Carnegie Fund which was never known to give save to small churches. The Carnegie Fund objected to round numbers. The old pipes, I said, were worth about $500. Although for a $5,000 organ, we would ask for $2,500 from Carnegie. The chief clerk made it $2,399. I raised the other half and we got the organ.

The new organ was installed by A. B. Felgemaker of Erie, Pennsylvania. The final cost was a little over $4,000. The console had three manuals, but the choir organ was never installed. Unfortunately, in less than ten years, this instrument began needing constant attention.

By the fall of 1916, the Treasurer's report was most disturbing, showing a deficit of about $10,000.*

An open letter was composed by the rector in September, 1916, and sent to all members:

> This is written for you; that you may know how we intend to work and grow. The church is here for a spiritual purpose . . . for the growth and healing of our Spirit and Soul, and the furtherance of the beautiful and good in life . . . YOUR life. Therefore, if you are one of us only for those things that you receive, we still wish you well and "God Speed." But we really want only those whose spirits are alive to our great opportunity, who wish to share in it.
>
> In the work before us to do, the church needs help and suggestions, not criticism. Criticism never has the heart in it. It is born of jealousy and envy. But we do want' you to work with us. We intend to work and grow. Are you with us, or are you not? Are you in the church for your-

---

*See Appendix K. Item 12.

self alone and for what you get, or are you in it for the good of all and to do your share? Are you really a Christian, which means consideration of others? We shall be interested to watch and know. H.K.D.

* * * *

But many in the congregation still disputed the propriety of the large $12,000 loan and the use made of the money. The lighting in the church was changed from gas to electricity early in 1917. The fixtures were of a very cheap order. The new heating plant, greatly needed and desirable, was never installed. The rector had proposed painting the exterior of the church and improving the beauty of the church yard by a new fence. These things were but partly done; most of the money borrowed had to be used for incurred indebtedness.

At a meeting of the vestry, June 14, 1917, the rector read a letter announcing his resignation to take effect on December 31, 1917. At a subsequent vestry meeting, December 14, 1917, Dr. Denlinger presented his formal resignation to take effect on the foregoing date.

The Junior Warden, Mr. George B. Covington, a personal friend and former classmate of the rector at Princeton University, then moved that the resignation be accepted "with deep and sincere regret . . . and with best wishes for his future work and welfare." The Bishop of the Diocese was informed.

The Chelsea Art Association was notified to discontinue the tenancy of the Art Room by January 1, 1918. The Senior Warden, Mr. Louis E. Schwab, offered the resolution that Mr. John Brooks Leavitt be employed by the vestry to act as their attorney in the proceedings brought by Mr. Jens Nelson (a member of the vestry) as to the legality of the present vestry and its right to represent the Corporation. This legal action started and continued by Mr. Nelson vs. the functioning vestry caused some concern and much annoyance, but never reached the courts.

In December, 1917, Messrs. Louis E. Schwab, Courtney Hyde, and George B. Covington were appointed to arrange for the calling of a new rector.

After leaving Holy Apostles, Dr. Denlinger became national lecturer for the Faith in American Foundations, visiting soldier camps in thirty states during the First World War. This work was under the National Educational Department of the Y.M.C.A., in which he was active for a year after demobilization. At this time, in 1918, he re-entered the "Presbyterian Group," feeling, as he said, "I could thus do more for the cause. However, I had never lost my love for the Episcopal ritual."

After his work in the Army camps, where he lectured to thousands of "doughboys," he became a member (1920-1932) of the faculty of the Connecticut Agricultural College, now the University of Connecticut. While there he became Assistant Professor in English and History, and at the direction of the President, he reorganized and became the head of the History Department, specializing in Moral Philosophy and Government.

In 1932, Dr. Denlinger removed to Hartford, Connecticut and taught public speaking, especially to insurance groups; and in 1934 he was made Director of the Hartford Federal College, set up by the Works Progress Administration (W.P.A.). He functioned in that position till 1938, when the college was closed by statute. His last position at seventy-seven years of age was real estate editor of the "Hartford Courant."

He died March 2, 1948, in his eighty-first year. His last words to the present rector were: "Pray for me. Keep your courage!"

THE REVEREND LUCIUS AARON EDELBLUTE

1918 - 1949

Bishops of New York:

The Rt. Rev. David Hummell Greer, D.D., 1908-1919
The Rt. Rev. Charles Sumner Burch, D.D., 1919-1920
The Rt. Rev. William Thomas Manning, D.D., 1921-1947
The Rt. Rev. Charles Kendall Gilbert, D.D., 1947-

* * * *

Suffragan Bishops of New York:

The Rt. Rev. Charles Sumner Burch, D.D., 1911-1919
The Rt. Rev. Herbert Shipman, D.D., 1921-1930.
The Rt. Rev. Arthur Selden Lloyd, D.D., 1921-1936
The Rt. Rev. Charles Kendall Gilbert, D.D., 1930-1947

1918. Armistice Signed After World War 1.
1920. League of Nations Organized.
1920. Seventh Avenue Interborough Subway Opened.
1927. Lausanne Conference on Faith and Order.
1929. Stock Market Crash and Era of Depression.
1933. "Bank Holiday."
1939. World War II Began in Europe.
1939. British King and Queen Toured the United States.
1941. Japanese Attack Pearl Harbor and United States Enters War.
1945. End of World War II.
1946. Proclamation by President Truman of End of World War II.
1947. "Boom Times."
1948. Golden Jubilee Commemorating Greater New York.
1948. Lambeth Conference of Anglican Bishops in London.
1948. Amsterdam Conference, "The World Council of Churches."

LUCIUS AARON EDELBLUTE

Rector, 1918 - 1949

Chapter XII

THE REVEREND LUCIUS AARON EDELBLUTE
1918 - 1949

The Challenge of the Present

The Reverend Lucius Aaron Edelblute was born on December 20, 1876, near Vernon, Indiana, today called "Old" Vernon —a "ghost town," since the days when the railroad built up North Vernon about two miles distant. He was the son of Lucius Samuel and Caroline (Redman) Edelblute, whose parents had settled near Delaware, Ohio, in the first part of the nineteenth century. In his youth he attended public schools in Cincinnati and at Sheboygan, Wisconsin.

In the fall of 1897 Mr. Edelblute entered Ripon Academy and later attended Ripon College, finishing his studies at Kenyon College and Bexley Hall, Gambier, Ohio. He was graduated from Kenyon College in 1904. Coming to New York in the fall of 1904 to complete his theological education, he entered the General Theological Seminary. While at the Seminary taking post-graduate work (1907-8), he received a Master of Arts degree from Columbia University and assisted at St. Peter's Church, Chelsea, where he became the curate in the spring of 1908.

The Rev. Mr. Edelblute was ordained a Deacon on the Fourth Sunday in Advent, December 22, 1907, at the Cathedral of St. John the Divine by the Rt. Rev. David Hummell Greer, D.D., Bishop Coadjutor of the Diocese of New York, and was advanced to the Priesthood on Trinity Sunday, June 14, 1908, at St. John's Chapel, Trinity Parish, by Bishop Greer.

From the fall of 1913 to May of 1914, the Rev. Mr. Edelblute taught at the West End School for boys, and while there was asked by Bishop Greer to take charge of St. George's Church, Williamsbridge, N. Y. In 1918 he was called to the rectorship of the Church of the Holy Apostles.

Below are the letters that were exchanged between the vestry and the Rev. Mr. Edelblute with reference to the call to the rectorship, followed by an appeal to the parish before Easter, 1918:

New York, February 26, 1918.

Rev. Lucius A. Edelblute,
661 East 219th Street, New York City.
Dear Mr. Edelblute:
The undersigned members of the pulpit committee of the Vestry of the Church of the Holy Apostles of the City of New York, in view of the authority reposed in them by virtue of a resolution of the Vestry dated February 13, 1918, a copy of which resolution is hereto annexed and made part thereof, do hereby issue to you a call to assume, undertake and fulfill the duties of rector of the Church of the Holy Apostles of the City of New York, a corporation organized under the laws of the State of New York, upon the terms and conditions as to salary and the furnishing and use of the rectory by you as in said resolution provided, which call is issued upon the understanding that you shall take charge and assume your duties as rector as aforesaid as soon as possible after the receipt of this paper but in any event on or before the first Monday of April, 1918; it being our desire that you shall be the Rector in charge of the Parish before and as soon before as possible, the next annual church election which is to be held on Easter Monday.

Very truly yours,

Louis E. Schwab,
George B. Covington,
Courtney Hyde.

* * * *

St. George's Rectory
Williamsbridge, New York

March 5, 1918.

To the Wardens and Vestrymen of the Church of the Holy Apostles, New York.

My dear Brethren:
After careful and prayerful consideration of the call to the Rectorship of the Church of the Holy Apostles, extended to me by the Pulpit Committee of said church, I beg to announce my acceptance of the call.

In accepting, I am not unmindful of the splendid work done in the past by the congregation of the Holy Apostles in old Chelsea; or of the devoted and consecrated pastors who have led and ministered at her altar. When I think upon these things, the flesh seems weak indeed, but not the spirit; for it is not our spirit, but God's Spirit, "that worketh in us to will and to do." His, then, is the work; His, the Spirit; His, the ultimate glory. It is only with the Christ working in and guiding me that I feel at all able to assume and try to fulfill the duties of Rector of the Church of the Holy Apostles

I know, for His dear sake, you will bear with me. I trust that my word of acceptance will be read to the congregation of the church, that they may know that their beloved church has again a spiritual head.

At present I will assume as many duties as time and distance will allow, and hope to be in residence not later than the first Monday after Easter, April 1, 1918. . . . .

On the first Sunday after Easter, April 7, I will officiate at the regular services in the church.

Wishing you all every blessing, I am

Yours sincerely,

LUCIUS A. EDELBLUTE.

*   *   *   *

Dear Friends (of the Parish):

Your Vestry has called Rev. Lucius A. Edelblute to be our Rector and Pastor. He comes to us with the highest endorsement and best wishes of our Bishop, Rt. Rev. David H. Greer, D.D. We ask you all to stand by the Church, help the rector serve the parish. The Church needs your help.

LOUIS E. SCHWAB, Senior Warden,
GEORGE B. COVINGTON, Junior Warden

It is hardly possible to exaggerate the anxiety in the mind of the unwary new rector when he began to encounter the unpleasant surprises in store for him. The air was often filled with vituperation and strife. The leader of a noisy group was Mr. Jens Nelson—he with a wicked look and fiery expression when aroused. One witnesses the same turmoil of undigested ideas at gatherings in New York's Union Square or London's Hyde Park. Mr. Nelson made his presence felt at most parish meetings by haranguing—not always contrary to facts—on many real and fancied grievances. After all, a questionable mortgage of $12,000 had been placed on church buildings, to name just one shining target for Mr. Nelson's shafts.

The new rector had little knowledge of the strife in the parish or its actual financial condition. While at the Seminary and during his curacy at St. Peter's Church, he had known this noble parish slightly under Bishop Paddock and the Rev. Appleton Grannis. Dr. Roche, on being told of Mr. Edelblute's acceptance of the rectorship, remarked, "Why? Does he want to ruin his ministry!"

On March 8, 1918, the rector received a letter from Miss Gertrude R. Cushman, daughter of Alonzo R. Cushman, one of the founders of the parish:

> Ever since I heard you had been chosen to be the Rector of the Holy Apostles, I have wondered if you know how changed the parish is. I have not been there for over a year and go to Trinity altogether, but I shall stir up some interest this year anyway if all goes well. Although this note sounds pessimistic, I don't want to be discouraging, but to let you know a little how matters are, which perhaps you might not have from the Vestry. If you bring it up even a little this year you will be doing good work.

Mr. George B. Covington, the Junior Warden, told the rector that as soon as legal matters were straightened out, he intended to withdraw from the parish. Miss Helen Jean Aitken, a liberal supporter, had definitely withdrawn her subscriptions. Other important members had temporarily withdrawn. Soon the organist, Mr. Scott Wheeler, and the sexton, Mr. John C. Futerer, took their leave. Messrs. George Cripps, Wm. Ballard, and Charles Hillock did the sexton's work during the summer months for which the vestry voiced their appreciation at their first meeting in the fall, October 10, 1918.

The societies of the parish had dwindled from fifteen to six. Many now met at the homes of members, such as the Woman's Auxiliary and the Parish Guild. The Altar Guild and the Choir still did their faithful duty, and the Dorcas Society, the Young Peoples' Union, and the Boy Scouts kept up their meetings in the Parish Hall.

The Rev. Mr. Edelblute was initiated into the sad conditions of the parish when he came down from St. George's Church, Williamsbridge, to take charge of the Annual Parish Meeting and Election, April 1, 1918. Sensing antagonisms, he began the meeting with a shortened form of Evening Prayer and an address. There were still violently contested "tickets" for the vestry: "The Ballot of the Church" and the "Ballot of the Congregation." Mr. Louis E. Schwab headed the "Ballot of the Church" as candidate for Senior Warden, and Mr. Jens Nelson was leader of the opposition.

The result of the election was that the old trusted vestry were retained: Wardens, Louis E. Schwab and George B. Covington and Vestrymen, Reginald C. Ballard, William Ballard, George A. Cripps, Noah Garrison, Charles Hillock, Courtney Hyde, George B. Kiely, and Wm. E. F. Smith.

The majority of the congregation, tired of dissension, were willing to support their new rector and his choice for the vestry, thus saving the parish further disaster. Mr. Nelson seemed to be a mental case and was actually so adjudged some years later when he forged a document of relationship to a wealthy Bowery recluse.

Immediately after the election, Mr. Nelson bombarded the rector with letters and documents. The following was typical:

April 9, 1918.

Reverend Sir:

On Monday evening, April 1st, 1918, at the Parish Meeting, I found it my duty to protest against the "nomination" of Louis E. Schwab for the office of Church Warden. Mr. Schwab could not be representing one Church in the State of New York and another in the State of Connecticut, as that is strictly against the spirit of Canon 12, part 2, of this Diocese.

(Mr. Schwab's summer home was at Sharon, Conn.)

I do also hereby demand that you issue to me a certificate of election as Church Warden for a two-year term of the said Holy Apostles Church, as it is a well known fact that both to you and all those present that I, Jens Nelson, was the only duly qualified and only unchallenged and only undisputed candidate for whom votes were cast for Church Warden at said election on April 1st, and I claim my right to be recognized as such. . . .

I have now demanded justice at your hands. It is now left to you to choose between Mr. Louis E. Schwab and the decision of the highest court in the state.

It is now left to you to do right or disregard right.

I shall expect to hear from you inside 48 hours.

JENS NELSON, 250 Tenth Ave., New York City.

Another letter (evidently written without assistance) followed:

Reverend Sir:

Thanks for the letter I received, for for the excuse it contains, I know before writting to you, whath yours answer would bee, for I know fulwel that, Mr. Schwab would not let you do otherwise. I only write the former simply as a matter of form, to be used latter, because there is moore to come abouth that Monday evening, April 1st, 1918 as yet. . . . There are still a lot of things to be cleared up, before the past can be discarded as you disired it to be, but there is many things wee may want, but whath wee get is a different thing and that always counts, as there is still many things to be replaced by some of the present vestry. I am Happy where i am now, Yust where I wanted to be. All of them that contribute to the support of the Church voted for me. While those that receive aid from the Church voted against me, oh I am proud of it. I am now free to act as I see fit, and I assure You I shall prove myself quite able to take care of the present Vestry.

It is my intention to remove them, and I shall succeed.

Hoping You and I will understand each other better, I am believe me,

Cincerely Yours,

JENS NELSON.

Mr. George B. Covington, an able lawyer, took these matters in hand and, during the trying ordeals of threats and legal proceedings that followed was of the greatest assistance, both legally and financially, to the rector and the parish. In less than two years the whole matter was forgotten.

*   *   *   *

The vestry and congregation tendered a reception to the rector and his mother in the Parish hall on April 25, 1918. The rector responded with thanks and said:

The reception given me, the redecoration of the rectory, the numerous expressions of good will, interest and hope, fill my heart with gratitude. I believe God will bless our parish and my ministry among you. For all the tokens of esteem and friendship to me and my mother. I thank you from the bottom of my heart.

However, Mr. Edelblute soon realized that the work to be done in the parish was beyond one man's time and energy, even with the valuable help of Mr. Louis E. Schwab as lay assistant.

To be sure, the active societies were under able leadership. Still, there were the three preaching services each week, the demands of the Sunday School, the Auxiliary No. 75 of the American Red Cross, and the returning veterans of the war.*

In September the rector fell ill, and though he recovered readily, he knew that he must give up the Wednesday evening service and have additional help for the Sunday School. His prayers were answered.

Early in the fall of 1918, the following letter was received:

My dear Mr. Edelblute:
    After prayerful consideration I have decided not to remain at St. George's after the first of July. I am looking for another position. Now that you are in the city, should you hear of anything to my advantage, will you please let me know as soon as possible. We all miss you so much. With much love to your mother. All good wishes and prayers.
    May the Lord bless and guide you is the prayer of,

Yours in His Name

MARGARET A. SQUIRE.

The rector immediately read the letter to Miss Helen Jean Aitken, asking her if she would not renew her interest and financial aid to Holy Apostles' Sunday School. Miss Aitken graciously and generously responded, making it possible for the parish to acquire the services of Miss Squire for the Sunday School and as Parish Visitor.

Miss Squire was well known in the diocese, having done splendid work at St. Bartholomew's Chapel, when Bishop Greer was rector of the parish. In 1913 Bishop Greer entrusted to her the oversight of All Saints Church, Henry and Scammel Streets. Later on, under Archdeacon Pott, she assisted in parish work and missions in the Bronx, and at St. George's, Williamsbridge. By her faithful work at Holy Apostles (1918-1925), she endeared

---

*See Appendix B (Veterans of World War I).

herself to all. Especially was she beloved by the children under her care in the kindergarten.

The summer of 1918 was the first in many years when the parish did not have to borrow money to meet current expenses.*

A year later Bishop Greer appointed Sunday morning, May 4, 1919, as the day for the institution of the rector into the parish, asking Bishop Paddock, who had recently returned from war service in Europe, to act for him. On May 3, 1919, Bishop Paddock received the following protest:

Reverend Sir:

You are requested to postpone the institution of Rev. Lucius A. Edelblute until after the Convention of this Diocese has been held this month of May, 1919. The ground for this is:

1: That informal complaint and report of action has already been placed in the hands of the Bishop.

2: That formal complaint and charges have been forwarded and now either are or will be in possession of the Bishop of the Diocese of New York before 10 o'clock on Monday morning, May 5th, 1919.

3: That request has gone forth to the committee on credentials of the convention of the Diocese not to recognize the Vestry dictated to this congregation by said Rev. Lucius A. Edelblute.

4: That this objection is formal and will be used in any proceedings that may hereafter be taken on this matter.

Copy of this protest will be forwarded to the Bishop of New York.

In Witness Hereof, I set my hand on this, the 3rd day of May, 1919.

(Signed) JENS NELSON.

*   *   *   *

The letter for the institution from Bishop Greer read:

DIOCESE OF NEW YORK

TO OUR WELL BELOVED IN CHRIST,

The Reverend Lucius Aaron Edelblute, Presbyter,

GREETING.

WE DO BY THESE PRESENTS, give and grant unto you, in whose Learning, Diligence, sound Doctrine and Prudence, we do fully confide, our LICENSE AND AUTHORITY to perform the office of a Priest in the Parish of the Church of the Holy Apostles, in the City of New York.

---

*See Appendix K, Item 13.

And also hereby do INSTITUTE you into said parish possessed of full power to perform every Act of Sacerdotal Function among the People of the same; you continuing in communion with us, and complying with the rubrics and canons of the CHURCH, and with such lawful directions as you shall at any time receive from us.

AND AS A PRIEST CANONICALLY INSTITUTED into the office of Rector of the Church of the Holy Apostles you are faithfully to feed that portion of the flock of Christ which is now entrusted to you; not as a man-pleaser, but as continually bearing in mind that you are accountable to us here, and to the CHIEF BISHOP AND SOVEREIGN JUDGE of all hereafter.

AND AS THE LORD HATH ORDAINED that they who serve at the altar should live of the things belonging to the altar; so we authorize you to claim and enjoy all the accustomed temporalities appertaining to your care, until some urgent reason or reasons occasion a wish in you, or in the congregation committed to your charge, to bring about a separation and dissolution of all Sacerdotal relation between you and them; of all which you will give us due notice; and in case of any difference between you and your congregation, as to a separation and dissolution of all Sacerdotal connection between you and them, we, your Bishop, with the advice of our Presbyters, are to be the ultimate arbiter and judge.

IN WITNESS WHEREOF, we have hereunto affixed our Episcopal Seal and Signature, at the City of New York this fourth day of May, A. D., 1919, and in the Sixteenth year of our consecration.

DAVID H. GREER, Bishop of New York.
ROBT. L. PADDOCK, Bishop of Eastern Oregon,
Acting on behalf of the Bishop of New York.

*   *   *   *

Just before the institution of the rector, the vestry met in April, 1919, and recorded a rising unanimous vote "of thanks and confidence to the rector for the very efficient manner in which he had conducted the spiritual and financial welfare of the parish during the first year of his rectorship."

On the Sunday morning of Institution, the church was well filled with members and friends of the parish. The rector to be instituted was fortified by the presence and counsel of Bishop Paddock who said, "If there be any protests or disturbances, no matter of what nature, keep silent. Let me handle any situation that may arise."

Naturally, in view of the dire threats of Mr. Nelson, apprehension was felt by many when the words in the Office of Institution were read: "If any of you can show just cause why he may not be instituted, we proceed no further." Silence! Relief!

Bishop Paddock preached a moving and forceful sermon, relating interesting experiences at the "Front," and pointing out lessons to be learned from the Great War. A special offering was taken for the Bishop's work in Eastern Oregon. The occasion became a most happy event, and although the services of Holy Communion, the Office of Institution, and the sermon necessarily took time, the solemnity, beauty, and brotherliness inspired by the Bishop were long remembered by those present.

During the early summer and fall many repairs were found necessary. The church windows (where tin had replaced the broken glass) were restored, and three new furnaces were purchased at a cost of $1,535. The Rev. Mr. Edelblute, supported by the vestry and congregation and the devoted leadership of Dr. James Pedersen, set about removing the mortgage of $12,000 placed on the rectory and 296 Ninth Avenue. Devotion was also shown by the sexton, Mr. Daniel Weymer, who spent himself till his death in 1920.

During the spring of 1919, Mr. Electus T. Backus, the son of the former beloved rector, Dr. Brady E. Backus, visited the rectory which had been his home as a boy. He volunteered his services to the church as organist and choirmaster, and also brought back to the parish his mother's interest and helpfulness. Mr. Backus had rare musical gifts and made the choir of boys, women, and men one of the outstanding choirs on the West Side of the city. He continued this service for his church until he made his home at Ridgefield, Conn., in 1934. Electus Taylor Backus died on March 10, 1938.

The close of the year 1919 filled the Rector with great sadness because of the death of his mother. The heartfelt sympathy of the parish was expressed by the vestry:

Resolved, that whereas, our heavenly Father has called to eternal rest and taken to His keeping, the dearly beloved mother of our rector: Whereas, her loss will be greatly felt by the church and the congregation: Be it—Resolved, that the vestry tender to our rector our heartfelt sympathy. Her death on December 15, 1919, in her seventy-second year, leaves behind her the remembrance of a lovely character, gentle and friendly.

A year hence, the mortgage of $12,000 was paid off amid great general satisfaction. On the Second Sunday in Advent, December 5, 1920, in the presence of one of the largest congregations for years past, a service unique in the history of the parish took place—"The Burning of the Mortgage"on the silver alms basin given by the Sunday School in 1871. After this ceremony, the Festival *Te Deum* of Dudley Buck was sung by the choir.

In presenting the mortgage to be burned, the Senior Warden, Mr. Louis E. Schwab, made these remarks:

Reverend Sir and dear Rector: I, Louis E. Schwab, as Senior Warden of the Church of the Holy Apostles do in the name and on behalf of the vestry, congregation and friends of this church, present to you this mortgage which has been paid by our generosity, and ask that it may be burned before us as a symbol of its being paid and as a pledge that we, congregation and vestry, will endeavor ever to keep these properties which are dedicated to God and given for the service of His church free from indebtedness.

To which the rector replied:

Mr. Senior Warden, I, Lucius A. Edelblute, as Rector of the Church of the Holy Apostles, thank the vestry for this kindness, and I also thank the congregation and friends of this church, who by their generosity have made this possible. It is with a supreme sense of thankfulness to Almighty God that I now set fire to this paper, and I ask that a fitting hymn of praise be sung.

The *Te Deum* was then sung.

The returning war veterans and some of the older men met the rector in January for the purpose of reorganizing the disbanded Men's Neighborhood Club. There were some misgivings among members of the vestry, but soon the club was well housed on the second floor of 296 Ninth Avenue, the men themselves taking in hand the refitting of their rooms. The club prospered for many years and was most helpful in its work and in the activities of the parish. But finally, in May, 1928, the affairs of the Men's Club were again taken up by the vestry who, with the rector's approval, expressed to them the opinion that the Club was now serving no real purpose and was hardly an asset to the life or work of the parish. In 1928, therefore, their rooms were rented.

The other parish societies functioning at this time were the Woman's Auxiliary, the Parish Guild, the Altar Guild, the Dorcas Society, Girls' Friendly Society, the Young People's Union, the Boy Scouts, a string orchestra, and the Sunday School Choir.

The Rector made over 600 calls in 1921, conducted 342 services, and preached and made addresses on 153 occasions. On the advice of the vestry, he sailed for Europe on the *Olympic*, June 25, 1921, and remained away till the middle of September.

The year 1922 opened most promisingly for the parish. Bishop Paddock had come to New York "to give an account of his Stewardship as Bishop of Eastern Oregon"—not to return West. His address before the Eastern Oregon League was, unusually for him, filled with statistics, soon understandable in the light of subsequent events and knowledge. He attended our Men's Club dinner, at which Bishop Shipman said grace. Bishop Paddock then made his address, carrying many back to the "old times" under his leadership.

Sunday evening, February 18, Bishop Paddock made an inspiring address in the church and, although a blizzard raged without, hearts were warm and aglow. People had come to hear him from the five Boroughs of the city. Ninety-seven persons of the "old days" at the Pro-Cathedral, Stanton Street, were present. After the service, all retired to the Parish Hall and there gave full vent to their joy and renewed fellowship. It was all in the spirit that keeps one young and spurs one to lead a better and brighter life.

A luncheon was given by Dr. James Pedersen in honor of Bishop Paddock on Monday, February 13, 1922. The rector has

never forgotten the place cards in the shape of a red heart, nor
the wording on them:

> This Luncheon:
> May be stag—but 'tisn't stagnant.
> Today is Monday—but NOT blue.
> It's the thirteenth—but it's lucky!
> Bishop Paddock—here's to you!

At the very time of the luncheon, the church narrowly
escaped being destroyed by fire. There was no little excitement
and a hurried departure. The lower floor of the Parish House and
the south transept of the Church were shrouded in flames and
scorching heat. Only the fact that the fire occurred in daylight
and was soon discovered by Miss Squire, together with the
prompt action of Chief Kenlon of the Fire Department, saved
this worthy landmark of old Chelsea from utter destruction. The
general damage done was considerably more than the insurance
received—$7,272.71. A twelve-foot hole was chopped through
the slate roof and the south transept was a wreck.

By the following Sunday, temporary repairs had so far pro-
gressed that, with little discomfort, the usual services were held.
Hymns of thanksgiving were sung and appropriate prayers
offered. In his address the rector recalled the fact that the church
was the oldest building along Ninth Avenue, and emphasized
how much it meant to the neighborhood and those accustomed
to worship here. On the following Easter Day, a "Thank Offering" ($2,531.77) was made by the congregation, one of the
largest Easter offerings in recent years. On the same Sunday,
Bishop Manning also made his first visit to the parish for Confirmation. His apt felicitations, followed by a forceful sermon,
cheered the hearts of the congregation. Later on Bishop Manning was instrumental in bringing the urgent need of the parish
to the attention of the Vestry of Trinity Church, and in obtain-
ing a gift of $3,000 toward the reconstruction.

After the fire, the sanctuary and chancel were entirely rearranged as well as beautified. Mr. W. Kerr Rainsford was the consulting architect. The organ was relocated with new screens on either side of the sanctuary. Mr. Rainsford designed the reframing of the picture, "The Ascension," above the altar, which was also retinted by the artist, Mr. Edward G. Unitt. Space was left immediately above the altar and below the picture for a reredos, also for side chapels in the empty bays of the transepts. Here Mr. Rainsford was trying to relieve the severity and bleakness of the spaces beyond the chancel by means of the dignity found in real beauty. The low wainscoting on either side of the altar was replaced by a higher motif so as to make the picture the dominant feature. The Tuscan character of the church was strongly emphasized in the picture's new frame. The detail here was adapted from the "Villa de la Pietra" at Florence, Italy. For sentimental reasons, the two Biblical inscription tablets were allowed to remain till 1941. The structural changes about the chancel and sanctuary were made for convenience as well as for effect. These consisted in widening the steps into the chancel, adding a parapet, and relocating the lectern and the pulpit. When the major work in the interior was finished, which had included the installing of new electric chandeliers, the releading of stained glass windows by J. & R. Lamb, and the cleaning and painting of the exterior of the church, the vestry had spent over $15,000.

Some time after the main work had been completed, Dr. Arthur H. Judge, Rector of St. Matthew and St. Timothy Parish, visited the church and wrote the Rev. Mr. Edelblute his congratulations:

I want to write you upon the transformation you have brought about in your fine old edifice. The new work is admirable. The whole aspect of the chancel is a delight, and I do feel that you have taken one of our most stately church interiors and given it just that perfect completion it lacked before. The view of the chancel from the west end is admirable, the arrangement of the choir, pulpit and lectern very decidedly an improvement, and, when the organ pipes to the right are in place, the work will be complete to satisfaction. You have done a fine thing and I think the whole diocese owes you a debt for taking in hand so reverent a restoration of the church.

This restoration and the fact that the church had been saved from destruction stimulated the whole parish to new zeal. A Healing Mission was held during Advent by the Rev. Van Rensselaer Gibson, and the following year (1923) "Ted" Mercer and Henry H. Hadley held a Witness Mission. Both were well attended with uplifting results.

On Sunday morning, November 23, 1924, a new reredos was dedicated to the memory of the Rev. Brady E. Backus, D.D., Rector of the Church from 1876-1901, by the Rt. Rev. Ethelbert Talbot, D.D., Bishop of Bethlehem, and Presiding Bishop. The reredos was given by Mr. Electus T. Backus in loving memory of his father.

On Christmas Day, 1924, a new processional Cross, blessed to the glory of God, was laid on the altar in loving memory of Marie Antoinette Whitlock. It was given by her surviving children, Miss Mary G. Whitlock, Mrs. Elwood Harlow, and Mr. W. P. Whitlock. The Cross measures twenty-one inches, and has a halo with twelve shields—symbolic of the twelve Apostles. R. & J. Lamb executed the design.

A new window, matching the others in the church, replaced one broken during the fire. This was dedicated to the memory of Miss Emma Vane Taylor, who had been an ardent worker and beloved by all. The window was given in February, 1925, by the Altar Guild and relatives and friends of Miss Taylor.

The rector and vestry were notified in March, 1923, of a large legacy of $17,000 bequeathed to the church by Anna J. Hilton, who for years was treasurer of the Fair and a member of the Dorcas Society. Two carved wooden candelabra of Italian workmanship, brought to this country about 1850, stand near the altar as a memorial to Miss Hilton, a generous benefactress of the parish.

The original intention of the vestry was to add this gift to the Endowment Fund, but the opinion soon prevailed that a better use of the money would be to purchase the building and lot of 294 Ninth Avenue (the Griffen property) in order to protect the south windows of the parish hall. The church was now paying $10 annually for light privileges. In October, 1923, this property was acquired for $24,000. For additional protection, the Peter McDonnell property, 367 West Twenty-seventh Street, was purchased for $11,500, the indebtedness assumed at this time was $22,000, and improvements soon to be made on these properties were to advance the indebtedness by $6,350.

The bequest of Mrs. Margaret Kennedy, whose death occurred on July 16, 1924, gave to the church almost her entire fortune, estimated at $112,000, but circumstances dissipated a large part of this legacy. Mrs. Kennedy was a life-long member, having been baptized in the church in 1847. Mr. Matthew Kennedy, her husband, was a vestryman from 1907 till the time of his death in 1916. Her brother, Mr. Robert Johnson, in a bequest, endowed a free bed in St. Luke's Hospital for the use of members of this church. Mrs. Kennedy endowed two more beds at St. Luke's for the same purpose; one in memory of her mother, Bridget Johnson, and the other in memory of herself. The power to appoint patients to these beds was vested in the rector.

Mrs. Kennedy's bequest brought about two long-drawn-out lawsuits, which were not adjusted till January, 1929. The first was by distant relatives, who contested her capacity at the time she made her will. The other, begun in May, 1926, was by Irwin Kotcher, respondent, vs. the rector, named in the will as executor, and the vestry of the church, appellants.

The plaintiff stated: option to buy two properties on Twenty-seventh Street valued at $60,000 for $36,000, as stated in a lease. On December 31, 1928, the Court of Appellate Division sustained the lease as a lease, but not the option to buy the properties at half their value after the death of Mrs. Kennedy.

After the satisfaction of a mortgage of $11,000 and the pay-

MEMORIAL REREDOS TO BRADY E. BACKUS

*The reredos is in the form of a triptych, suggestive of the Trinity.
It was designed by W. Kerr Rainsford. Below is a description in detail.*

The right side—Christ receiving the crown of thorns from the Roman soldier; above—the Paschal Lamb. Left—"Ecce Homo" and Pilate about to wash his hands; above—a fish meaning "Jesus Christ, Son of God, the Saviour." In the centre—two sleeping soldiers before the tomb of the Resurrection. The Person of the Redeemer is suggested by a Latin Cross surmounted by the imperial wreath that contains the monogram of Christ (XP). Two doves—the souls of believers—stand upon the arms of the cross and feed upon the leaves of the Tree of Life that compose the wreath. On either side of the centre are two angels of the Resurrection, above them peacocks—symbols of the Resurrection. On the extreme sides above are two cherubs holding a branch from the Tree of Life.

CENTER OF REREDOS, 1936   MEAD ALTAR MEMORIAL

INTERIOR OF CHURCH AND NEW ORGAN

MARGARET A. SQUIRES
AND SUNDAY SCHOOL CHILDREN

MEMORIAL ALTAR
TO MARGARET A. SQUIRES

BY REGINALD A. BALLARD

VESTRYMAN 1818-1829

It stands alone, and mounting high,
Its steeple pointing to the sky,
Through frowning clouds and sunshine clear—
The edifice we hold most dear.

And entering in, may we all pray
That it may stand for many a day
To spread the Gospel, teach the Word
Of Him whom the Apostles heard.

So come ye faithful, may your light
So shine that ye make others bright,
And He who said, "For you I die,"
Will take you to your rest on High.

COMMUNION SILVER, 1935

ment of fees of $10,951 to the law firms of Hoes & Miller and
Harrison, Elliot & Byrd, the church received the properties at
316 and 322 West Twenty-seventh Street unencumbered, but
now needing many repairs.

The chimes in the new Casavant organ were placed in the antiphonal
organ in the church gallery as a memorial to Mrs. Margaret Kennedy for
her munificence to the parish.
Other memorial gifts at this time were given for the enhancement of
the interior of the church. A memorial reredos was placed in the south
transept by Miss Nettie Hartman, in memory of the deceased members of
her family; four small sanctuary chairs were made a memorial to Mr. Charles
W. Knight; and a red silk, damask chalice veil and burse, also a pulpit
antependium of the same material, were given as memorials by Mrs. Anna
C. C. Carll, in loving memory of her husband, Albert Carll.

Early in March, 1925, the rector, as President of the Junior
Clergy Missionary Association of the City of New York, was
delegated to represent Bishop Manning in welcoming the first
group of Church Army men to the United States from England.
The party was led by Captains B. F. Mountford and C. C. Casey.
As they had traveled third class, they were detained for some
time on Ellis Island, but took the delay in good part. All ended
cheerfully as the rector and his guests had luncheon at the Seamen's Church Institute. In May the rector was given the privilege of addressing Church Army men from the outdoor pulpit
on Cathedral grounds, after which the first Church Army Mission vans were dedicated by Bishop Manning.

The parish suffered a sad loss in the death of its faithful
parish worker, Miss Margaret Alice Squire, on July 8, 1925. It
had been her wish that she might be found worthy to do her
Master's work till the very end of her life. Her wish was granted.
She suffered a stroke of paralysis on the morning of June 6. Next
Easter Day, 1926, a beautiful church banner, presented by the
children of the Sunday School, was dedicated to her memory.
Friends and members of the congregation also gave a suitable
altar for the Baptistry in her memory. At the blessing of the

altar, on June 12, 1926, the rector brought to the attention of the congregation the joy expressed in Miss Squire's life:

I feel that I can touch the heartstrings of that joy found in the life of our late parish worker. It was in her love for children. They seemed to have made up her very life. There was always a glow of great joy when she felt that she had been instrumental in bringing a child for baptism. So, on this Sunday, Trinity Sunday—the Sunday of Divine Love, for "God is Love"—let us pause in our prayers and remembrances of a soul dear to our Blessed Lord, Who said, "Suffer the little children to come unto Me, and forbid them not: for of such is the Kingdom of God."

Encouraged by the recent large legacies to the parish, the rector and vestry purchased 292 Ninth Avenue for $32,500, assuming a mortgage of $20,000. They also had every reason now to expect a favorable decision in the remaining Kennedy suit. It was their intention to assemble a blockfrontage facing Chelsea Park for future development. But the Wall Street crash of 1929 was not far ahead.

A joyous and prosperous year seemed in the offing for 1926, when the church appointed a committee in April to make preparations for the celebration in the fall of the Ninetieth Anniversary of the beginning of the Sunday School in 1836. At this time, each month, the treasurer of the parish was showing a balance of $500 to $1,000.

In the fall of 1926, Miss Lillian G. Stafford was engaged as parish worker. Miss Stafford had been employed in church work at Christ Church, Bedford Avenue, Brooklyn, with Canon Chase. She brought to the parish unusual ability, conscientious devotion, and an untiring zeal for the cause of Christ and His Church in the mission fields of the world. She became greatly admired and beloved in the parish; and deep regret was felt when, in the fall of 1947, Miss Stafford decided to leave Chelsea and become Parish Worker at the Chapel of the Holy Communion, Parish of Holy Apostles and The Mediator, Philadelphia, Pennsylvania.*

The Ninetieth Anniversary proved a most happy occasion, for, at the special Thanksgiving Service on the morning of

November 21, our Bishop, the Rt. Rev. William T. Manning, D.D., was present and preached the sermon. His felicitations to the rector and congregation were greatly appreciated.

At the Festival Reunion Service at 8 P. M., Dr. Arthur H. Judge was the preacher. Dr. Judge recalled his interest in and affection for the parish and its people since the time he became the Assistant to Dr. Backus in 1887. After the service, a social half hour was spent in the Parish Hall.

Anniversary week was followed by meetings in the church and hall, ending with Thanksgiving Day, November 25. The Chairman of the "Celebration" was Dr. James Pedersen. Others associated with him were the Wardens, Louis E. Schwab and Courtney Hyde; Mrs. Brady E. Backus, Miss Gertrude R. Cushman, Miss Grace M. Whitlock, Mr. Edmund L. Baylies, and Mr. William E. F. Smith.

Two years after the Ninetieth Anniversary celebration in 1928, the vestry and congregation tendered a reception to the rector on Saturday afternoon, May 5, at the rectory. It was his Tenth Anniversary. The following Sunday forty-five young people of the church attended an early Corporate Communion. At the other services, May 6, large congregations gathered to wish their rector Godspeed. At the eleven o'clock, the vestry followed the crucifer and, at the chancel steps, a testimonial was read by the Clerk of the Vestry, Mr. Wm. E. F. Smith.

The Churchwardens and Vestrymen of the Church of the Holy Apostles desire at this time to publicly extend to our beloved rector their hearty congratulations on this the Tenth Anniversary of your rectorship at this church.

Our united people, our flourishing Sunday School, and our beautiful edifice all bear witness to the realization of your high ideals of purpose and achievement.

May our mutual affection, esteem, and co-operation continue for many years, and may God's richest blessings attend your work and you.

---

*Appendix K, Item 14.

The following telegram was read from the Bishop of the Diocese:

> Warm and affectionate greetings to you and your vestry and people on this happy anniversary. May God's blessings continue to be with you all.
> (Signed) William T. Manning.

Another comment harked back to the early days of the rectorship:

> Mr. Edelblute took up the work at Holy Apostles with courage, ardor, and persistence. He found the church divided and in debt, but in two years, harmony was restored and a mortgage of $12,000 burned.

After the vestry's felicitations and the reading of the Bishop's telegram, a beautiful service followed, which had been arranged by Mr. Backus, organist and choirmaster. Before the sermon by Dr. Arthur H. Judge, the rector spoke a few words of greeting and appreciation to those present:

> I cannot resist the impulse of saying a few words of greeting and welcome at this point in the service. For, besides being the tenth anniversary of my rectorship here, it is also the twentieth anniversary of my ordination to the Priesthood. It, therefore, has a double significance for me.
> I want first of all to express my deep thanks to the vestry and congregation. As I looked back over the past ten years, I felt no hypocrisy when I began the morning service with "Dearly Beloved Brethren."
> You have been more than friends, comrades, brothers. Indeed, I believe that this, our anniversary together, will weld hearts to God and His Church. Working together in His Name we cannot fail.
> You have made me very happy many, many times, but at no time more so than at this our festival together, vestry and friends, congregation and pastor, priest and people, rejoicing before the Lord in happy relationship in His Name. May God bless you all.

Following the rector's greeting, Dr. Judge preached an eloquent and convincing sermon on "The Church, the Body of Christ," and then referred in these terms to the Rev. Mr. Edelblute's ten years of service:

> He is a true pastor of his people, a true priest of the Church of God. When he came here ten years ago he must have been appalled for a moment

when he realized the situation; but when he meets with difficulties his heart rises above them. He has been the general, and the parish the battalions which follow him. When the present rector came, public worship was carried on in the parish hall on very cold days because the furnaces emitted smoke and were inadequate for heating the church. Much thought had to be given to the work done immediately under the church—as well as the outside and yard fence. Then the fine harmonious windows, literally falling out in places, were restored. Next came the paying off of the debt of $12,000. Shortly after the fire damage, there was the consequent renewal and beautification at an expenditure of over $20,000. Then property was acquired to the south of the church as a protection from business encroachments. All this has been accomplished in a material way, as well as all the spiritual administrations.

At the evening service, Dr. John F. Steen, a neighbor and friend of the parish for over forty years, made an address. Before this address, the rector again entered the pulpit to greet and thank the large congregation. And so the ceremonies were concluded.

Late in January of the following year, an estimated hundred-mile gale lashed the city and did considerable damage to the church steeple and roof. Two pieces of the copper ridge-lines were torn off, hurled onto the church roof and into the street. The sidewalks about the church had to be roped off. The steeple was severely tested. It was fortunate that no one was injured, as it all happened at the noon hour, when many school children were passing the church. After examining the damage done and the condition of the steeple, a member of a firm of steeplejacks remarked that it did his heart good to see the kind of workmanship displayed in the tower and steeple. John Kavach & Co. repaired the damage at a cost of $1,100. The last repair work done on the steeple before 1929 was during the rectorship of Dr. Grannis, when $4,000 were spent. No real repair work has had to be done since.

The Vestry were notified in March that the church had received by legacy $10,000 from the estate of the late Mary Grace Whitlock. This sum was added to the Endowment Fund of the parish.

Miss Whitlock entered Life Eternal at the close of Easter Day, April 17, 1927. Thus ended the mortal life of a soul precious to the Risen and Glorified Christ. She had been a loyal and deeply devoted communicant of the parish all her life, admired and beloved by all.

The following March, her sister, Antoinette Whitlock Harlow, gave $1,000 to a fund to be known as "The Whitlock Flower Fund."

Early in 1929, the wrought iron Rood Screen, formerly in the Church of the Beloved Disciple, was given to the parish by Dr. Henry Darlington, Rector of the Church of the Heavenly Rest.

Upon the advice of Mr. Kerr Rainsford, the Rood Screen was made into two choir screens, one for each side of the chancel. In adorning these screens, Mr. Rainsford added finials and eight sconces. The screens were in place by Easter, 1930.

The church was also indebted to Dr. Darlington and the Vestry of the Church of the Heavenly Rest for the gift of ten pictures, which included "Christus Consolator," "The High Priest," and "The Four Evangelists." Most of these pictures were unsuitable for the Holy Apostles except the "Christus Consolator," which was placed as an altar piece in the Chapel of Rest. The other nine pictures were presented to the Rector of St. Martin's Church, Lenox Avenue and 122nd Street.

Before Advent, 1929, a number of new groups had been added to the societies already using the church buildings. The Willing Workers were a group of young girls who helped children in St. Mary's Hospital. The Junior Scouts were placed under the leadership of Edward Ferre and Mr. Joseph Ebbers, Scoutmaster. There were also the Young Peoples' Fellowship and the Junior Fellowship Club of which Mr. Frederick E. Boes was president.

A Prayer Group, The Children's Church, and the Junior Altar Guild had been formed, and were under the able leadership of the Parish Worker, Miss Stafford. The Girl Scout Troop 89 had Miss Sarah (Dolly) Every as Troop Leader.

The Sea Scouts, a Boys' Yacht and Hunting Club were organized by Mr. William I. Battin, Jr. In 1928, Scout Troop 338 under the leadership of Scoutmaster Mario E. La Penta, arranged for a summer Scout Camp (Bo-Lap) at Tomkins Cove, N. Y.

The camp was near the House of St. John at the "Cove" where hundreds of children and mothers from this parish and the city were given a two weeks' outing.

During the summer months, the children remaining in the city attended the "Children's Church" at 10 A. M. Bouquets of flowers from the garden of the Senior Warden, Mr. Louis E. Schwab, were often sent to the children.

At the children's Christmas Festival, the Sunday School, if the weather permitted, was gathered about an illuminated out-door Christmas tree in the church yard where carols were sung.

The comparatively new but incomplete Felgemaker organ placed in the church in 1916, largely through a gift from the Carnegie Fund, had become somewhat noisy, emitting "statics" not intended by the organist. A lady, somewhat hard of hearing, was heard to say as she left the church, "What a shame that someone snored through the beautiful service."

The plan in 1925 was to rebuild and complete the organ. By 1930, this plan was discarded when an organ fund for a new first-class instrument was started through the generous gift of $8,000 from an old friend of Dr. and Mrs. Backus, Mr. Edward Severin Clark, of Cooperstown, N. Y.

Mrs. Backus often recalled the Biblical warning: "Be not forgetful to entertain strangers: for thereby some have entertained angels unawares":

Soon after their arrival at Cooperstown, young Mr. Clark, wishing to welcome the rector and his young bride, called at Christ Church rectory. The front door-bell was out of order. The call terminated in the kitchen where Mrs. Backus was busily engaged in baking cookies. Freshly baked cookies and milk were enjoyed at the kitchen table by Mr. Clark. Mrs. Backus made happy by entertaining (as she supposed) a village young man who had dropped in to say "Hello!" The kitchen grew into a place of lasting concern and friendship during the rest of their lives.

The organ fund grew by other contributions and the parish raised $3,985. The names of donors were inscribed in a "Golden

Altar Book.''* Soon it was felt that it would be a mistake to incorporate any part of the old organ with the new. Prominent New York organists and organ builders were consulted, and it was found that to place in the Church one of the best organs of commanding proportions would cost something over $23,000. After two years more of intensive study, an order was finally placed with the Casavant Freres Organ Co. of St. Hyacinthe, Quebec, Canada. As a first step, the organ chambers were lowered four feet upon steel and concrete foundations so to accommodate a larger and heavier instrument. The old Felgemaker organ was sold for $500 to Grace Church at City Island.

On December 22, 1931, the new Casavant organ was completely set up. On that day, at 9:30 A. M., the rector was called into the church by the builders to hear the new organ breathe forth its first wonderful tones as the electricity was turned into the motor. It was like a mighty giant coming to life—really exciting.

The Inaugural Recital was given by Dr. F. Tertius Noble, organist of St. Thomas Church, New York, on the evening of February 29, 1932. Many pronounced the organ one of the finest in the city, and the recital by Dr. Noble as one of the best ever heard. Dr. James Pedersen remarked to the rector, "Why! We have now a regular cathedral organ in our dear old church." So it then seemed, and so it has continued to delight many eminent music lovers. Concerts were arranged and given by such outstanding organists as Messrs. David Williams, Clarence Dickinson, Lynwood Farnam, Seth Bingham, Kenneth Walton, Robert Bedell, Harold Friedell, Vernon de Tar, and Miss Lillian Carpenter.

Mr. William E. F. Smith, who for many years was Clerk of the Vestry, died on September 11, 1935. Mr. Smith had been on the vestry for over twenty years. He was a faithful and devoted member of the church, and always attended morning serv-

---

*See Appendix I (Names recorded in "Golden Book").

ice when he was in the city. As a good citizen he set a shining example, taking a keen interest not only in his church but also in the Mayflower Society, the Sons of the American Revolution, the Seventh Regiment, and the Mendelssohn Choral Society. Our late brother was always ready to give of his best to further worthy causes. In tribute to the esteem in which he was held, the following resolution was spread upon the minutes of the vestry:

Resolved, that in the passing of William E. F. Smith, the Church of the Holy Apostles has lost a good and faithful servant, and that the Rector, Wardens and Vestrymen extend to Mrs. Eleanor Smith and their family their deep sympathy.

On October 29 of the same year, the beloved and generous Senior Warden, Mr. Louis E. Schwab, was suddenly stricken with a heart attack and died. The whole parish was shocked. He had devoted practically his entire life to social welfare and religious work. Mr. Schwab had been with Bishop Paddock at the Pro-Cathedral before coming to the church of the Holy Apostles, where he became lay assistant and was especially helpful in the Church Office, as well as in the Sunday School and the Men's Club. The vestry set aside a Memorial Page in their minutes to his memory:

"We preach not ourselves, but Christ Jesus our Lord; and ourselves your servants for Jesus' sake."—so did Louis E. Schwab, our late beloved Senior Warden, by his life. His gentleness of character and loving service to the Church of the Holy Apostles will long be remembered by his fellow-vestry-men and the congregation of this church. For the past eighteen years during the present rectorship, and long before that time, he was instant in season and out of season thinking and planning for its welfare.

With infinite tact and gentlemanliness he was always ready to suggest ways and means of furthering the interests of his church. His whole life was given to the service of his Master.

The death of two such faithful and helpful men was a serious loss, especially when the problems of the parish were increasing from year to year. The rector and vestry in 1936 felt the time had come to bring forcefully to the congregation's attention the serious financial condition of the parish. A committee was appointed to devise a "Crisis Drive" in connection with the one hundredth anniversary of the beginning of the Mission Sunday School. A concert was held in April and a Fair in the fall. A general appeal was sent out by July to all friends of the parish, stating the indebtedness—$14,168.00. The mortgages were not considered in the statement.

From all these efforts, $2,148 was realized. Two persons lent the parish the sum of $4,000 without interest. Miss Emily Schwab generously canceled a loan of $3,815 which had been made to the church by her brother. And so for the next year or so, with high hopes for a better day, financial worries were put aside. The church was now living within its budget, but owing to the "depression" and the shrinking of interest rates, its Endowment Fund was not yielding as high an income as before.*

The commemoratory services of the Hundredth Anniversary were held on Sunday, November 15, 1936, with special hymns, festival *Te Deum*, and sermon by Dr. Arthur H. Judge. At the eleven o'clock service, Bishop Paddock was also present in the sanctuary and, at the close of the service, pronounced the Blessing. The rector read a telegram from Bishop Manning:

Congratulations and all good wishes to you and your vestry and people on the One Hundredth Anniversary of the beginnings of the Church of the Holy Apostles, God's grace and blessing be with you all.
(Signed) WILLIAM T. MANNING.

After a word of welcome to our visiting guests, Bishop Paddock and Dr. Judge, the rector said in part:

It is, I assure you, with great pleasure and rejoicing of heart, that I, as rector, greet you on this our Hundredth Anniversary celebration. We have gone through a number of depressions in the past—as we all so well know—and have come through them as a parish and people, and, I hope, not too seriously injured, for which we rejoice and give thanks today. And, what is more important, we are looking to many more years of usefulness in this neighborhood. We still have a feeling that our lot is cast right here.

---

*App. K, Item 15

As I stand in this pulpit this morning, it is humbling but also stimulating as I try to visualize our inheritance. And I pray that God's blessings may still rest upon us in this parish.

Dr. Judge took for his text, *Joshua* 1:7. "Be thou strong and very courageous."

At the eight o'clock Festival Reunion Service, Dr. Henry Darlington, Rector of the Church of the Heavenly Rest, was the special preacher and assisted the Rev. Mr. Edelblute in the dedication of the Chapel of Rest and the replacing of the picture, "Christus Consolator," which was formerly over the main altar under the baldachin in the old Church of the Heavenly Rest, Fifth Avenue and Forty-fifth Street.

The picture was painted in Italy, at the request of the Rev. Robert S. Howland, D.D. The artist was Joseph Mazzolini, a celebrated Italian painter. It was completed in the autumn of 1873.

It is a copy of the noted "Christus Consolator," painted by Ary Scheffer in 1837. The original now hangs in the Museum Fordor, Amsterdam, Holland, and illustrates *St. Luke* 4:18. In the original painting, the Christ is seated on a cloud, with outstretched arms, His face showing love, tenderness and compassion. Surrounding Him are the poor, the blind groping in darkness for the light of life, a brokenhearted mother placing her dead child at Jesus' feet seeking life through faith, and prisoners holding up their fettered arms to be released and made free to serve.

At the top of the picture are the words which gave the artist his conception of the subject:

Misit me sanare Contritor Corde. Praedicare captivis Remissionem.

During the processional hymn, "The Church's One Foundation is Jesus Christ her Lord," the choir halted in the vestibule of the church, where followed proper versicles and responses with the prayer:

Almighty and merciful God, Who hast granted grace unto Thy Priests; have respect unto our prayer and to our supplication. Hallow this Chapel of Rest, that those who visit it may be cheered and comforted by Thy Presence—*per Christum Consolatorem. Amen.*

Then followed the *Twenty-third Psalm* and *Gloria,* after

which the choir and clergy resumed procession to the chancel. A shortened evening service and sermon followed. Dr. Darlington in his sermon said in part:

> I bring to you not only my own greetings but the official greetings of the Vestry of the Church of the Heavenly Rest to the members of the Church of the Holy Apostles, the greetings of a daughter to a mother, because the Church of the Holy Apostles is the parish from which the Rev. Dr. Howland went out in 1868 to found the Parish of the Church of the Heavenly Rest. When the church was erected on Fifth Avenue near Forty-fifth Street, it was at the extreme northern limits of the city. The painting "Christus Consolator," was placed in our church by Dr. Howland and when, many years later, our church erected a new building farther uptown, the type and construction of the building provided no appropriate place for this picture. Therefore, with the approval of the rector and vestry and the written consent of Dr. Howland's heirs, the "Christus Consolator" was presented to the Church of the Holy Apostles. Your rector paid me a delicate compliment by inviting me to dedicate the picture tonight; and I am deeply touched by the thought that it is placed in your *Chapel of Rest*, for in that name, is implied the association with the Church of the Heavenly Rest.

In a little over two years, among losses sustained by death, few were more deeply felt by the rector and many in the congregation than that of Jean Aitken Paddock on January 31, 1937. Mrs. Paddock, over many years, had been ready always to use her influence and gifts for the furtherance of the work of the church.

A resolution of the vestry, February 14, 1937, reads:

> Resolved: That the Vestry of the Church of the Holy Apostles has heard with sorrow of the death of Jean Aitken Paddock, the wife of our beloved former rector, Robert Lewis Paddock, retired Bishop of the Missionary Diocese of Eastern Oregon. During her life, Mrs. Paddock was a sympathetic and generous contributor toward the many charities and benevolences, as well as to the general work of this parish.
>
> Her passing is felt a distinct loss to the parish, and we extend to Bishop Paddock and her family our sincere sympathy in their bereavement.

In May, 1937, the rector and vestry gave their approval to the ordination of Mr. Maurice W. Venno, who as a Seminary student had assisted in the church. Mr. and Mrs. Venno were most helpful in the work of our Sunday School and among the young people.

The Rev. Mr. Edelblute had now been the rector of the parish for twenty years. June 5, 1938 was chosen as the Sunday for the recognition of this fact. It was in form a "Spiritual Tribute" of prayer and thanksgiving by the congregation. A large four-layer anniversary cake was lighted with memorial candles in the Parish Hall after the evening service. The candles were so many that, when all were lighted, it appeared for a time that the whole cake might go up in smoke. The heat was surprisingly great from several hundred candles. Each candle represented one dollar or more of offerings, and the money so secured was used to help pay off the indebtedness on the organ. The net result was $1,276. The following sonnet was written as a tribute by Mabel Newton Betticher, who was most helpful in our Church School.

THE SUSTAINING CROSS

Where city problems, woes, unhappiness,
Oppress and burden with confused commands,
The Church of the Holy Apostles stands,
As witness, to the power and righteousness
The *Cross of Christ* develops and sustains.
As decades come and go, and needs increase,
The Church reveals the Power Christ called
     His Peace
Enables, in whate'er to life pertains.

We pause to-day and contemplate the view
Of twenty years; dispensing God's own Word
And Sacraments, as faithful stewards do,
A messenger and watchman clearly heard,
The Holy Spirit calls us all anew
To show the Cross makes known the *Way* preferred.

Whitsunday, 1938.   M. N. B.

* * * *

The following year the rector was honored by being elected president of the New York Churchman's Association. At the Mid-Lent Devotional Service, The Rt. Rev. Benjamin M. Washburn, Bishop of the Diocese of Newark, gave an hour of spiritual retreat to the members of the association.

Before the summer of 1939, the rector felt it necessary to open up a center for "Released Time from Public School" to pupils desirous of weekday religious instruction. It was called "The Louise Robison Center," in memory of the late principal of Public School 33, on West Twenty-eighth Street. Since then, it has been meeting each week from October to May, the group being under the auspices of the Protestant Teachers' Association of New York.

Owing to unsettled conditions before World War II and then the War itself, the church was now unable to meet the upkeep on its properties, especially with stabilized rent control. Recurring deficiencies followed in the church's finances, and legacies were used to meet these deficiencies. By 1945 the vestry planned to sell, at a considerable loss, all recently acquired real estate.

The year 1939 was filled with anxious forebodings by the people of Europe because of the breath-taking aggression of the Germans under Hitler. Uncertainty characterized the policy of most nations, as the question of war or peace oppressed the public mind. President Roosevelt and Congress had passed a "Neutrality Law" to prevent the United States being dragged into a war. By preserving our liberty of action, we could either decide to remain neutral in the event of actual war in Europe or to take sides on the objective merits of the situation. By March, 1941, Congress had transferred to the President absolute power over our domestic and our foreign affairs. Virtually, we were at war. On Sunday, December 7, 1941, came the Japanese attack on Pearl Harbor, soon followed by our formal declaration of war.

So World War II finally had come upon us. Its effects were quickly felt by every family in our land, and of course were reflected in church activities. By the summer of 1942, twenty-five young men, brought up in this parish, had been called into the service of their country. Upon their return, many never again took an active part in regular religious duties. By the end of the war, over one hundred young men had gone from our midst.* Early in the war the evening service had to be abandoned because of the darkened streets. This service was not resumed after the close of the war because of the general indifference.

Members of the vestry, conscious of the weakening forces of Christianity through disunion, passed a resolution at their January meeting in 1940 asking that delegates from this Diocese favor the proposed union of the Episcopal and Presbyterian Churches, commonly known as the Concordat:

Resolved: That it is the sense of the Rector, Churchwardens and Vestrymen of the Church of the Holy Apostles that, at the Diocesan Convention of New York, there should be elected to the General Convention of the Protestant Episcopal Church to be assembled in Kansas City, Mo., Deputies, Clerical and Lay, who will give sympathetic consideration to the proposed union of the Presbyterian and Episcopal Churches, commonly known as "The Concordat"; and, to that end, it urges its Parish Delegates to the Diocesan Convention to use every proper and appropriate means to accomplish this result.

The interior of the church was now badly in need of retinting. Mr. Robert Kinnier and the sexton, Mr. Daniel Brown, undertook the redecoration of the interior as a labor of love. This was accomplished during the summer and early fall. Also at this time the removal of the two rather heavy tablets situated on either side of the altar enhanced the beauty and subtle grandeur of the sanctuary with its dominating painting of the "Ascension" over the altar. On the first Sunday in October, 1941, at the eleven o'clock service the sexton and Mr. Kinnier were presented with handsome gold Elgin watches. The presentation was made by the rector on behalf of the vestry and congregation in recognition of their splendid work.

Eventually all the other interior enrichments, as suggested by Mr. Rainsford after the fire of 1922, were carried out. A new side altar in the south transept was dedicated with prayers and

---

*See Appendix B (Men in Service—World War II).

blessing, and named the Chapel of the Christ Child. The service of dedication took place on Maundy Thursday evening, April 10, 1941. The altar of brown Vermont marble was a gift of Mrs. Catherine Mead—"To the glory of God and in loving memory of the Mead family." The Hartman memorial reredos above the altar was retinted with bisymmetrical designs.

Earlier in the year, Mr. Louis E. Ferguson, a former vestry-man and parish treasurer for many years, died. Mr. Ferguson bequeathed $5,000 to the Endowment Fund. He and the Ferguson family were loyal church supporters and much interested in the welfare of the parish. Dr. Arthur H. Judge and the rector conducted the last funeral rites.

A year later, the parish suffered another great loss by the death of Miss Gertrude Ruthven Cushman, baptized at the church in 1858. Her father was among those on the Board of Incorporation in 1844. Miss Cushman and her sister Adelaide were faithful supporters of all that pertained to the welfare of the parish. They were interested especially in the Women's Auxiliary, the Altar Guild, and the Sunday School. Her bequest to her beloved church was $10,000. She entered into the Paradise of God on September 29, 1942. Bishop William T. Manning, Dr. Frederic S. Fleming, Dr. Arthur H. Judge, and the rector officiated at the funeral in the church. *Resurgam.*

The next few years of the war period were times of intense financial worry, which have lasted to the present on account of "absenteeism," deaths among earnest church supporters, and the rising cost of current expenses. The disposal of church properties was paramount in the minds of the vestry, and not without reason. The Kennedy properties were disposed of at a real sacrifice. In 1945 all parish real estate holdings, including the parish hall, were to be sacrificed to the moloch of expediency. But the rector and the congregation were not in accord with the proposal. In consequence, a few resignations occurred in the vestry.*

---

*See Appendix K—Item 16.

LUCIUS A. EDELBLUTE
25th Anniversary

CHURCH CHOIR, 1930

COMMUNION SETT, 1845

CHURCH INTERIOR WITH WINDOWS, 1858

CHURCH CHOIR, 1935

CHRISTUS CONSOLATOR

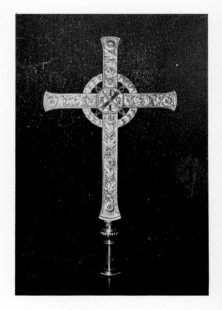

PROCESSIONAL CROSS, 1924

In June, 1943, the church received a "Certificate of Merit" from the United States Citizens Service Corps for "patriotically and generously contributing to the protection of the City of New York by freely providing office space for Civilian Defense workers and activities."

Earlier in the year, the vestry proposed celebrating the rector's Twenty-fifth Anniversary in the parish and his Thirty-fifth in the Ministry. A Festival Reunion Service was held Whitsunday, June 13, 1943. Simultaneously, an appeal for funds— "Keep My Doors Open"—was placed in the hands of the congregation and friends of the parish. This plea for financial aid seemed necessary because the City of New York has assessed the parish the sum of $2,205 (with interest at 7 per cent) for the removal of the Ninth Avenue Elevated structure in front of the church properties. Later on, the city remitted this assessment. The vestry gave a dinner to the rector at the King Arthur Room in London Terrace and presented him with a pair of gold cuff links "to attest their affection and esteem."

The following year, the rector announced that the church as a corporate body would be one hundred years old in November, 1944, and that the celebration of this anniversary was to commemorate the forming of an independent parish with a rector and a vestry to function under the "Religious Corporation Act of the State of New York. The offerings at the celebration were to be for the increase of the Endowment Fund. This memorial anniversary took place on Sunday morning, November 19. Bishop Manning had kindly consented to preach the sermon, and took for his text: "Stand fast in the Faith."

Bishop Manning referred to the influence of the parish in the last hundred years, and pointed out that the work of the parish was never more needed and never more spiritually effective than at this time. He called for renewal of faith, strength, and loyalty, and asked each individual to do his part faithfully, steadfastly, and loyally in his own parish; saying, "We must be real in our religion, real in our faith in life in the church, real in the things that keep us near to Christ and to God."

* * * *

The following poem by the rector dealt with the theme of triumph over the anxieties of the times:

OUR "V" FOR VICTORY

The skylark from the clods of earth
Soars heavenward with melodious mirth
    That rends the air;
And there aloft he wakes the morn,
The master of his fate and song,
    Free from all care.

There is a brightness in the sky,
A radiance towards which I fly
    Up to the blue.
This conquering attitude of life,
Dispelling gloom and earthly strife,
    Will keep me true.

Earth's clods but lightly touch man's feet,
If in his soul he rise to greet
    The dawn of day;
New heights and powers of soul will bring
New visions of the Christ, his King,
    To light his way.

Earth's common problems, yours and mine,
Blind us to VICTORY sublime,
    Fettering our mind.
To Freedom's call—be this your dare,
To strive this higher faith to share,
    God's Will to find.

L. A. E.

Entering upon its second century of usefulness, the church received many encouraging and congratulatory letters during its week of rejoicing. However, none was more pleasing to the rector and the congregation than the following:

WHEREAS the Church of the Holy Apostles in New York City is celebrating the One Hundredth Anniversary of its organization on Sunday, November 19th, 1944; and WHEREAS the said Church of the Holy Apostles is the Mother Parish of the Church of the Heavenly Rest.

RESOLVED by the Rector, Wardens and Vestrymen of the Church of the Heavenly Rest that they heartily congratulate the Rector, Wardens and Vestrymen of the Church of the Holy Apostles on the completion of a century's efficient work in the cause of Christianity and pray that God may pour out His blessing on the work of the Parish in the years to come.

WE HEREBY delegate the Reverend Herbert J. Glover, Vicar of our Parish to officially represent us at the Centennial Service.

(Signed) HENRY DARLINGTON, Rector.

What future have the next hundred years in store for the Church of the Holy Apostles? In an ever-changing environment one cannot prophesy, especially today, with rising costs and shrinking church income. Encouraging is the new Elliott Housing development, facing Chelsea Park, which opened for tenants on December 31, 1946. Other proposals for both public and private housing in old Chelsea are being considered by the Chelsea Association for Planning and Action. That this church will remain here as a sanctuary of spiritual witness and uplift there is no doubt.

During World War II the rector received many letters from our boys in all parts of the world. Trying to cheer and help, he spent two nights each week answering by long hand these messages to him as pastor. Someone suggested that he write a form letter and thus save the demands upon his time. But a priest of the church must never forget that his life is not that of a business man. He is the pastor of a flock no matter how widely scattered, and is needed especially in times of great spiritual and mental stress such as befell many a young man at the "front."

Here, for example, is a part of a letter received by the rector from Germany, June 16, 1945:

We've lost our Commanding Officer. He was strict. He had his faults like all of us have, but on the whole I think, he tried to do his best for us. I believe we've lost the best officer we had. I felt sorry for him because he had all he could do to say "Good-bye" to us. He managed to get through his address, and he had his cry.

Some day I must have a good cry and get rid of all the hardness that I've had to build up in order to go through this long period of repression and service. On second thought, I don't believe anything could break through the armor which I've clothed myself in—in order to survive. No one of our generation has been spared in this war. We can only hope that the coming generation will never be called upon to witness man in all his bestial brutality in the future generations to come. Thanks for all your cheery words.

The letter and an enclosed snapshot moved the rector to write:

A MAN IN UNIFORM

Why not say frankly who I am?
Do not "the clothes make the man"?
The brass buttons, a stripe here and there—
I wondered—as I looked.
Come now—look me o'er from head to toe.
The girls do, and love me so;
Safe with me? Genteel? Why, say
Uncle Sam's Army—it's Okay!

I thought, the Glorious Army!
You see, said I, my eyes are thoughts
And look beyond what clothes have wrought,
Would fathom what was in the soul,
What aims and mastery mark thy goal
TO WIN—Enduring VICTORY.

L. A. E.

The war period had a disruptive influence on the home and in social life. After the war, many returning veterans found it hard to readjust themselves to either. The youths returned more matured and disciplined, and now felt quite able to command their own way of life irrespective of loved ones' feelings. Naturally many heartaches were caused and mistakes made.

Normal parish life was weakened by the war. The stuffy, self-satisfied, stay-put Christian Soldiers annoyed the returned war veterans. Inarticulately they turned away from church doors. Young people's groups were in vogue, but after individuals got acquainted, danced together, and participated in some form of religious or social service, they paired off into interests that concerned "two only." The constant demands on the ingenuity of leaders to stimulate interest and excitement was most disheartening. Of the one hundred men of this parish who saw service, few upon returning retained their former interest in parish work, or contributed systematically to church support.

Pastoral supervision by a rector ought to revert to its original spiritual foundation. A priest in charge of souls ought to be freed from business responsibilities, and above all, he should be freed from the necessity of devising social entertainment schemes of a material character for the purpose of raising money.

The apostles early saw the necessity for the Gospel not being hampered by their having the economic oversight of the churches which the witnessing for Christ had brought into being. (*Acts* 6:2) "It is not reason that we should leave the Word of God, and serve tables." So they appointed a devout, specialized staff for doing "this business"; and the consecrated labor resulted in no small spiritual usefulness to those workers as well as to the churches.

Wherefore, brethren, look ye out among you seven men of honest report, full of the Holy Spirit and wisdom, whom we may appoint over this business.

But we will give ourselves continually to prayer, and to the ministry of the word.

And the saying pleased the whole multitude; and they chose Stephen, a man full of faith and of the Holy Ghost, and Philip, and Prochorus, and Nicanor, and Timon, and Parmenas, and Nicholas, a proselyte of Antioch:

Whom they set before the apostles: and when they had prayed, they laid their hands upon them.

And the Word of God increased; and the number of the disciples multiplied in Jerusalem; and a great company of the priests were obedient to the faith.

EPILOGUE

On Friday night June 4, 1948, the Thirtieth Anniversary of my rectorship was recalled by an anniversary cake. The occasion took place at the Strawberry Festival under the auspices of the Altar Guild, Miss Sophie R. Olmstead, Directress for thirty years. Looking back over those thirty years, the rector expressed the hope that his ministry at the Church of the Holy Apostles was but a link in the chain between the past and an enlarging future.

It has been said that a rector who stays long enough in a parish will outlive the difficulties and disadvantages which are the lot of a newcomer. However, the difficulties for a rector in a downtown parish in New York never cease. He hardly knows at the close of one year who his parishioners will be in the next. Often the question arises in his mind whether or not to stay. Why not move to fairer fields where no city problems exist? Then the bonds of his pastoral relations, involving growing knowledge and affection, lengthen and multiply the years, and he stays on: for they have become as strong as life. Indeed, they have become his life.

My long rectorship, amid all the difficulties that have at times beset the parish during these last thirty years, has been blessed for the most part by a faithful and devoted people. A mutual understanding and love have survived the strain of church difficulties, in the same manner that a family weathers the storms that would shatter its peace and harmony. Your rector has had many hours of joy and blessing for which he is truly thankful.

My God's blessings rest upon you all and the Church of the Holy Apostles in the years that are ahead.

231

October 14, 1948.

To the Wardens and Vestrymen, Church of the Holy Apostles,
My dear Brethren:

I have now completed more than thirty years as Rector of the Church of the Holy Apostles. On March 5, 1918 after prayerful consideration, I accepted the call to this parish. My first official act was to conduct the Annual Parish Meeting and Election on April 1, 1918. On the First Sunday after Easter, April 7, I ministered at its altar. To me, this has been a long and happy rectorship.

During the last three years, I have felt again and again that the interests of the parish would be better served if I retired, but conditions were such that I have been induced to remain. Now, things have changed somewhat.

Today, my general health is not what it ought to be for the work that lies ahead. The calls upon my time and strength are beyond my physical powers and endurance. I feel that a younger man should take the leadership in this exacting time, especially as conditions are now in this immediate neighborhood.

So, fully conscious of my obligations to you and the parish, I want, at this our first meeting in the fall, to announce that I will retire as rector of the Church of the Holy Apostles as soon after January 1, 1949, as circumsances will allow.

In the near future, I will notify the Bishop of the Diocese of my intention.
With appreciation of your loyalty and many kindnesses, I remain

Yours sincerely,
(Signed) Lucius A. Edelblute.

* * * *

NEW YORK AS VIEWED FROM 27TH STREET
SHOWING CHURCH OF THE HOLY APOSTLES

Courtesy—"Seventeen Magazine"—1948

REV. LUCIUS AARON EDELBLUTE

APPENDIX A

RECTORS OF THE CHURCH OF THE
HOLY APOSTLES

Rev. FOSTER THAYER, November 26, 1844 to May 1, 1847.

Rev. ROBERT SHAW HOWLAND, D.D., June 2, 1847 to November 30, 1869 and Rector Emeritus, 1869-1887.

Rev. GEORGE JARVIS GEER, D.D., December 7, 1858 to April 30, 1867. Co-Rector.

Rev. JOHN PATTERSON LUNDY, D.D., November 30, 1869 to October 28, 1875.

Rev. BRADY ELECTUS BACKUS, D.D., March 19, 1876 to August 2, 1901.

Rev. ROBERT LEWIS PADDOCK, D.D., January 1, 1901 to December 18, 1907.

Rev. APPLETON GRANNIS, D.D., January 27, 1908 to November 30, 1910.

Rev. HENRY K. DENLINGER, D.D., February 17, 1911 to December 31, 1917.

Rev. LUCIUS A. EDELBLUTE, M.A., March 5, 1918-1949.

APPENDIX A

ASSISTANT MINISTERS OF THE CHURCH OF THE HOLY APOSTLES

Rev. WILLIAM HUNTINGDON, January to April, 1849.

Rev. WILLIAM EVERETT, May, 1849 to September, 1851.

Rev. CHRISTOPHER B. WYATT, Sept. 14 to Oct., 1852.

Rev. GEORGE JARVIS GEER, October, 1852 to 1867.

Rev. GEORGE L. NEIDE, May, 1859 to 1866.

Rev. DAVID L. SCHWARTZ, 1863 to 1867.

Rev. THOMAS K. CONRAD, June, 1867 to March, 1868.

Rev. THOMAS SEIBT, December, 1867 to December, 1868.

Rev. W. F. LEWIS, December, 1870 to June, 1872.

Rev. EUGENE L. FOY, 1872 to March 18, 1873.

Rev. O. VALENTINE, July, 1874 to August, 1875.

Rev. THOMAS B. NEWBY, October, 1875 to February, 1876.

Rev. GEORGE A. KELLER, August, 1876 to August, 1879.

Rev. B. F. LASSITER, 1879 to August, 1880.

Rev. JOSEPH B. SHEPHERD, 1882 to 1884.

Rev. VICTOR C. SMITH, May 1, 1884 to February 1, 1886.

Rev. W. F. DICKINSON, D.D., Feb., 1886 to Sept., 1886.

Rev. WILLIAM R. WEBB, Dec., 1886 to Oct. 23, 1887.

Rev. ARTHUR H. JUDGE, October, 1887 to 1890.

Rev. J. H. YOUNG, July, 1890 to September, 1891.

Rev. HENRY McCREA, October, 1891 to December, 1891.

Rev. ROBERT HUDSON, December, 1891 to March, 1892.

Rev. W. T. FITCH, April, 1892 to 1893.

Rev. GEORGE G. HEPBURN, April, 1892 to 1893.

Rev. ISAAC J. STURGES, July, 1892 to 1894.

Rev.. W. J. ROBERTS, November, 1893 to 1894.

Rev. HENRY MITCHELL, February and March, 1894.

Rev. THOMAS McCLINTOCK, October, 1894 to April, 1898.

Rev. WM. D. WILLIAMS, May 31, 1898 to December 15, 1899.

Rev. WM. JOSLIN EHRHARD, Jan., 1900 to Sept., 1900.

Rev. D. VAUGHAN GWILYM, Dec., 1900 to Nov., 1901.

Rev. WILLIAM M. MIX, March, 1901 to January, 1902.

Rev. HENRY B. OLMSTEAD, June, 1902 to January, 1904.

Rev. W. HAMILTON BENHAN, Nov., 1904 to April, 1905.

Rev. L. M. A. HAUGHWOUT, July, 1905 to Nov., 1906.

Rev. THOMAS J. CROSBY, January, 1907 to January, 1908.

Rev. GEO. L. ADRIANCE MOORE, Apr., 1907 to June, 1910.

Rev. ROYAL RANSOM MILLER, Oct. 1, 1908 to June, 1910.

Rev. H. K. DENLINGER, D.D., Dec., 1909 to May, 1910.

Rev. MAURICE KAIN, 1910 to 1911.

Rev. GEORGE M. GEISEL, November, 1910 to July, 1912.

Rev. JOHN H. HEADY, September, 1912 to July, 1914.

Rev. KEN. S. GUTHRIE, Ph.D., Jan., 1915 to Apr., 1915.

Rev. FREEMAN DAUGHTERS, April, 1915 to June, 1915.

Rev. VAN RENSSELAER GIBSON, Feb., 1916 to Aug., 1916.

Rev. DONALD J. MacDONALD, 1916 to 1917.

Rev. F. ALLEN SISCO, July, 1917 to January 1, 1918. Locum
tenens, 1918.

Arthur Horner Judge was born August 11, 1859, the son of Cornelius and Harriet (Horner) Judge. He was by birth a Canadian, spending his young life in Montreal, Canada. Later on he attended school in Quebec and became a member of St. Matthew's Church there.

As a youth he attended Bishop's College, Lennoxville, Quebec, and in 1882 was graduated with a B.A. degree; and from Bishop's College he also received a Master's degree. He then studied theology at Bishop's College and was ordained a Deacon at St. Matthew's Church, Quebec, on September 24, 1882, by Bishop James W. Williams, who also ordained him to the priesthood on December 9, 1883.

His first curacy was at Cookshire, Quebec, 1882-1887, and from there he was called to assist Dr. Brady E. Backus as Curate of the Church of the Holy Apostles, 1887-1890. And from this parish he was called to assist Dr. Howland at the Church of the Heavenly Rest. Later (1900) he became Rector of St. Matthew's Church, New York. In 1916 he received the honorary degree of Doctor of Divinity from St. Stephen's College, N. Y.

After twenty-seven years as Rector of St. Matthew's Church, he retired and was made Rector Emeritus of the Parish of St. Matthew and St. Timothy, New York. Dr.. Judge was a lifelong friend of the Church of the Holy Apostles.

WARDENS, CHURCH OF THE HOLY APOSTLES

Since Its Incorporation in 1844

John Smith	1844-1867	Clement S. Parsons, Jr.	1895-1897
Again	1870-1871	George W. Ferguson	1897-1902
Elias Drake	1844-1845	James Pedersen	1903-1914
Alonzo R. Cushman	1845-1850	J. Walter Lyman	1907-1914
Walter Roome	1850-1866	Louis E. Schwab	1914-1935
Samuel Newby	1867-1870	Brandeth Symonds	1914-1915
John F. Seymour	1867-1870	George B. Covington	1915-1920
John P. Collord	1870-1875	Courtney Hyde	1920-1940
William Borden	1871-1882	Oscar W. Ehrhorn	1935-1945
Daniel B. Whitlock	1875-1888	William Matthews	1940-1945
Robert H. Goff	1883-1907	John W. Moffett	1945-
Edmund L. Baylies	1888-1891	Charles H. Smith	1946-
James T. Wright	1891-1895		

VESTRYMEN, CHURCH OF THE HOLY APOSTLES

Since Its Incorporation in 1844

John Snowden	1844-1847	Again	1867-1871
Christopher D. Varley	1844-1871	John F. Fisher	1850-1855
Francis Many	1844-1869	Adolphus Gorham	1851-1853
Worthington Romaine	1844-1846	Samuel Wiswall	1851-1854
Alonzo R. Cushman	1844-1844	Richard Sterling	1852-1854
John Brandigee	1844-1844	Samuel Newby	1854-1866
James Blackhurst	1844-1847	Charles F. Osborne	1854-1855
Henry Onderdonk	1844-1845	Henry O. Freeman	1854-1855
Walter Roome	1845-1850	Hopkins P. Hall	1855-1860
William Baker	1845-1846	Anson T. Colt	1856-1862
Joseph Nowill, Sr.	1845-1849	Elliott W. Gregory	1856-1857
Thomas Hardcastle	1845-1845	Schuyler Hamilton	1857-1858
J. D. Ogden	1846-1847	Again	1864-1866
David H. Dick	1846-1847	Edgar Logan	1857-1859
Lewis Many -	1846-1850	Chauncey P. Winans	1858-1862
William H. Roome	1847-1848	James B. Glentworth	1859-1864
John P. Collord	1847-1870	John F. Seymour	1860-1867
John A. King, Jr.	1847-1854	Daniel B. Whitlock	1862-1875
J. D. Gill	1849-1850	Willett N. Hawkins	1862-1864
Orrin Terry	1849-1852	George Moore	1865-1870
Again	1855-1857	Again	1880-1886
William Borden	1850-1851	Charles Hall	1867-1869

Henry Griswold	1867-1875	Matthew Kennedy	1907-1916
Again	1881-1883	John B. Duncan	1908-1910
Robert H. Goff	1869-1883	Frederick M. Pedersen	1909-1911
William Orton	1871-1878	Alvin G. McCallion	1910-1914
Henry Ivey	1871-1879	Brandeth Symonds	1911-1914
John M. Buckingham	1874-1878	George F. Mills	1912-1918
Enoch Chamberlin	1871-1877	Oliver Tims	1916-1916
A. S. Roe	1875-1878	Louis E. Schwab	1914-1914
Charles S. Fischer, Jr.	1875-1883	Jens Nelson	1914-1918
Benoni Lockwood	1877-1883	William J. Ballard	1914-1928
Thomas J. Hall	1878-1878	Frank Garrison	1914-1917
George Reton	1878-1879	William H. Hookey	1915-1916
Lawson B. Bell	1878-1881	William E. F. Smith	1915-1935
James T. Wright	1879-1890	Charles F. Hillock	1916-1933
John R. Walker	1879-1885	Franklin Johnson	1916-1918
Clement S. Parsons, Jr.	1883-1895	George A. Cripps	1917-1920
James W. Clark, Jr.	1883-1887	George B. Kiely	1917-1920
Edmund L. Baylies	1883-1888	Reginald C. Ballard	1918-1929
Robert H. Goff, Jr.	1884-1885	Noah Garrison	1918-1929
Alison G. Mills	1885-1891	Thomas Hickey	1919-1927
Charles P. Champion	1886-1893	Joseph J. Boes, Sr.	1920-1934
George W. Ferguson	1887-1897	Again	1936-
Charles F. Richards	1888-1891	William G. Irving	1920-1923
Augustus W. Colwell	1888-1892	William T. Fowler	1921-1931
Robert S. Fowler	1890-1891	Clifford V. Cooper	1923-1924
Again	1914-1916	Electus Taylor Backus	1925-1936
William J. McDonald	1891-1900	David Morton	1927-1930
Levi H. Squire	1891-1892	Richard B. Kimball	1928-1933
Edwin J. Winson	1892-1896	John W. Moffett	1929-1945
James Pedersen	1892-1903	John W. Beatty	1929-1938
Charles S. Beardsley	1893-1894	Thomas Clark	1930-1942
William M. Farrar	1893-1895	John L. G. Green	1931-1935
Andrew H. Kellogg	1894-1903	Henry C. Doretta	1933-1946
James H. Richmond	1895-1897	Henry H. Ritter	1933-1937
Victor C. Pedersen	1895-1901	Mario E. La Penta	1935-
John A. Custons	1896-1897	George Phillips	1935-1937
Again	1903-1914	William Matthews	1936-1940
George W. Ferguson, Jr.	1896-1901	George Evans	1937-1940
Charles E. Hubbard	1897-1914	George Wilson	1937-1944
John F. Bush	1897-1903	Vincent J. D'Onofrio	1938-1948
John E. Smih	1899-1902	Edwin D. Ganong	1940-1945
James Walter Lyman	1900-1907	Charles H. Smith	1940-1946
Louis Ferguson	1902-1913	John B. Stevens	1942-1947
William N. Wilmer	1902-1907	George Loughran, Jr.	1944-
Ross C. Van Bokkelen	1902-1909	Floyd J. Huth	1945-
John C. Wolfe	1903-1912	John Walker	1945-
Courtney Hyde	1903-1920	Everett D. Shenk	1946-
Oscar W. Ehrhorn	1904-1916	Herbert C. Hertfelder	1946-
Again	1934-1935	Walter Moore	1947-
		Walter Carter	1948-

CLERKS OF THE VESTRY

Worthington Romaine	1844-1845	John F. Bush	1898-1903
Francis Many	1845-1848	Charles E. Hubbard	1903-1904
Walter Roome	1848-1866	Oscar W. Ehrhorn	1904-1908
Daniel B. Whitlock	1866-1884	Courtney Hyde	1908-1915
John R. Walker	1884-1885	Frank L. Garrison	1915-1916
Edmund L. Baylies	1885-1887	William E. F. Smith	1916-1935
Clement S. Parsons, Jr.	1887-1897	John W. Moffett	1935-1936
James Pedersen	1897-1898	Mario E. La Penta	1936-

TREASURERS

Alonzo R. Cushman	1844-1845	Oscar W. Ehrhorn	1912-1913
Again	1846-1850	Brandeth Symonds	1913-1914
John Snowden	1845-1846	Courtney Hyde	1914-1936
Francis Many	1850-1869	John W. Moffett	1936-1941
George Moore	1869-1873	Edwin D. Ganong	1941-1946
Robert H. Goff	1873-1907	George Loughran Jr.	1946-1947
Louis Ferguson	1907-1912	Herbert C. Hertfelder	1947-

ORGANISTS AND CHOIRMASTERS

Mr. Miller	1845-1849	Eugene Woodhaus	1903-1904
Mr. Johnson	1849-1850	H. N. Ruland	1904-1905
Mr. Burdett	1850-1850	George T. Banker	1905-1911
William E. Beames	1850-1852	Winfield Scott Wardell	1911-1917
W. H. Sterling	1852-1860	Summer of	1931-
G. G. Rockwood	1860-1873	Scott Wheeler	1917-1918
Charles S. Fischer, Jr.	1874-1883	Mr. Bausman	1918-1919
Mrs. Allen	1883-1889	Electus Taylor Backus	1919-1935
Sheldon W. Ball	1889-1895	Samuel Quincy	1935-
Albert Alexander Wild	1895-1903		

SEXTONS

Tunis Bennett	1845-1851	Daniel William Weymer	1918-1920
Robert Bennett	1851-1870	John McVey	1920-1920
Samuel Hays	1871-1909	George Louis Goodare	1921-1923
Charles A. Hays	1909-1914	Mario E. La Penta	1923-1925
Walter Hayes	1914-1916	John Bedell Byrd	1923-1925
John C. Futerer	1916-1918	Daniel Brown	1925-

PARISH WORKERS ON STAFF—MEN

Louis E. Schwab	1905-1935	Joseph Ebbers	1927-1934
Horace E. Clute	1907-1908	Maurice W. Venno	1933-1937
Edward T. Schoch	1908-1914	A. Wesley Konrad	1948-
Humphrey Lee	1916-1917		

DEACONESSES

Edith Charlotte Smith	1902-1909	Margaret S. Peet	1911-1914
Alice J. Knight	1905-1908	Jane F. George	1914-1915
Pauline L. Neidhardt	1907-1908	—— Schodts	1925-1926

PARISH WORKERS ON STAFF—WOMEN

Mrs. Williams	1877-	Florence E. Dunn	1910-
Adeline ʒ. Bendt	1885-1889	Louise Harrison	1910-1914
Gillespie	1889-	Pansy H. Butler	1915-1917
Lillian Babcock	1894-	Mucy K. Kenan	1915-
Mrs. Chilvus	1897-	Margaret A. Squire	1918-1925
Mrs. Frank Ealy	1899-1909	Levia Shero	1925-1926
Julia T. Loomis	1906-1908	Isabel Baker	1925-1927
Hermione A. Baldwin	1907-1908	Lillian G. Stafford	1926-1947
Ida Merrett	1909-1911		

WORLD WAR II

RECTOR AND CHURCH WORKERS

Left to right, top row: Bottom row:
HORACE E. CLUTE, ROBT. L. PADDOCK,   DEACONESS KNIGHT, MISS LOOMIS,
LEFFERD M. A. HAUGHWOUT.   DEACONESSES NEIDHARDT AND SMITH

REV. ARTHUR H. JUDGE, CURATE—1887-1890

DR. JAMES PEDERSEN

AND

MRS. ANNA PEDERSEN

*At the time when the Endowment Fund of the
Church of the Holy Apostles was first started*

SCOUT TROOP 89, 1931

BOY SCOUTS TROOP 338

Extant Records of Members of the Church of the Holy Apostles who served in the Armed Forces during the Civil War, 1861-1865.

Babcock (Killed in action) John Price (Killed in action)
John Burrows (Died of wounds) Purdy (Killed in action)
Andrew Dow (Died of wounds) Ramsey (Killed in action)
James Green (Died of illness) Charles Stafford (Killed in action)
Jones (Killed in action) James Tiebout (Killed in
Look (Died of sickness) battle in South Carolina)
Samuel Malloy (Defense of Joseph Weddus, Sailor
the Capitol, Washington, D. C.) (Died of illness)
Nanes (Drowned in the Mississippi) Wilson (Died in action)
Henry Monroe (Killed in battle) Daniel Wylie (Died of sickness)

(There are no church records of those who served this nation during the Mexican and Spanish-American Wars).

WORLD WAR I

A letter:

Somewhere in France, November 8, 1918.

We have been very busy and results are beginning to show. Each man in my outfit has given a good account of himself. Today I am training an entirely new outfit—just over.

I find the people of France very interesting and their country is well worth fighting for. It is truly a great incentive to know that the people back home are backing us up. Some of my best friends have been killed. Their fate spurred their fellows on to make a finish fight of it.

We now look at an Englishman or a Frenchman in a much different light than in the old days, that in itself is sufficient.

A long period of reconstruction is going to keep many of us over here for some time, I feel assured.

COL. WM. H. EDELBLUTE, F.A.

LIST OF THOSE WHO SERVED IN WORLD WAR I

J. Armstrong
Henry Beck
Hugh Bownes
Charles Boyd
David Burns
Malcolm F. Camp
William Corbett
Edward Duffy
Francis Duffy
William Duke
William Dunn
Edwin Durlacher
William Feil
Cyrus Fields
Charles Gerke
Max Gerke
Joseph Goldstein
Edward Graves
Francis Guermonprez
Albert Hadley
Lester Haines
Edward Hamilton
Herbert C. Hertfelder
Joseph Inslee
Howard Johnson
James Leonard
Robert Leonard

Arthur Mann
Charles McCarthy
William McCarthy
Charles Milligan
Herbert Nichols
George Pappin
Enoch Petterson
William Petterson
Howard Schaefer
Carlton Schroeder
Clifford Scott
Frank Snavely
John Sohl
Arthur Stone
William F. Stothers
William Talbot
George Vreeland
William Walton
William Warnock
Edward Wells

John Whaley
Charles Weyman
Robert L. Wood
David Woods
Lester Woods

Alice J. Knight, Deaconess—Died in service.

On Sunday evening, April 27, 1919, a fitting memorial service was held in memory of Deaconess Alice J. Knight, who died in France serving her country. Because of her work in the parish (1905-09), Deaconess Knight was much beloved by all. Before coming to the parish, she was a member of the Salvation Army. At the memorial service, Comdr. Erickson of the Salvation Army sang. A touching eulogy was given by Bishop Arthur S. Lloyd, President of the Board of Missions.

LIST OF THOSE WHO SERVED IN WORLD WAR II

Louis Angelos
Edward J. Applegate
Francis Applegate
Barry G. Batchelder
Charles Wm. Beck
Peter Beck
Eugene Bergen (Killed in action)
Ernest H. Bickel
Walter H. Bone
Edward Braden
Robert Charles Braden
Joseph C. Bray
Albert A. Brown
Frank Brown
James A. Brown
James Brown, Jr.
William G. Burke
Peter J. Cairnie
George Robert Callas
William Callas
Henry C. Campbell
Malcolm C. Campbell
Richard B. Campbell
George Carnie
Donald Wells Catlin
Michael J. Cermenello
Mildred M. (Whythe) Clapp
Samuel T. Coombs
William C. Cornell
Robert F. Cornell

James Davidson
Kenneth S. Davidson
Reginald Davidson
Robert J. Davidson
Raymond Davidson
James S. Ditty
Raymond F. Dorry
Thomas Duke
Oscar W. Ehrhorn Jr.
Arthur Every
Howard W. Eubank
Frank Eubank
John Fenton
William F. Ferre
Lester Frato
William F. Frato
Edwin D. Ganong
Stephen George
James L. Griffith
George Haines
William Haynsworth
Harry J. Hurley
George Hutchison
Floyd J. Huth
Thomas L. Kane
Roy R. Keely
Roy A. Kinnier
William Klein
Robert G. Kohler
Thomas E. Kuhn

George M. Kuzmanovich
Charles Loew
William R. Loew
Henry Lord
George T. Loughran
Richard Mahon
Victor Mahon
Richard Mertz
John Metaxotos
William G. Metaxotos
Andrew Robert Meyncke
William B. Mohl
Walter R. Moore
Melville A. Murry
Donald A. Mutford
David MacAdam
John C. MacKean
Thomas David MacKean
Richard F. Perkins
Thomas C. Perkins
Roy Petersen
Frank Phelleppa

Henry Rausch
Henry Restel
Harry W. Reynolds
Wilbert B. Richardson
Albert Robinson
Robert Robinson
Douglas Rohde (Killed in Service)
James A. Scott
William J. Scott
Harold R. Seickendick
Raymond Seickendick
Robert Shepherd
Arnold Sigrist
Clarence J. Smith (Killed in Action)
George A. Stewart
Fred Tirado
Charles Todd
Frank Vogl
Winfield S. Wardell, III.
Raymond A. Weber
Arthur Williams

APPENDIX C

THE STORY OF THE PARISH OF THE HOLY APOSTLES

A STATEMENT AT THE TWENTIETH ANNIVERSARY
NOVEMBER, 1864

By R. S. HOWLAND, Rector

Text: St. Mark IV. 30, 31, 32.

The Twentieth Anniversary of this parish exhibits as the result, direct or indirect, of the seed sown twenty years ago: Three Churches, a staff of four clergymen, over six hundred communicants, nearly a thousand children under Sunday School instruction, and about twelve hundred visits to sick and dying, in the course of the current year.

We have, as belonging to the parish proper, a church building, twice enlarged, and now entirely free from debt—a building which, for chaste beauty and pleasantness for worship, is not surpassed by any in the city. We have besides a Mission Chapel and Sunday School House.

We have the occupancy and spiritual oversight of a field of immense extent: a missionary harvest ground, in which are living full five thousand men, women, and children, professing allegiance to our Church, but with no episcopal minister to care for their souls, except the clergy, supported in whole or in part by the liberality of this parish.

We have a large and harmonious congregation, and a band of zealous, self-sacrificing laymen, stretching out their hands to work in all directions —in Parish Vestry, in Missionary Association, in Sunday School, and in a brotherhood for visiting and caring for the sick.—Here certainly is a great, a magnificent result—a result to satisfy the pride of any founders—a result to fill every Christian heart with gratitude to Him who has brought it to pass. . . .

Accordingly, what, think you, was the original force of the movement which commenced this parish twenty years ago? And commenced the work, remember, in a district which, to this day, is deserted, because of its pecuniary unprofitablesness as a field of church enterprise; so much so, that while on a given square mile about Fifth Avenue there are a dozen Episcopal churches, on the corresponding square mile about Ninth Avenue there is not one. The only parish organization which has existed in the district alluded to, after many years of persevering effort, has deserted the neighborhood. And if, even at this present date, this northwestern part of the city is so uncongenial a soil for the planting of self-supporting Episcopal churches that old congregations desert it; if even now it is, as we find it, almost entirely missionary ground, what are we to say, how shall we not admire those who, twenty years ago, when so much of the neighborhood was waste, and the population so much poorer and more sparse—put their seed into the ground with a good trust in God, and a confiding expectation that He would bring forth first the blade, then the ear, after that the full corn in the ear.

This planting was three years before my time, and I can speak only therefore by report; but also I am enabled thereby to speak more freely.

They were the teachers, male and female, of a small independent Sunday School: a school started by themselves in view of the great destitution of the neighborhood. This Sunday School became the mother of churches. The male teachers were so few that they had to beg members of a distant parish to connect themselves nominally with them in order to make a show of so many as ten men to fill up the necessary number for a vestry. . . .

And yet you see the result. You are living in the enjoyment of the accomplishment. They have achieved more, much more than they—sanguine as they were—had ventured, even in day dreams, to look forward to.

What is the meaning of this? What the explanation of the success?

They were working for God, and He brought His work to pass. He, not they, made bricks without straw. . . .

For three years the small congregation was a wanderer in the city, having no settled abiding place; first worshipping in their school-house; driven thence by faction, they took refuge in their clergyman's house in Fiftieth Street; thence they removed to the chapel of the Blind Institution, where they remained a year; thence to a basement in Twenty-eighth Street, and afterwards to a loft in Twenty-seventh Street—where, for the first time, I was admitted to share their struggles and their triumphs.

Meanwhile, a liberal gift of land and money from private individuals, some subscriptions, and a small contribution from Trinity Parish, enabled them to commence a church building; not, however, the edifice, as you see it. As originally constructed, the pews commenced back of the present transept line, back of the columns that are now halfway down the aisle. A few years later, the subscriptions of the congregation then worshipping within the walls enabled the Vestry to make a large addition to the building. Still later, these extensive transepts were thrown out; and finally, on Easter day last, whatever of debt, floating or mortgaged, remained, was, by God's blessing and your liberality, entirely swept away.

One other thing I wish to say in conclusion, viz., that the work has always been met and mastered under a pressure; that there never has been a time during the last twenty years when everything went smoothly, when no effort was required, when no anxiety was felt, and no sacrifices called for. The heat and burden of the day has lasted full twenty years, and still lasts, and, I trust, always will last.

. . . Let this church stand, then, to the end of time, as a convincing encouragement to Christian labor and Christian sacrifice; as an evidence of what men can do for Christ, even with but one talent; of what men can do whose opportunities are small, but whose hearts are large; of what Christian men can do when they work together with a will, as remembering for whom they work, and at what price He purchased the right to ask for their self-sacrifice.

Appendix D

(Letter of Appeal to Trinity Church)

New York, January, 1871.

To the Rector, Wardens and Vestrymen of Trinity Church:

Gentlemen and Brethren:

We are in receipt of a communication from your honorable body under date of 14th, July last, denying our former application for aid in behalf of the Church of the Holy Apostles. We nevertheless make this further appeal to you . . . for the same object; being moved thereto by the necessity of the case, and sense of the responsibility resting upon ourselves in the premises. . . . The only encumbrance upon the church is a mortgage held by your honorable body for $6,000. . . . And a lot on the Ninth Avenue adjoining the church plot, about 24 feet wide by 122 feet deep, in the rear of which and connected with the church is our Sunday School and Mission House. . . . making mortgages amounting together, to $18,000. The dwelling and store on the front of this lot is rented for $1,000 per annum.

Current Expenses	$10,013.00
Yearly Resources	6,657.00
Showing a deficit of	3,356.00
Floating Debt at present	$ 2,000.00

Our appropriation and expenditures are, we think, as economical as good judgment will warrant and some we feel might be increased to advantage.

The Church contains 167 pews, and will accommodate about 700 persons, but although the attendance upon the services is large, not one half of the pews have been rented at any time within the last five years.

An investigation of the circumstances of the neighborhood people by our Rector shows that the great bulk of them are not able to contribute to any material extent toward the support of the church. The investigation further shows that in 1,013 families visited in the district say, from 26th Street to 36th Street, from Eighth Avenue to the River, comprising over 4,500 persons, and believed to be a fair criterion of the entire district, there are:

        331 Episcopalians
      1,816 Roman Catholics
        355 Methodists
        344 Presbyterians
        656 German Reformed and Lutherans
        193 Baptists
         36 Congregationalists
         23 Quakers

>16 Universalists
>8 Unitarians
>1 Swedenborgian
>197 Jews
>587 Infidels, or Nothingarians.

—and is certainly a good field for our Church to work in. . . .

In the last few years, in the population of this part of the city, we have lost a large proportion of those who formerly mainly contributed to the support of this Chursh, and whose places in the neighborhood have been filled by those who lack either the ability or the inclination to assist in the work. . . . Our former Rector was a man of liberal means and most generous heart, who for many years gave us his services with little or no compensation. . . , His withdrawal from the Parish took from it more of those who had continued to aid in its support. There is still one other point, which we feel in justice to ourselves ought to be presented to you; although from the delicacy of the subject, we approach it with hesitation. We refer to the fact that the only other church in our immediate vicinity, *i.e.*, St. Peter's Church in West 20th Street, is able, by certain fortunate circumstances, such as owning a rectory, and being in receipt of a stipend from your honorable body, to undersell us in the matter of pew rents in a way that has been to our decided disadvantage.

Trusting that you will appreciate rightly our motives in the last allusion and hoping that you may find in the foregoing good and sufficient reason for extending to our church the same measure of assistance which you have so generously accorded to our sister parish and thereby enable us to continue its work in the neighborhood, where it is so eminently needed.

We are, very respectfully yours,

(Signed) JOHN P. LUNDY, Rector

JOHN P. COLLORD, ⎫ Wardens.
JOHN SMITH, ⎭

Appendix E

To the Rector, Wardens and Vestrymen of Trinity Church, New York City:

Gentlemen and Brethren:

We, the undersigned, the Rector, Wardens and Vestrymen of the Parish of the Holy Apostles, respectfully present to your honorable body the following petition, humbly, and yet urgently, praying that the request we make will commend itself to your earnest consideration and favorable action.

This Parish is situated on the far West Side of the city, in the midst of a thickly settled community of people of only moderate means. Many of these people are Irish and English Protestants. . . . They are favorably disposed to the Church, and naturally in their sorrows and necessities hold out their hands to us for relief. . . . The Rector, during the past seven years, has baptised 650 children and adults, held 325 funeral services, solemnized 220 marriages, and presented for confirmation 265 persons.

We have 250 regular communicants, and 350 communicant names on record. The Holy Communion is celebrated twice a month. A mother's meeting has regularly cared for the spiritual and physical wants of fifty poor women—all we could receive. One hundred twenty-five young girls have been regularly taught sewing in the Industrial School, and a Workingmen's Club of sixty members has been organized and provided with reading and recreation rooms, which are open every evening. We have about 300 families on our visiting list . . . and between 500 and 600 children in our Sunday School.

This work has been carried on by the Rector over and above his other duties of holding services, preaching, attending meetings of various other parochial organizations. . . . In view of these facts, and the burden of the work laid upon us, and the grand opportunities open to us in our neighborhood for doing a blessed and noble work for the Church, we turn to you as our only hope in this emergency. Our Parish obliged to struggle as it is against the movements of well-to-do-people uptown, and the losses we have sustained by the death of our elder and abler members, makes it impossible for us to engage the services of a Missionary and Assistant. Our income from all sources, including the $2,000 stipend already given us by Trinity Parish, is $7,000, and our expenses, under the most economical management, exceeds by some $500 that amount, which we have to find ways of making up at the end of the year. . . .

Under the circumstances, dear Brethren, we most urgently ask you to grant us an additional appropriation of $1,000 a year to provide a Missionary and Assistant in our neighborhood and parish. . . . This parish in past years always has had an Assistant Rector or a Missionary and Assistant. Now, when we most need one, we have none. . . .

We want an earnest, energetic, active young man in Priest's orders to aid us in this important field. . . . We are here, with Church and Mission buildings, ready to do the Master's work. We can do it if you will help us

249

in this special way, and we therefore heartily pray that you will find it in your power, as we believe you will in your hearts, to grant this our needful and worthy request.

REV. BRADY E. BACKUS, D.D., Rector.

At the Vestry meeting, April 17, 1884, a committee was appointed to approach Trinity Church again to increase the annual stipend given this parish.

To the Rector, Wardens and Vestry of Trinity Parish, New York City:

We, the undersigned, the Rector, Wardens and Vestrymen of the Parish of the Holy Apostles, New York City, beg leave respectfully to present again to your honorable body the enclosed petition, laid before you last season, which we are assured then received your kind and cordial consideration, but which, as you advised us, you were unable for adequate reasons to grant.

We venture thus again to urge our special need upon you, feeling confident of your sympathy and interest in the work of our Parish, and in the hope that circumstances may now be such as to enable you to extend to our petition a more favorable consideration.

To show that we are in earnest in doing all we can in carrying out for ourselves the spirit of our request, we would state that since sending in our request, we have succeeded, through the generous donations of a few friends in this city outside of our parish, in raising the sum of $500, which with a like amount raised among our own parishoners has enabled us during the past year to employ an Assistant and Missionary in the parish only for one year, and is a source of aid to which we can not further appeal.

We therefore are brought again this spring face to face with the old problem: Can we retain or employ any clerical assistance to meet the spiritual needs of the many poor in our neighborhood? We have to confess, with regret and some fears, that we are not able so to do, and so we come again to you for relief in our emergency, asking, as before, for a special appropriation of $1,000 for this purpose.

There is no better missionary field in the Diocese of New York than the West Side of this city, and, as indicating its character and the work we have accomplished, especially the past year, we append the following report:

REPORT

Baptisms	125
Burials	85
Confirmed	41
Marriages	50
Families visited	450
Individuals	1,500
Sunday School Children	500
Communicants	400

ENDOWMENT FUND TRUSTEES, 1894-1914

Sponsored by the "Be Ready Ten"

DR. JAMES PEDERSEN, Chairman	1894-1914
MR. CLEMENT S. PARSONS, JR., Secretary	1894-1897
MRS. HELEN M. KELLOGG, Secretary	1897-1914
MISS ELLA F. WHITLOCK, Treasurer (Mrs. H. Ivey)	1894-1909
MISS M. B. CONKLIN, Treasurer, (Mrs. Geo. Ferguson)	1909-1910
MRS. ANNA PEDERSEN, Treasurer	1910-1914
MRS. CLEMENT S. PARSONS, JR.	1894-1900
MR. WILLIAM J. McDONALD	1894-1900
MISS ADELAIDE CUSHMAN	1895-1911
MISS GERTRUDE R. CUSHMAN	1895-1914
MISS A. ZENAIDE GOFFE	1895-1914
MR. GEORGE W. FERGUSON, JR.	1896-1910
MR. ANDREW H. KELLOGG	1897-1914
MRS. ANTOINETTE (WHITLOCK) HARLOW	1894-1914
REV. ROBERT L. PADDOCK	1902-1907
MISS MARY GRACE WHITLOCK	1902-1914
MR. LOUIS FERGUSON	1902-1914
MRS. NATHALIE E. BAYLIES	1907-1913
MISS ANNE M. HYDE	1911-1914
MISS CAROLINE B. AUSTIN	1911-1914
MRS. W. H. CLARK	1910-1914
REV. HENRY K. DENLINGER, D.D.	1911-1914
LOUIS E. SCHWAB	1913-1914

Members of the "Be Ready Ten" met on March 6, 1894, to organize and form a committee, as trustees, for subscriptions toward an endowment fund for the Church of the Holy Apostles.

Their objective was a fund of $10,000.

They met at the home of Mrs. D. B. Whitlock, where most of the subsequent meetings were held. It was voted that the trustees elected deposit the monies received in a savings bank in New York City. By May 15, 1894, the trustees reported that they had deposited $6,400.

The first INDENTURE was made in June, 1894. It states that the trustees have now in hand $6,400, and the interest therefrom shall be applied to the principal until the fund receives $10,000; then the interest therefrom is to apply to such uses and purposes of the said church so long as the edifice of said church wherein Divine Services are held shall be located at the southeast corner of Ninth Avenue and Twenty-eighth Street in the City of New York. In case the parish goes out of existence, it is to be given to Trinity Parish, the income to be used at their discretion for the purpose of a downtown parish.

The sums given were not large at first, but amounted to about $500 a month. By November 18, 1895, the total was $10,297.48. The $10,000 objective had been reached. The "Tithe Gleaners" were very active at this time and numbered about 100 under the direction of the "Be Ready Ten."

By June, 1896, the "Ten" reported contributions amounting to $12,112.00
By June 1897, the amount invested was 12,810.00
By April, 1898, the invested funds had reached . . . 13,604.75
By December 20, 1899, the sum was 14,000.00
By March, 1900, the fund had reached the sum of . . 15,124.98

The discussion that now held the attention of the trustees was how best to place the funds beyond the reach of any vestry of the church—the interest alone to be applied to parochial purposes. It was finally decided to place the funds in the hands of the Trustees of the Estate and Property of the Diocese of New York.

The objective now set for this first fund was $20,000. This agreement was reached on December 2, 1901.

The INDENTURE again states that in case, at any time in the future, the corporate existence of Holy Apostles shall terminate, the said income shall be hereafter paid to the Rector, Church Wardens and Vestrymen of Trinity Church, to be used for mission work in the lower part of Manhattan.

By April 10, 1901, the amount reported was $15,735.17
By May, 1902, the sum had reached 16,325.00
By October, 1903, the amount was 17,350.80
By December, 1904, $20,000 was reported by the Treasurer   20,000.00

The Endowment Sundays in the spring of 1904 follows:

CHURCH OFFERINGS		SOCIETIES	
Jan. 31, 1904 . . .	$181.07	Rector's Aid	$100.00
Feb. 28, 1904 . . .	98.88	Helping Hand . . .	10.00
Mar. 30, 1904 . . .	53.35	Parish Guild	20.00
Apr. 20, 1904 . . .	115.38	Dorcas Society . . .	10.00
Apr. 20, 1904, Dr. Pedersen	25.00	Girls' Friendly . . .	5.00
Easter Offering, 1904 .	15.94		

During the ten years of the First Fund, no gift over $200 is reported.

SECOND AGREEMENT: $30,000.

Toward the end of the year 1904, the Committee was instructed to write the Vestry of the Church urging them to defer using the interest of the fund ($20,000) and return it to the general fund.

February 24, 1906, balance in the hands of the Treasurer . $1,073.28
February 16, 1906, collected on Endowment Sunday . . 1,225.53
December 31, 1907, fund had reached the sum of . . . 3,349.40

The SECOND INDENTURE was made on December 17, 1907, with the objective of $30,000, between the Trustees of the Church and the Trustees of the Estate and Property of the Diocesan Convention of New York. It states that if the existence of the Church should terminate, the said income shall be hereafter paid to The Church House Foundation in the Diocese of New York. . . . If the Church House Foundation in the Diocese shall terminate existence, then the same shall be paid to the Rector, etc., of Trinity

Church in the City of New York, the income to be used and applied by said Rector, etc.—in the manner, and for the purpose, aforesaid.
Reported:

February 8, 1910, the Second Fund was	$10,073.14
February 8, 1910 Estate of Marie Antoinette Whitlock	10,000.00
February 8, 1910, Estate of Mary J. Johnson	5,000.00
February 8, 1910, Estate of W. N. Wilmer	2,000.00
By March 22, 1911, the Sum had reached	30,000.00
March 22, 1911, Balance in Savings Banks	1,606.23

* * * *

THIRD ENDOWMENT FUND: $50,000.

The INDENTURE, made on May 2, 1911, had as its objective $50,000.00. The same disposition to be made of the interest as stated in previous funds.

It states that the balance toward the Third Fund was now $7,115.00, largely through the ($5,000) by Richard Conklin in memory of his wife, $5,000.

Legacy from the estate of Adelaide Cushman	$5,000
Gift in memory of the late Mrs. Joseph Pedersen	1,000
Gift by Louis Ferguson	5,000
Gift by Prof. Frederick Pedersen	500
Gift by Mrs. George Ferguson, in memory of her husband and children	5,000
Gift in Memory of the mother of Mrs. Lizzie B. Van Vorst Colwell	200
Gift of Mrs. Auchmuty	2,500

By March, 1914, the Third Fund had reached the sum of $38,648.80.
The Endowment Fund Association of 1914:

> The Rector, Rev. Henry K. Denlinger, D.D. (ex-officio)
> Dr. James Pedersen, Chairman
> Mrs. Andrew H. Kellogg, Secretary
> Mrs. James Pedersen, Treasurer

Other members: Miss Caroline Austin, Miss Gertrude R. Cushman, Mr. Louis Ferguson, Mrs. Ellwood Harlow, Miss Anne M. Hyde, Mr. and Mrs. Andrew H. Kellogg, and Miss Mary Grace Whitlock.

Legacies and subscriptions to the Endowment Fund by June, 1915:

Previously acknowledged ($10,000 legacy) total	$92,000
Otis Elevator Company	1,000
In memory of H. C. Post by J. C. Schwab, Henriette M., Emily, and Louis E. Schwab	500
Miss Anne Morgan	500
J. B. A. Fosburgh	300
Mr. and Mrs. Herbert L. Satterlee	200
Mr. Brandreth Symonds	100
Mr. Francis Lynde Stetson	100
Total to date, June 15, 1915	$94,700

No further records are available, except that by 1916 the Third Fund of $50,000 was completed.

Since 1916, the following legacies have been designated to the Consolidated Endowment Fund of the Church of the Holy Apostles:

1927—Mary Grace Whitlock $10,000
1935—Louis E. Schwab 10,000
1941—Louis Ferguson 5,000

* * * *

SPECIAL FUNDS CREATED BY MEMBERS FOR PARTICULAR CHURCH WORK

In January, 1867, Mrs. John P. Collord gave the vestry the sum of $1,000, to be held in trust by them with the understanding that the interest of said fund should be applied to the purchase of books for Sunday School library.

* * * *

In 1886, Mr. Edmund L. Baylies, then a vestryman of the parish, together with his brother, Mr. Walter C. Baylies, and his sister, Mrs. Frances C. Lowell, gave to the church the sum of $2,000, to constitute a fund known as the "Ruth Baylies Fund," the income of which, according to the terms of the gift was to be used annually in sending poor women and children of the parish to the country for a portion of the summer.

"WHITLOCK FLOWER FUND":

On March 22, 1928, Antoinette Whitlock Harlow, gave to the Rector, Churchwardens, and Vestrymen of the Church of the Holy Apostles the sum of $1,000. The interest of this sum was to purchase flowers to be placed on the altar rail and pulpit on All Saints Day, Christmas, and Easter. These perpetual gifts of flowers are memorials to the donor's father, Daniel B. Whitlock.

"MEMORIAL FLOWER FUND" ENDOWMENT

The Memorial Fund for flowers on the Altar, on a given date of each year, had its beginning in 1927 by a gift of $50 to the church from the remaining estate of Lina Georg, and was presented to the Church by Mrs. Winfield Scott Wardell, at a Memorial Service held on Trinity Sunday, 1927, in memory of Margaret A. Squire.   Other memorial gifts have since been made.

Date of Gift	Donors	In Memoriam	Date of Commemoration (or Sunday nearest the date)	Amount
1927—Mrs. Winfield Scott Wardell		Lina Georg	February 15th	$ 50.00
	Louis E. Schwab	Lucy S. White	2nd Sun. in March	100.00
	Trinity Sunday Offering	Margaret A. Squire	July 7th	65.00
	Miss Susan Greene	Charlotte Kelly	3rd Sun. in June	50.00
1928—Louis E. Schwab		Henrietta M. Schwab	4th Sun. in March	100.00
	Gertrude R. Cushman	Members of Cushman Family	Easter Day and All Saints' Day	400.00
	"Whitlock Flower Fund"	Members of Whitlock Family	Easter Day and All Saints Day	1,000.00
	Mary Grace Whitlock,			
	Miss Susan Greene	Mary Moffett	3rd Sun. in June	50.00
	Mrs. George Stirling	Anna Fowler	2nd Sun. in May	100.00
1933—Estate of Clara J. M. Jones		Clara J. M. Jones	January 28th	
		Frederick K. Jones	4th Sun. in April	300.00
1937—Mrs. Katherine Mead		Isabella and John Mead	December 14th	100.00
1938—Mr. Frank Miller		Elizabeth J. Miller	December 1st	100.00
1939—Mrs. Katherine Mead		William Mead	2nd Sun. in Nov'mb'r	100.00
1940—Estate of Mary O'Connor		Mary O'Connor	Easter Candles	100.00
1941—Mr. Orwin H. Cripps		George A., Ellen and Selina Cripps	1st Sun. in October	100.00
1943—Estate of Dimey Williamson		Dimey Williamson	2nd Sun. in July	100.00
	Rev. Lucius A. Edelblute	Caroline Redman Edelblute	May 25th	100.00
1945—Rev. Lucius A. Edelblute		Lucius Samuel Edelblute	September 13th	100.00
1946—Mrs. Anna C. C. Carll		Alfred F. Carll	May 3rd	100.00
1949—Nettie (Hartman) Starkenbury Family			October 16th	100.00

Total Memorial Flower Fund (1949) $3,215.00

Appendix G

DR. SMITH'S SERMON

Just sixty years ago last Tuesday night this parish was organized. I count
it a special privilege to be asked to share today in your anniversary joy.
My mind naturally goes back, first of all, to the Rectors, all of whom I have
known excepting Mr. Thayer. How greatly blessed you were in Dr. Howland.
I see him now as I often met him with Dr. Weston, his intimate friend who
looked somewhat like a knight of the days of chivalry. Dr. Howland was a
charming, Christian gentleman, a man who gave his money and himself to
you all during twenty-two years of faithful rectorship, and then founded
another church, which thus in a certain sense became your offspring, the
Church of the Heavenly Rest. And side by side with him, first as Assistant
and then as Associate, was Dr. Geer, who always seemed to me to have
enough enthusiasm for ten ordinary men. His Christian life seemed to be a
perpetual joy. I think that he must have carried people right along with him
by the magnetism of contagious delight in his friends, in his church and in
his religion. Oh, the dull people who find everyday life stupid! I cannot
understand them, they ought to have talked half an hour with Dr. Geer.
While he was with you he became interested in reviving the St. Timothy
parish which had become very decrepit, and finally he left you to build it
up and thus you gave again of your very substance to establish on strong
foundations another parish. Dr. Lundy became your next rector. We all
recollect his scholarly mind and rich voice and substantial eloquence. He
used to take us under the arch of Titus and point to the golden candlestick
upon the wall and vividly describe the destruction of Jerusalem. Again he
would carry us to Mars Hill where we would listen to St. Paul's sermon on
the Unknown God, and see the Greeks listening to him with profound attention. It is a good thing when a preacher helps us to realize that our faith has
come down the ages and won victory in all centuries and all climes.

And then came our very dear Dr. Backus, my own intimate friend who
worked with me at St. James' parish before you knew him, a pastor such as
men dream of but don't find every day, a royal man among men, one whom
strong men loved, a good preacher, a fine musician, a sweet singer, by the
side of the choir he loved so well.

Beginning his rectorship in 1876, he gave his very best to this parish for
twenty-five years and at the Silver Anniversary—what a festival we had
together and how plainly you all showed your love for him and he showed
his love for you. Under his ministry your organizations flourished, your
church was beautified, your rectory was purchased and your endowment, a
most important, nay, vital thing in this parish, was finally begun. The best
of all, one of God's own men was living among you in your hearts and in
your homes.

Now pardon me what seems to be a slight diversion but really is not.
When I was a boy in a boarding school in Hamden, Connecticut, once a
year there came from Cheshire, ten miles away, good Dr. Paddock to preach
in the village church the kind of a sermon we loved to hear. He had three
sons who afterward showed by their life that they came from good stock.

257

One became a Christian physician, two became clergymen who rose and rose in usefulness and power until one was called to be the Bishop of Massachusetts, the other, who have been the successful rector of the flourishing parish of St. Peter's in Brooklyn, became the Bishop of the State of Washington. His son was not long ago heard of by us all as a young man in charge of the Pro-Cathedral work, who had taken a bold stand on behalf of purity amidst the corruptions of a great town. I do not wonder that you wanted him to become your rector and that he came and has found so many supporters here. Let me give to you, my young brother, a text of promise, taken from the 180th Psalm of the Psalter:

"The Lord from out of Zion shall so bless thee that
thou shalt see Jerusalem in prosperity all thy life long."

There isn't any greater joy than this, for the Hebrews to see his Holy City flourishing, for the child of God to see his parish prosper. Jerusalem stood among all the cities of the earth as sponsor for faith in one good God, for spiritual wisdom, for justice, truth and righteousness and for kindness towards the poor. That was at least the ideal holy city, that the kings of the earth should walk around about her, count her towers, mark well her bulwarks and then enter the temple, listen to her majestic singing, see her altars smoking, recognize the presence of Jehovah and go forth saying "This God is our God forever and ever. He shall be our might unto death."

Such should also be our ideal of the parish church, it should be a house of God in the midst of all other houses, a center of spiritual magnetism for a whole neighborhood. We remember the sacred purity of Trinity Church in Boston under Philips Brooks, the gathering of multitudes of strangers who knelt around that semi-circular chancel on the Sunday mornings and the immense congregations who listened spellbound to the eloquence that came to them through those rushing words and glowed in those dark flashing eyes.

And today, at St. George's Church, under the ministry of Dr. Rainsford, we can see how the great throngs of rich and poor are gathered together and 1,700 people kneel together at the early Easter communion. We recall the work at St. Bartholomew's under the ministry of Dr. Greer and the great parish house where 2,000 people are to be found every day of the week receiving the blessings which that institution affords.

We think of the Brick Church under the ministry of Dr. Babcock, under whose wonderful preaching the church was so crowded that people would be seated upon the very pulpit steps. We remember the wonderful rural ministry of the Rev. Mr. Hoir at Lake Placid, and the beautiful influence by which he not only reached the souls of the country people within a distance of ten miles, but also filled their everyday lives with genial influences that before were unknown to them.

And who that knew the Holy Communion under the ministry of Dr. Muhlenberg can ever forget those early Easter Services, when the sun came through the chancel window and the good rector himself seemed radiant with all the joy of the festival?

In such parishes we find an ideal spectacle, Jerusalem in prosperity, the world rushing to the churches to be thrilled with God and to be taught to live day by day purely, honestly and truly. But it is not every parish that can expect to do this magnificent work. We cannot all attain these pinnacle-glories. They occur only when churches have those very exceptional rectors who act upon a community just as a magnet does upon sands. I think after all God best loves those parishes that do good and regular and beautiful work without having a light in the pulpit of ten thousand candle power, but instead of that a man of God who gives a true message and is a faithful and warm-hearted pastor in the homes and hearts of his people. If you have gotten as much as that in your pastor, you are very rich. It is these parishes that do the great work of the church. They labor against obstacles, they are not borne along by the helpful gale of forty miles an hour. But in such parishes as here in the Church of the Holy Apostles, you will find for sixty years and more an Apostolic Succession, noble laymen and Christian women who come to God's house in rain and shine whether there are many or whether there are few. Faithful choir masters deserving far more credit than many who have larger salaries, surprise one with the good results reached, sometimes surpassing those attained by others at large expense. Bright-eyed young men are regularly at their posts as ushers, scores of Sunday School teachers every Lord's Day do the beautiful work that the angels know. A Mr. Whitlock, for instance, leads the way, multitudes of givers following the lead of Founders like Mr. and Mrs. Robert Ray, Mr. John Smith, Mr. John King, Miss Maria Robins, the Cushmans and Collords and Bordens and Wrights and Baylies and Goffs, and I know not how many others (perhaps I am failing to mention some of the best of all, but God will not forget, their reward is with the Most High).

I tell you it is not the pulpit geniuses who chiefly build the churches, but the best Apostolic Succession in all this world, the Succession of the people good and true who give to their parishes (without the spur of excitement) their attendance, their money, their love and their work. There are no flashes of electric splendor radiating from these churches, but there is a steady quiet glow that lights the whole neighborhood, carrying God's truth, God's morals and God's love into thousands of homes.

My dear Brother, perhaps you will do even better than this, you may be electric. We have heard good things concerning you; you have one great advantage, the gift of the morning: "Thou hast the dawn of thy youth." Oh, I should like to be in the ministry again at your age. There are great opportunities just before us in this new-born twentieth century. May all of them open before you, but especially may you have one help. It is said of Archimedes that he exclaimed, "Give me a place where I may rest my lever and I will move the world." The one great need of this parish, which if supplied would give it a mighty power, is a great endowment. If any person of wealth in this world's goods wishes to know what is about the best thing that can be done to bless those who are to come after him, I would say, let him ask himself whether he can do anything better than this, give a great lift towards raising the present endowment of this parish to $200,000—it surely needs that much. I do not know of any investment promising a larger interest from generation to generation, diffusing perpetual blessing centuries hence, the giver's hand thus continuing to give to God himself in spite of the fact that that hand has been dust for many generations. I tell you this would be a sublime victory over death, to seize such an opportunity before going into that country into which no money can be taken.

In closing I will simply invoke for this dear parish the gift to stay in this spot for ages, a blessing on the homes which surround it, singing the song of Tennyson's Brook, "Men may come and men may go, but I go on forever."

CONSECRATION OF BISHOP PADDOCK

THE CONSECRATION SERVICE

The Rector's Consecration as Bishop of Eastern Oregon took place in our own church on the morning of the 18th day of December, 1907, at 10:30 o'clock.

The Consecrator was presiding Bishop Tuttle. He was assisted by Bishop Potter and Bishop Satterlee, of Washington, D. C. Bishop Greer was the Preacher; Bishop Scadding of Western Oregon, and Bishop Wells of Spokane, the Presenting Bishops. The Rev. Dr. Huntington of Grace Church, and the Rev. Dr. Nicholas of Holy Trinity, Harlem, the Attending Presbyters. The Rev. Dr. Grosvenor had been appointed to act as Registrar, but was prevented by illness, and the Rev. James Freeman took his place. Archdeacon Nelson was to have been the Master of Ceremonies, but owing to illness he was unable to be present, and the Rev. H. R. Hulse took his place. He was assisted by the Rev. Dr. Crowder, and the Rev. Ellis Bishop, the Rev. M. H. Gates and the Rev. W. T. Crocker.

The processional hymns were: "The Son of God goes forth to War," and "The Church's One Foundation is Jesus Christ, her Lord."

The service began with the Ante-Communion, Morning Prayer having been previously said at nine o'clock by the Rev. Mr. Judge, assisted by the Rev. Mr. Haughwout.

The hymn before the sermon was, "When Morning Gilds the Skies."

At the close of his sermon, turning to the Bishop Elect, the preacher said, ' It is because men have seen the Divine Presence in you, my brother, that you have been able to do for those with whom you have come in contact, and for this city and the community in which you live, what you have, and for that reason that you have been called to this new service. You will carry into this larger work the same Divine Presence. Through the power of the indwelling Christ you will be able to do in your mission field what you have done here, and more and greater things."

Immediately after the sermon the Elected Bishop was presented to the Presiding Bishop by Bishop Wells and Bishop Scadding, and the testimonials were read.

Dr. Van de Water, of St. Andrew's Church, Harlem, read the permission of the House of Bishops for the Consecration to take place. Bishop Johnson, assistant Bishop of South Dakota, the certificate of election by the House of Bishops, and Mr. John Wood, secretary of the Board of Missions, the certificate of election by the House of Deputies.

The Litany was read by the Rev. Dr. Kimber, associate secretary of the Board of Missions.

After the Litany, the Presiding Bishop put the required questions to the Bishop Elect, to which he responded, and hymn 586,

"Lord, speak to me, that I may speak
In living echoes of Thy tone."

was sung.

During the singing of this hymn the Bishop Elect retired to the robing room, accompanied by his Attending Presbyters, where he was vested in the full Episcopal habit, returning and taking his place before the Presiding Bishop, just as the last verse was being sung.

Hymn 289, "Come, Holy Ghost, our Souls inspire," was then sung, the Presiding Bishop singing one line and the choir and congregation the next.

The Consecration then took place. The Presiding Bishop, with his assistants and all the other bishops present with them, laying their hands upon the head of the Bishop Elect, while the words of consecration were pronounced.

After the Consecration, the newly made Bishop took his place with the others, within the Sanctuary, and the Presiding Bishop proceeded with the Communion Service.

The offering was devoted to the needs of Bishop Paddock's Missionary District of Eastern Oregon.

The Recessional hymns were "Ancient Days," and "Go forward, Christian Soldier."

The entire service was most solemn and impressive, though marked throughout by the utmost simplicity.

After the service Bishop Paddock held a brief and informal reception in the Parish House, especially for the out-of-town friends.

* * * *

PARISH PAPER LITERATURE

A part of an article and poem which appeared in the parish paper upon the death of Sergeant Oliver Tims, a vestryman who died June, 1916, is given below:

Not every life leaves a single impression. Most lives are confused and distracted. But here and there a life is lived singly. It is centered and moves like a great steamer on a sure course from port to port. . . .

Mind is the servant of the soul; and the soul cannot achieve its task save through keen and mental interest. Sergeant Oliver Tims was a mind. He was guided at once by faith in Reason and by an enthusiasm growing from that faith, which ever sought its light in the solution of human problems. May his example help us to resolve more fully to have our love abound more and more in knowledge "to approve the things that are excellent."

Who was it said the reason is cold?
He's o'erbold.
There are no fires that burn with such
Fervor and glow
As the fires of the brain, in desire to know;
His Truth on the world and mankind to bestow.

I know this is true
Because I knew you.

Who was it said the Mind was hard?
His truth is marred.
She is ever discovering the way of the right,
For mercy and kindness she furnishes sight,
For the good and true she shines as the light.

I know this is true
Because I knew you.

H. K. D.

This is another poem as printed in the parish paper in 1916:

PALM TREE AND THORN TREE

The Palm Tree and the Thorn Tree
Were waiting by the way
To meet and greet the King.
Said the Thorn Tree to the Palm Tree:
"What message do you bring?"

Then the Palm Tree said to the Thorn Tree
"I've long been waiting here
To greet and hail the King!
Soon the children with glad voices
In whose soul the King rejoices
Will seize my branches low—
The breezes told me so—
And loud Hosannas sing."

The Thorn Tree said to the Palm Tree:
"I, too, am waiting here
To hail and crown the King.
I hear the maddened crowd
With hoarse shout lifted loud,
My thorns that brow shall press
With sharp pain's swift caress
And lo! the sad world ring!"

The King passed by
The Palms waved high
The thorns left their crimson crown;
No longer Palm and Thorn.
For in crowning the King
Came this marvellous thing
The Union of Thorn and Palm.

H. K. D.

THE BOOK OF REMEMBRANCE

*This Golden Altar Book is dedicated to the Service of God
and in loving memory of all those who contributed to
The Organ Fund from 1930 to 1941.*

O God, forasmuch as without Thee we are not able to please Thee; mercifully grant that Thy Holy Spirit may in all things direct and rule our hearts; through Jesus Christ our Lord. Amen.

John Andrews
Susie Andrews
Margaret M. Andrews
William H. Armstrong, Jr.
Mrs. Hamed Ali
Joseph Anthony
Charles Anthony
Margaret Anthony

Joseph Boes
Elizabeth Boes
Frederick E. Boes
Joseph Boes, Jr.
Mrs. Peter Beck
Caroline L. Beck
Arthur Brewer
Edmund L. Baylies
Mrs. Sarah Brown
Mr. and Mrs. Frederick Barhold
Mrs. W. Blackshaw
Mr. and Mrs. Joseph Bennett
William I. Battin
Elsie Edelblute Battin
Wm. I. Battin, Jr.
Mrs. Brady E. Backus
Electus T. Backus
George Brown
Edna V. Benson
James A. Benson
Wm. E. Brown
W. H. Baldwin
Mrs. M. Baerenbach
Mrs. J. Baerenbach
Mrs. F. Bopp
Mrs. A. Baerenbach
Miss J. Baerenbach

W. Bolt
Mr. and Mrs. R. W. Brownson
Amy Burlingame

Thomas Clark
Mrs. Thomas Clark
Annie Clark
Mrs. Anna C. Carll
Miss Gertrude R. Cushman
Mrs. Lillian A. Cooper
Mrs. Thomas Conroy
Sam Conroy
Sadie Caker
Mrs. S. Cohen

Anna Davis
Mary E. Drum
Mrs. W. Deimling
Thomas F. Dalton
Mr. and Mrs. Henry C. Doretta
Percy Diver

Rev. Lucius A. Edelblute
Mrs. Edwin Every
Arthur Edminston
Olivia Elliott
Sarah A. Every
Gertrude Every
Laura Every
Edwin Every, Jr.
Mrs. George Evans
Mr. and Mrs. Henry Emmer
Mrs. Frank Ealy

William T. Fowler
Mrs. William T. Fowler
William T. Fowler, Jr.

THE BOOK OF REMEMBRANCE

Louis Ferguson
Mrs. J. E. Ferdinand
Mrs. V. Fuchs
Mrs. J. Forster
Margaret Frizzell
Mrs. J. Foster

W. J. Ganong
Elizabeth Ganong
Betty Ganong
Edwin D. Ganong
R. H. Goffe
Robert Grunert
Mr. and Mrs. J. E. Gleason
Harold L. Gantner

Courtney Hyde
Charles F. Hillock
Mrs. Daniel Hutchison
Mrs. A. E. Hutchison
William J. Hewston
Margaret T. Hewston
Mary A. Hewston
William Hookey
Alick Hamilton
A. J. Hawthorne
Mrs. J. Hoffman
Mrs. James Arthur Hammond
Herbert C. Hertfelder

Margaret Inslee
John Inslee
Wm. H. Inslee
John J. Inslee, Jr.
Robert Inslee

Florence Johnston
Mrs. Frederick K. Jones
Mr. and Mrs. George W. Jackson
Julia Jenkinson

Mary Keegan
Mrs. O. Kane
Harold G. Kuhn

Mario E. La Penta

Amelia Mann
Mahon Family
Mr. and Mrs. William Matthews
Mr. and Mrs. William Mead
Minnie Meyberger
Mr. and Mrs. Paul Morich
Mrs. Mary Moffett
David Morton
Bessie Inslee Merckey
Mrs. John Mead
Mr. and Mrs. A. Wm. Mohl
Mrs. Elizabeth Menacho
Mr. and Mrs. Henry Dunlap Morrison
Miss E. Martin
Mrs. A. Marshall
Miss F. Murray

Mrs. Anna McFarland
Jane McAuliffe
Margaret L. McClean
Mrs. H. McCast

Rev. Harry Nichols, D.D.
Mr. and Mrs. T. S. Newman
Philip T. Newman
Mrs. L. Nehr
Eliza Neumann
Annette Norberg

John Francis O'Connor
John Francis O'Connor, Jr.
Leala Owen
Mary S. Olmstead
Sophie R. Olmstead
Susan Hawley Olmstead
Mary O'Connor

Charlotte Paine
Rt. Rev. Robert L. Paddock
Mrs. Robert L. Paddock
Bishop Paddock Memorial Gifts:
Rev. Brady E. Backus, D.D.
Mrs. Edmund Lincoln Baylies
Mr. and Mrs. Geo. W. Ferguson
Victoria Pedersen (Mrs. Jos. S.)
Elizabeth Adeline Cushman

THE BOOK OF REMEMBRANCE

Dr. James Pedersen
George A. Phillips
Peter C. Phillips
Eleanor Poste
Elizabeth M. Phillips
Mrs. George A. Phillips
A. V. Roe
Frank Palsgraf
Mrs. F. Platz

Mrs. Ogden Reid
Mr. and Mrs. Henry H. Ritter
A. V. Roe
Elizabeth H. Rorke
Frances Rohde

Louis E. Schwab
Emily Schwab
Rev. John F. Steen, D.D.
    (Memorial: Miss M. B. Wade)
Emily Andrews Schneider
Emily Audrey Schneider
Louis Allen Schneider
Mr. and Mrs. Robert Shepherd
Margaret Shepherd
Robert Shepherd, Jr.
Barbara Beth Shepherd
Mary E. Smith
Emily L. Sarders
George J. Schmidt
Martina Schultz
Marie Sodemann
Mr. and Mrs. John Schroeder
Mr. and Mrs. Carlton Schroeder

Margaret Seguine
Miss L. Southard
Alex Scott
Evelyn Simmonds
Rose Shepherd
Ida M. Schaefer
Earl Schaefer
Mrs. E. Schaefer
Lilliam G. Stafford

Mrs. Margaret Thompson
Mrs. G. Tighe
Georgina M. B. Taylor

Mrs. G. Ulmer

Grace Vaughan

Dimey Williamson
Mrs. Edward Wells
Lena Margaret Wade
Charlotte T. Whiteside
Betty M. Whiteside
Alexander Whiteside
Mrs. J. Winckelbach
Sarah S. Watts
Mrs. J. Wolfer
J. Wolfer
Ellen Wilkinson
Emily Wilkin
Maria Bennett Wade
Robert Williams

Ada Scott Yeatman

APPENDIX J

ST. MICHAEL'S CEMETERY

List of names and year of interment in the Plots of
THE CHURCH OF THE HOLY APOSTLES

They shall hunger no more, neither thirst any more; neither shall the sun light on them, nor any heat. For the Lamb which is in the midst of the throne shall feed them, and shall lead them unto living fountains of waters: and God shall wipe away all tears from their eyes.—REV. VII: 16, 17.

✠

Henry Thornberry	1853	Jane Collins	1862
Benjamin R. Lowde	1854	Thomas Bryant	1863
Christopher Rooker	1854	Catherine Brooks	1863
Melinda Beattie	1854	Margaret Wood	1863
Mary Ann Sheridan	1855	Mary Jane Breen	1863
John James Rice	1855	Abraham Bryant	1863
George Fox	1855	George Boll	1863
Ann Maria Base	1855	Ella McNulty	1863
Arthur Fleming	1855	William Kirkland	1863
Bessey McCann	1856	Maria Bryant	1864
Cordelia Mills	1856	Ishmael Allen	1864
David Freeland	1858	Robert Collins	1864
Elizabeth Small	1859	Ann Stanley	1864
William Fox	1859	Susanna Bryant	1864
Margaret Jane Patchel	1859	Henry Johnson	1865
Jane Reed	1859	Sarah Johnson	1865
Elizabeth Stanley	1860	Walter Tarbell	1865
Ann Bottle	1860	Bryce C. Blair	1865
Edward C. Morton	1860	Alice E. Bright	1865
Ida Vale	1860	Jane McNeeland	1865
Lansa Philips	1861	Francis Grainger	1866
Selmo I. Chambers	1861	Joseph Kimbly	1866
Jeremiah Trimble	1861	Andrew McCullough	1866
John Kirkland	1861	Alice Eliza Howard	1867
Sarah Kimberly	1862	James Parks	1867
Francis J. Kimberly	1862	Mary Wood	1867
James Stanley	1862	Catherin Fox	1867
Mary Jane Patterson	1862	Charles E. Tarbell	1868
Stephen Mitchell	1862	Elizabeth Thompson	1869
Francis Garrett	1862	Carrie Emma Thompson	1869
John Dance	1862	Mary Howland Small	1870
Jane Tremble	1862	John J. Smith	1870
Charlotte Garrett	1862	John Smith	1870
Elizabeth Wark	1862	Elizabeth Churchill	1871
George Kimberly	1862	Jane A. Crocus	1871
Anna L. Foster	1862	Robert Blair	1871

Francis W. Murtha	1872	Jane Courtney	1889
Henry Marshall	1872	Lillian Long	1889
James Sawyer	1872	Mary Cole	1889
Charles Murtha	1873	Ellen McElwee	1890
Annie Johnson	1873	Alexander Sutherland	1891
Lucy C. Hall	1873	Elizabeth Titterinogton	1892
John Murtha	1874	Emma Crespini	1892
Elizabeth Thompson	1874	Isabella Stewart	1892
William F. Blair	1874	M. W. Van Dyke	1893
Elizabeth Flanigan	1875	Catherine Davis	1890
Robert McCormack	1875	Mary F. Mellifont	1893
Thomas E. Butler	1875	Thomas Conroy	1894
Benjamin F. White	1876	Jennette S. Conroy	1894
George W. Rogers	1877	Mary McDowell	1894
Jane Redfeow	1877	Violet Follis	1904
Mary E. Miller	1878	Annie Tobiason	1909
Thomas G. Mallifont	1878	Edith C. Miller	1909
William Moore	1879	Annie L. Tausey	1911
George Moore	1879	Waltraub Miller	1914
Mary Senterm	1879	Caroline Lundgren	1915
George A. Wesselgner	1880	William Davis	1916
Alice E. Carpenter	1880	Margaret Gilmore	1916
Mary Hughs	1881	William B. Lyons	1916
Eliza Stanley	1881	Sven P. Wesselgren	1917
August Smith	1881	Carl F. Lundgren	1919
William Walsh	1882	Edna Vernon	1921
Gertrude Richmond	1882	Charlotte Blake	1922
Dora Switzer	1882	Raymond Vernon	1924
John Richmond	1882	Margaret Alice Squire	1925
James Williams	1882	Lina Georg	1927
Ruben McKenna	1883	Ellen Wilkinson	1930
David Mellifont	1884	Elva Johnston	1931
Susan E. Cowen	1886	Walter Briden	1931
Anne Falz	1886	John Diniz	1931
James Davis	1888	Douglas Williams	1934
William Davis	1888	Blanche Vogl (Wilson)	1939
Richard Davis	1888	France D. DeLong	1939
Lillie Scully	1888	Daniel Haines	1940
John McKain	1888	Jane Elliot (ashes of)	1941
Edith F. Rayment	1889		

✠

Into Paradise may the Angels lead thee, at thy coming may the Martyrs receive thee, and bring thee into the holy city of Jerusalem. May the choir of Angels welcome thee, and with Lazarus, who once was poor, mayest thou have eternal rest.—Amen.

APPENDIX K

BUDGETS AND EXPENDITURES

ITEM 1

Due on Bills, January 13, 1846

Rector's salary	$ 189.76
Ground Rent	24.00
Wm. S. Hunt	51.00
Care of S. S. Room	9.00
Balance in Treasury	$ .96

* * * *

ITEM 2
Yearly Expenditures—1847

Rental for room, West 27th Street	$ 85.00
Sexton	50.00
Insurance	36.00
Coal and Lights	24.00
Interest on Mortgage	280.00
Rector's Salary	500.00
	$975.00

* * * *

ITEM 3
Receipts—1849

Pew Rents	$ 743.24
Plate Offerings	246.74
Gift—Trinity Church	300.00
Sinking Fund	149.00
Donations	155.00
Specials	63.45
Loans	300.00
Balance (1849)	63.41
	$2,020.84

* * * *

ITEM 4
Standing Committee Report—1856

Pew Rentals	$2,126.00
Offerings	992.58
Floating indebtedness	7,913.00

* * * *

Item 5

Year	Pew Holders	Rentals	Families	SS. Scholars	Salary
1848	40	$ 885.00	150	200	$ 673.00
1854	67	1,815.00	164	245	2,160.00
1858	106	2,847.00	200	250	3,100.00

* * * *

Item 6

Liabilities, 1871		Resources, 1871	
Salary of Rector	$4,000.00	Pew Rents	$3,857.00
Salary of Assistant	1,000.00	Offerings (estimate)	1,400.00
Music	1,250.00	Rentals	1,400.00
Sexton	500.00		
Fuel and Gas	531.00		$6,657.00
Repairs	690.00		
Taxes, Insurance	405.00		
Interest on Mortgage	1,387.00		
Incidentals	250.00		
	10,013.00		

Item 6½

Expenditures Year Ending May 1, 1883		Income Year Ending May 1, 1883	
Rector's Salary	$2,500.00	Pew Rents	$1,834.00
Music	1,250.00	Pledges	900.00
Sexton	800.00	Offerings	825.00
Clerical Services	300.00	Easter	676.00
Coal and Gas	571.95	Rent, 296—9th Ave.	800.00
Repairs	399.35	Trinity Stipend	2,000.00
Insurance	208.00		$7,035.00
Taxes, Rectory and 296 9th Ave.	321.06	Deficit	525.36
Interest, ($12,450)	710.00		
Incidental Expenses	500.00		7,560.36
	$7,560.36		

Item 7

The Treasurer Reported after Easter, 1892

Receipts

Offerings	$1,224.97
Pew Rents	981.50
Pledges	853.23
Trinity's Gift	3,000.00
	$6,059.70

Of the 350 communicants, about 90 were regular subscribers through the church envelopes. A special appeal was made in 1894 to increase the weekly support of the parish, and to a mailing of 313 packages of envelopes, about 200 persons responded.

* * * *

Item 8
The Standing Committee's Financial Report, 1897

Expenditures		Receipts	
Rector's Salary	$2,500.00	Trinity Church	$3,000.00
Assistant Minister	1,000.00	Pledges	2,256.50
Sexton	1,000.00	Pew Rents	584.50
Music	1,000.00	Easter and Christmas	1,825.74
General Repairs	3,145.12	Contributions	198.75
Sundries	1,584.47	Rent, 296—9th Ave.	1,000.00
Interest	610.53		
			$8,865.49
	$10,840.12		

Deficits	. . . . . .	$1,974.63
Notes	. . . .	2,450.00
Balance	. . . . .	118.48

* * * *

Item 9
Treasurer's Report, December, 1902

Receipts		Expenditures	
From Trinity Church	$3,000.00	Rector's Salary	$3,000.00
Plate Offerings	2,314.81	Music	1,263.97
Pledges	1,441.68	Sexton	1,000.00
Pew Rents	322.00	Assistance	669.50
Sundries	1,134.10	Repairs	1,606.60
Rents, 296—9th Ave.	1,000.00	Gas	391.20
Charities	152.00	Taxes and Insurance	679.77
Missions	378.50	Advertising	164.39
		Sundries	265.51
	9,743.09	Missions	395.20
Other Charities	233.00	Charities	397.50
	$9,976.09		$9,833.64

ITEM 10
Report, May 1904

Receipts		Pledges	
1901	$ 9,000.00	1901	$1,600.00
1902	11,705.94	1902	2,300.00
1903	13,498.70	1904	3,000.00

* * * *

ITEM 11
Report of the Treasurer, December, 1908

Receipts		Expenditures	
Balance on hand (1907)	$ 971.13	Salaries	$6,420.71
From Trinity Church	3,000.00	Music	1,375.99
Loose Offerings	1,092.81	Repairs	1,919.45
Pledges	3,438.13	Gas, Electricity, Coal	840.37
Christmas and Easter 1907	2,333.00	Taxes	507.37
Donations for S. S.	1,000.00	Insurance	643.51
Specials	837.13	Interest	409.03
Pew Rents	206.00	Expenditure for S. S.	1,000.00
Christmas Sale	510.00	Poor Relief, etc.	360.61
Communion Alms	360.61	Printing, etc.	174.50
For Missionary in Mexico	784.07	Missionaries in Mexico	784.07
Women's Auxiliary	300.00	Missions	476.97
		Women's Auxiliary	300.00
	$14,832.88		$15,212.58

* * * *

ITEM 12
Treasury Deficit, September, 1916

Note to Greenville Banking and Trust Co.	$ 2,900.00
Notes to Mr. Louis E. Schwab	3,800.00
Indebtedness on new organ	2,369.20
Unsecured loans	575.00
Other loans from funds, otherwise designated	434.88
	$10,079.08

* * * *

ITEM 13

Receipts, 1918		Expenditures, 1918	
Endowments	$4,558.36	Salaries	$3,925.00
Loose Offerings	404.44	Repairs	1,027.71
Pledges	767.30	Gas and Electricity	473.71
Christmas and Easter	798.96	Coal	622.50
Rents	814.25	Taxes and Insurance	1,137.05
Fair	630.63	Interest on Loans	678.75
Special Offerings	629.42	Sundries	448.55
Missions	191.40	Missions and Specials	519.40
	$8,794.76		$8,832.67

ITEM 14

In December, 1929, the main necessary yearly expenditures were:

Salaries	$ 5,100.00
Music	2,250.00
Insurance and Taxes	5,889.56
Repairs	5,634.25
Coal, Gas and Electricity	1,190.75
Expense A-c.	5,372.89
Interest (mortgages)	3,310.54
Other Expenses	2,327,27
	$31,075.26

The full effect of the financial depression was most severely felt in the years 1932-1934. The church had overexpanded, and parish finances were strained to the uttermost by its realty investments, its reduced rentals, expensive repairs necessitated by the demands of the city, and the interest on its indebtedness. The total real estate indebtedness was then $48,500 at 5 per cent.

In 1934, a regrettable though necessary, reduction in salaries was made. The sexton's salary was reduced from $1,500, with apartment, to $1,000. The music, with an expenditure of over $2,000, was reduced to $1,500. The parish worker, who came to us at a yearly salary of $1,000, was now to receive $900. And the rector's salary was reduced from $2,700 to $2,400.

* * * *

ITEM 15

Financial Report—1935

Receipts, 1935		Disbursements, 1935	
Envelopes	$1,589.40	Salaries	$4,575.00
Plate Offerings	1,944.95	Music	1,678.67
Donations & Sun. School	791.89	Fuel, Light and Power	1,006.07
Fair	1,023.44	Printing, etc	351.29
Endowments	3,654.30	Current Expenses	657.96
Rentals	9,825.33	Parochial Expenses	1,391.60
Missions	619.36	Interest	1,539.54
Alms	136.72	Taxes and Insurance	2,472.49
Improvements	754.35	Permanent Improvements	8,900.18
Loans	3,200.00	Missions	816.38
		Poor	136.72
	$23,539.74		$23,525.90

* * * *

ITEM 16

Receipts, 1945		Expenditures, 1945	
Endowment, interest	$4,085.97	Salaries	$ 5,010.00
Pledges	1,411.67	Music	1,138.36
Plate Offerings	1,521.82	Coal, Light, Water	945.84
Fair, Organizations	1,000.54	Printing and Stationery	140.95
Donations and S. S.	577.85	Repairs	368.45
Gifts outside parish	81.74	General Expenses	776.37
	$8,679.59		$ 8,379.97
Missions	728.21	Missions	728.21
Special gifts	111.28	For Specials	111.28
	$9,519.08		$ 9,219.46
Real Estate (Rentals)	$8,398.29	Real Estate (Expenses)	$12,534.12

* * * *

BIBLIOGRAPHY

Retrospections of America by John Bernard

The Topography and Hydrology of New York by Egbert L. Viele

Manual of Old New York by Valentine

Historical Churches in New York by Clyde F. Rehrig—1941-1943

History of the Church of Zion and St. Timothy of New York by David Clarkson—1894

Historical Sketch of the Church of the Holy Apostles by Charles Knapp—1894

Cradle Days of New York by Hugh Macaramney—1909

Dock Walloper by Richard J. Butler and Joseph Driscoll—1933

Dictionary of American Biography

Immigration and Growth of the Episcopal Church by Walter Herbert Stowe—1942

"Benjamin Tredwell Onderdonk," *Historical Magazine* by E. Clowes Chorley—1948

Church Magazine

The Churchman

Gospel Messenger

Journal of Christian Education

The Living Church

General Sunday School Union

Journals of the Diocese of New York

The Episcopal Recorder

The Protestant Episcopalian

Secular Newspaper of New York

Minutes, Standing Committee Reports, Eighth Avenue Sunday School—1836-1844

Minutes of the Vestry, Church of the Holy Apostles—1844-1848

Standing Committee Reports of the Vestry—1844-1935

Minutes, Societies of the Church of the Holy Apostles—1844-1948

Publications by the Rectors of the Church of the Holy Apostles —1856-1948

Letters, Statements received by the Rectors

Sermons preached in the Church of the Holy Apostles

INDEX